Interpersonal Meaning in Multimodal English Textbooks

Bloomsbury Studies in Systemic Functional Linguistics

Series Editors:
David Caldwell, University of South Australia, Australia
John S. Knox, Macquarie University, Australia
J. R. Martin, University of Sydney, Australia

Advisory Board:
Thomas Andersen (The Danish Language Council, Denmark)
Chang Chenguang (Sun Yat-Sen University, Guangzhou, China)
Priscilla Cruz (Ateneo de Manila University, Philippines)
Meg Gebhard (University of Massachusetts Amherst, USA)
Isaac Mwinlaaru (University of Cape Coast, Ghana)
Teresa Oteíza (Pontifical University of Chile, Chile)
Mary Scheppegrell (University of Michigan, USA)
Akila Sellami Baklouti (University of Sfax, Tunisia)
Miriam Taverniers (University of Ghent, Belgium)
Orlando Vian (Federal University of Sao Paulo, Brazil)
Li Zhangzi (National University of Defence Technology, Nanjing, China)

Among functional approaches to language and related semiotic systems, Systemic Functional theory stands out as an evolving paradigm, constantly developing new systems to accommodate descriptive challenges. Bloomsbury Studies in Systemic Functional Linguistics responds to this ever-developing field, speaking to instances of evolution at the frontier of the discipline.

Publishing contemporary, cutting-edge research in Systemic Functional Linguistics, this cohesive series unites complementary developments into an integrated multiperspectival whole. Titles focus on specific themes to explore emerging new fields of research in Systemic Functional theory alongside innovations within long established areas of SFL research. Placing emphasis on new voices and directions, Bloomsbury Studies in Systemic Functional Linguistics demonstrates how a disciplinary singular like SFL continues to evolve and subsume its past into possible futures.

Interpersonal Meaning in Multimodal English Textbooks

Yumin Chen

BLOOMSBURY ACADEMIC
LONDON • NEW YORK • OXFORD • NEW DELHI • SYDNEY

BLOOMSBURY ACADEMIC
Bloomsbury Publishing Plc
50 Bedford Square, London, WC1B 3DP, UK
1385 Broadway, New York, NY 10018, USA
29 Earlsfort Terrace, Dublin 2, Ireland

BLOOMSBURY, BLOOMSBURY ACADEMIC and the Diana logo are trademarks of
Bloomsbury Publishing Plc

First published in Great Britain 2022
This paperback edition published 2024

Copyright © Yumin Chen 2022

Yumin Chen has asserted her right under the Copyright, Designs and Patents Act, 1988, to be identified as Author of this work.

For legal purposes the Acknowledgements on p. xi constitute an extension of this copyright page.

Cover image © Magnia / Shutterstock

All rights reserved. No part of this publication may be reproduced or transmitted in any form or by any means, electronic or mechanical, including photocopying, recording, or any information storage or retrieval system, without prior permission in writing from the publishers.

Bloomsbury Publishing Plc does not have any control over, or responsibility for, any third-party websites referred to or in this book. All internet addresses given in this book were correct at the time of going to press. The author and publisher regret any inconvenience caused if addresses have changed or sites have ceased to exist, but can accept no responsibility for any such changes.

A catalogue record for this book is available from the British Library.

A catalog record for this book is available from the Library of Congress.

ISBN: HB: 978-1-3500-7494-1
PB: 978-1-3503-0024-8
ePDF: 978-1-3500-7495-8
eBook: 978-1-3500-7496-5

Series: Bloomsbury Studies in Systemic Functional Linguistics

Typeset by Deanta Global Publishing Services, Chennai, India

To find out more about our authors and books visit www.bloomsbury.com and sign up for our newsletters.

Contents

List of illustrations		vi
Foreword		ix
Acknowledgements		xi
1	Introduction	1
2	Research background: Multimodality, multiliteracies and EFL education in China	11
3	Theoretical foundations	31
4	Heteroglossic harmony: Multimodal ENGAGEMENT resources and voice interaction	57
5	Attitudinal accumulation: Verbiage-image complementarity and co-instantiation	91
6	Contestable reality: A multilevel perspective on modality in visual communication	129
7	Conclusions and recommendations	161
Appendices		171
Notes		175
References		179
Index		202

Illustrations

Figures

3.1	Language and its semiotic environment	34
3.2	Cline of instantiation	35
3.3	Functional diversification of language and social context	39
3.4	An overview of APPRAISAL resources	40
3.5	The ENGAGEMENT system	44
3.6	Interactive meaning in images	49
3.7	Visual focalization	50
4.1	Multiple voices in multimodal EFL textbook discourse	61
4.2	Labelling in multimodal textbook discourse	63
4.3	Labelling in a junior secondary textbook	64
4.4	Dialogue balloons in lending support to editor voice	66
4.5	Dialogue balloons in explaining rules of games by demonstration in a primary textbook	67
4.6	Dialogue balloons in explaining rules of games by demonstration in a junior secondary textbook	67
4.7	Dialogue balloons in giving directions to readers	70
4.8	Jointly constructed drawing exercise	71
4.9	Multimodal jointly constructed herald page	73
4.10	Jointly constructed verbal text with accompanying images	75
4.11	Image as the link between verbal texts	78
4.12	Illustration of improper behaviours	79
4.13	Background and foreground illustration	80
4.14	Highlighting in visual image	82
4.15	FORCE of three types of dialogue balloon in realizing [attribute] value	84
4.16	FOCUS of three types of jointly constructed text in realizing [attribute] value	85
4.17	FORCE of two types of illustration in realizing [attribute] value	86
4.18	Voice interaction in multimodal EFL textbook discourse	89
5.1	Verbal strategies for inscribing and evoking ATTITUDE	95

5.2	Inscribed happiness of English-learning	98
5.3	Gradability in affectual inscription	101
5.4	Logogenetic recontextualization in multimodal textbook discourse	103
5.5	Recontextualizing feelings in a cartoon	104
5.6	A multimodal text without logogenetic recontextualization	105
5.7	Co-instantiation and putative reading	107
5.8	Co-instantiation in JUDGEMENT invocation	112
5.9	Invoked APPRECIATION of reaction	115
5.10	Co-instantiation in encoding APPRECIATION	117
5.11	Co-instantiation in jointly constructed text	121
5.12	JUDGEMENT and APPRECIATION as institutionalized AFFECT	126
6.1	Modality scale for colour saturation	135
6.2	Articulation of detail	135
6.3	Technological coding orientation	139
6.4	Sensory coding orientation	140
6.5	Abstract coding orientation	141
6.6	Sensory coding orientation in *We Love Animals*	143
6.7	Abstract-sensory coding orientation in *Why Do You Like Koalas*	144
6.8	Naturalistic coding orientation in *Wildlife Protection*	147
6.9	*New Senior English for China Student's Book 2*	149
6.10	Photograph for representing actual scene	151
6.11	Drawing for illustrating mythology	154

Tables

2.1	The World That a Pedagogy of Multiliteracies Needs to Address	21
3.1	The Gradability of Attitudinal Meanings	44
3.2	The Gradability of Engagement Values	45
3.3	Multifunctionality for the Modalities of Verbiage and Image	46
4.1	Cline of Instantiation – Evaluation	59
4.2	Speech Functions and Their Corresponding Visual Patterns in Figure 4.6	68
5.1	The Distribution of Visual Styles in EFL Textbooks for Different Levels of Education	97
5.2	Types of AFFECT in the Cartoons of Figure 5.1	99
5.3	ATTITUDE Analysis of the Verbal Texts in Figure 5.5	109

5.4	Inscribed and Invoked ATTITUDE in the Verbiage of Figure 5.6	112
5.5	Inscribed and Invoked ATTITUDE in the Verbiage of Figure 5.8	119
5.6	Inscribed and Invoked ATTITUDE in the Verbiage of Figure 5.9	122
5.7	Emotion and Attitude Goals for Grades 2, 5 and 8 in *Curriculum Standards for English*	125
6.1	The Narrative Structure of *The Story of Atlanta*	156

Foreword

Two of the most striking developments in linguistically informed discourse analysis during the noughts had to do with multimodality and appraisal. As far as multimodality was concerned, work by Kress and van Leeuwen on images inspired discourse analysts to increasingly turn their attention to the multimodal texts in which language was supported by other modalities of communication (paralanguage, images, sounds and music etc.). With respect to appraisal, largely inspired by Martin and White's appraisal framework, discourse analysts increasingly focused on attitudinal meaning in texts, alongside an ongoing concern with ideational and textual resources. In this volume Chen Yumin takes these developments as her foundation and moves discourse analysis into the teens by showing how images and appraisal work in tandem in a corpus of Chinese English-language teaching textbook materials.

In accomplishing this project, Chen Yumin makes three innovative contributions. For one thing, following up on Martin and White's recontextualization of Bakhtin's work on heterglossia, she explores how voices are introduced and aligned inter-modally, across verbiage and image, in her data. This provides us with a very innovative extension of the engagement dimension of appraisal across modalities. In addition she demonstrates how verbiage and image co-instantiate attitude in her materials, showing how different syndromes of feeling unfold for students of different ages – with the enjoyment of language learning activities foregrounded for younger students. Finally she draws on Kress and van Leeuwen's insights into sensory modalities to investigate the shift in coding orientation from what she refers to as the 'pleasure principle' of the early years towards the more abstract modality of the senior years.

Alongside these invaluable contributions to multimodal discourse analysis as far as the 'languaging' and imaging of evaluation are concerned, Chen Yumin makes important observations about the English-teaching curriculum she is investigating – including the childist ideology at play in the material for young children and the sensitivity of intermodal relations to the field of discourse (the topics chosen for consideration). This makes her book as important a contribution to educational linguistics as it is to cutting-edge discourse analysis.

All of these achievements are, of course, predicated on a deep understanding of systemic functional linguistics and semiotics, including the very latest developments as far as multimodality, appraisal and instantiation theory are concerned (including coupling, commitment and logogenesis). As such this monograph is as important for up-and-coming students of functional linguistics and multimodal discourse analysis as it is for seasoned practitioners in the field. I commend the book to all concerned as a token of the exciting contributions we are now enjoying from the new generation of Chinese scholars entering our field.

Professor James R. Martin

Acknowledgements

First and foremost, I am immensely grateful to Professor Huang Guowen in South China Agricultural University, whose constant support and encouragement have been crucial in guiding me from the very first day of my linguistic journey.

A huge debt of gratitude is also owed to Professor J. R. Martin in The University of Sydney. I am greatly indebted to him for his inspirational guidance and insightful comments on the first draft of the book, which have continuously challenged my thinking and encouraged me to push the boundaries of my work.

My heartfelt gratitude is also due to Professor Fang Zhihui in the University of Florida, who generously shared with me his scholarly insights and expertise on language and literacy education during my visit in the University of Florida.

I have benefited enormously from being part of two brilliant and enthusiastic academic communities in Guangzhou and Sydney. My sincere thanks go to all the members of the Functional Linguistics Institute at Sun Yat-sen University for their generous help. I am equally indebted to my valued colleagues and friends in Sydney for their valuable intellectual support.

Special thanks go to the series editors Dr David Caldwell in the University of South Australia and Dr John Knox in Macquarie University, whose critical and practical advice made the publication of the book possible.

I would also like to acknowledge the original appearance of part of my research reported in this book in the academic journals including *Visual Communication, Linguistics and Education, Foreign Language Education, Journal of World Languages* and the edited volume *Appliable Linguistics*. The encouraging feedback from the reviewers and editorial boards has given me the confidence to pursue this study. I am also thankful for the fund from the 'the Fundamental Research Funds for the Central Universities, Sun Yat-sen University' for the support for the current research.

1

Introduction

1.1 Multimodality and semiotics

Multiple representational and communicative modes are commonplace in our everyday communication. Evidence can be found by looking into the evolution of human language as well as the reality of information transmission and distribution in the modern world. Human beings are believed to have had pictographic representation and communication long before the emergence of the earliest scripts such as the cuneiform script of the Sumerians in Mesopotamia around 3500 BC (Diringer 1968; Gelb 1963; Ong 1982: 83). While most of the ancient scripts, including Mesopotamian cuneiforms, Egyptian hieroglyphics, Mayan scripts in Mesoamerica and Chinese characters, have been developed independently of each other (Ong 1982: 85), each of these writing systems are considered to have pictographic origins (Coulmas 2003: 192–7). As Coulmas (2003: 209) comments, 'the development of writing systems must be explained in terms of how visual signs are interpreted.' Along with its manifestation in writing systems, the 'inherent multimodality of language' (Matthiessen 2007: 4) is also revealed in oral communication, as shown through 'body language' (e.g. gestures and facial expressions) and 'paralanguage' (e.g. vocal features) (Matthiessen 2007: 6). Linguistic multimodality has also been investigated in research on the protolanguage of children (see Halliday 1975; Painter 1984).

Language evolution and individual language development reveals that human language has an intrinsic potential for multimodality. This orientation to multimodality in human communication has been further enhanced through the advances in modern digital and multimedia technology. Contemporary layout design and printing techniques allow pages to be produced as combinations of language, images and diagrams, with a great variety of choices in typeface, font and coloration. Moreover, the wide application of computer-enabled tools and the proliferation of web-based resources further promote the phenomenon of multimodality to an unprecedented level.

This increasingly multimodal reality has been one of the central topics for linguistically informed discourse analysis over the past two decades (Baldry and Thibault 2006; Bateman 2008, 2017; Kress and van Leeuwen 2001, 2006, 2020; Lemke 1998a, 2000, 2012; Martin 2001, 2008a; Martin and Rose 2008; Norris and Jones 2005; O'Halloran 2005; O'Halloran et al. 2016; O'Toole 1994; Scollon 2001; Scollon and Scollon 2004; Unsworth 2001, 2008, 2017). There is a growing consensus that the messages drawing on more than one semiotic resource do more than language alone can do, and 'are assuming their central role in information dissemination in the modern world' (Bateman 2008: 2; see also Thibault 2001: 294). As Kress (2000: 337) states, 'it is now no longer possible to understand language and its uses without understanding the effect of all modes of communication that are copresent in any text'.

Before the current discussion proceeds, the term 'multimodality' requires brief clarification. The use of 'multimodality' here refers to the diverse ways in which a number of semiotic systems (i.e. linguistic, visual, audio, spatial, gestural) 'are both co-deployed and co-contextualized in the making of a text-specific meaning' (Thibault 2000: 312), or 'the combination of different semiotic modes . . . in a communicative artefact or event' (van Leeuwen 2005: 281). There is increasing awareness that the examination of meanings in multimodal discourse[1] should focus on the interaction or 'the simultaneous orchestration' (Bateman 2008: 1) among different semiotic modes (Baldry and Thibault 2006; Lemke 1998a; Martin 2008a; Norris 2004). Detailed discussion and review of the major approaches to multimodality will be provided in Chapter 2.

Among the different communicative contexts in which multiple modes are co-deployed, multimodal pedagogic practices have claimed scholarly attention from educators and researchers. More and more communication in pedagogic context takes place through the interplay of various semiotic resources rather than by relying on a single semiotic mode in isolation (Jewitt 2002; Kress et al. 2001; Lemke 1998b). These developments have been discussed under the titles of 'visual literacy' (Dondis 1972; Messaris and Moriarty 2005; Seppänen 2006) and 'multiliteracies' (Cope and Kalantzis 2000; New London Group 1996; Kalantzis and Cope 2001; see Section 2.2.2 of Chapter 2 for an overview).

In order to systematically describe and explain the multimodal resources in a given pedagogic context, the current research draws on the theoretical framework of semiotics informed by linguistic theory. To be specific, it is social semiotics (Halliday 1978; Hodge and Kress 1988; Kress and van Leeuwen 2006, 2020; van Leeuwen 2005) that this study is aligned with.

There has long been a tradition of scholarship of applying semiotic theory to the study of signs. The concept of 'semiotics' originates from the terms 'semainon' and 'semainomenon' used by the Stoic philosophers in ancient Greek linguistics, which mean 'signifier' and 'signified' respectively (Halliday 1985: 3; emphasis in the original). These ideas were further developed by the Swiss-French linguist Ferdinand de Saussure 2,000 years later, for whom semiotics is the study of 'the role of signs as part of social life' (de Saussure 1916 [1983]: 15). There have been two main traditions in semiotics, that is structuralism including the Eastern European tradition and the Paris school, as well as a more philosophical approach developed by the American philosopher Charles Sanders Peirce that extends the reasoning and logic in natural sciences to semiotics (Stenglin 2004: 25–33). Semioticians in both traditions have investigated multimodality in multiple aspects, covering photography (Barthes 1981), theatre (Bogatyrev 1938; Honzl 1940), cinema (Metz 1974), film (Mukarovsky 1978), fashion (Barthes 1985) and architecture (Broadbent 1977; Eco 1972; Jencks 1984).

In the history of semiotic studies, however, the conception of sign has tended to be viewed as 'isolate, as a thing in itself' (Halliday 1985: 3). In examining the artefacts that involve more than one semiotic system, we need to comprehend not only the ways in which the componential elements are pieced together but also what the arrangements or combinations mean in a given communicative context. To facilitate this understanding, a social theory of semiotics is needed to empower analysts to grasp the meaning of semiotic choices in relation to the context in which semiotic configurations are embedded. Moreover, this semiotic theory needs to be able to offer 'something like a grammar', which as Nodelman (1988: x) suggests might enable us to better understand images in picture books. The social semiotics developed by M. A. K. Halliday (1978) and his colleagues, which is strongly associated with the linguistic theory known as Systemic Functional Linguistics (henceforth SFL), provides such a robust tool for analysing multimodal texts. As Eggins (2004: 21) states, 'what is distinctive to systemic linguistics is that it seeks to develop both a theory about language as social process *and* an analytical methodology which permits the detailed and systematic description of language patterns' (emphasis in the original). This functional-semantic orientation of SFL affords semioticians a vantage point from which a systematic discussion of contextual demands is made feasible, and a detailed linguistic and semiotic analysis is enabled (see Chapter 3 for further explanation). Drawing upon the Systemic Functional approach, the current research explores the semiotic configurations of meaning in multimodal textbook discourse.

1.2 The interpersonal aspect of EFL pedagogic context

As compared with the growing body of work carried out in Western educational settings, a limited amount of multimodality research has been conducted within the context of teaching English as a foreign language (henceforth EFL) in China. Acknowledging the evolving multimodal teaching and learning environment in the present-day educational context in China, the current research examines the multimodal features of EFL textbook discourse, and will suggest ways in which discourse analysis may help textbook editors and users better understand and interpret how meanings are construed through the co-deployment of linguistic and visual meaning-making resources.

The teaching and learning environment in China has become increasingly multimodal (Fu 2005; Zhang 2009, 2010, 2018). A close reading of multimodal pedagogic materials that takes into account multiple semiotic systems will enable deeper understanding of how semiotic resources may 'multiply' (Lemke 1998a) meaning potential, which may in turn have implications for designing and utilizing pedagogic materials.

It is argued that EFL textbooks for primary and secondary education are far less investigated than textbooks for other school subjects (Zhang 2005: 11–12). Given the common adoption of textbooks as one of the essential teaching and learning resources for primary and secondary schooling, this study explores different dimensions of interpersonal meaning realized by linguistic and visual meaning-making resources in EFL textbooks.

The choice of focus on interpersonal management among other possible aspects is based on one recent influential development in curriculum standards. As stipulated by Ministry of Education, curriculum standards provide guiding principles for the editing and compiling of pedagogic materials for every school subject. The eighth curriculum reform in 2001 is recognized as 'an important milestone in our country's curriculum development history' (Zhong 2006: 373), one reason for which is the unprecedented highlight of the attitudinal goal for developing students' positive emotions in the corresponding curriculum standards for all school subjects (Zhu 2006: 193). This 'emotion and attitude' goal is clearly articulated as one of the essential five aspects of the overall goal in EFL education (see Section 2.3.3 in the following chapter for a detailed discussion). Nevertheless, the relative lack of research on how this emotion and attitude dimension is incorporated in primary and secondary textbooks has been identified as another drawback in textbook studies in China (Zhang 2005: 11). Language teaching and learning, among many other subject areas, is acknowledged as 'far more closely related to emotion and attitude education than other school subjects' (Cheng 2002: 32). By investigating both the verbal component and the visual medium in EFL textbook discourse, this book shows how the attitudinal concerns are realized through the visual as well as linguistic semiotic choices.

In addition to the emotion and attitude dimension emphasized in the curriculum standards, two other aspects in interpersonal management call for further exploration. In the given pedagogic context, dialogic processes are advocated throughout classroom teaching, and textbooks are considered to be an essential component in this process (Chen and Ye 2006; Zhong 2006). Multimodal modes of communication may further enable diversity in editor-reader alignment. Nonetheless, the way multimodal resources can be manipulated to mediate the heteroglossic space in textbook discourse remains under-researched. Still another aspect that demands attention is the fact that certain visual choices in EFL textbook discourse are constrained by the perceived needs of the readers. The extent to which these visual treatments are appropriate in the given pedagogic context is yet to be fully examined. Knowledge structure and the nature of pedagogic discourse (Bernstein 1990, 2000) needs to be considered when assessing visual design in pedagogic materials.

The aforementioned three aspects of interpersonal meaning (i.e. editor-reader alignment, attitudinal dimension and visual design in relation to contextual factors) constitute the major pedagogic concerns of this book. Further explanation of the interpersonal management in the given EFL education context is provided in Chapter 2. It is hoped that by seeing more clearly how linguistic and visual semiotic choices work in tandem to construe the dialogic setting, to hint at the intended evaluative stance, and to respond to the discerned readers' needs, we may arrive at a better understanding of the functions fulfilled by linguistic and visual semiotic resources in pedagogic context.

1.3 Data and methodology

The data examined in this book comprises eighteen mandatory EFL textbooks for primary education, junior and senior secondary education, edited and published by People's Education Press (henceforth PEP) between 2002 and 2006, which include an entire series of the edition after the eighth curriculum reform. Altogether 118 teaching units are involved (i.e. 47 in the primary textbooks, 46 in the junior secondary ones and 25 in the senior secondary textbooks). All teaching units contain images as well as verbal texts, ranging from those multimodal texts with a relatively small amount of verbiage for primary schooling through to those with a greater proportion of verbiage for secondary education. Some statistical summaries show that 1,398 images of different styles (see Table 5.1 in Chapter 5) are employed in the EFL textbooks under discussion. The large number of images involved in the textbooks indicates a pressing need to grasp the meanings encoded in the multimodal texts for pedagogic context. EFL textbook discourse can be viewed as a typical configuration of semiotic choices from both linguistic and visual semiotic systems. However, EFL textbooks for primary and secondary education are yet to be fully examined at the micro, discursive level (Zhang 2005: 11–12), and far less understanding has been achieved in terms of the semiotic description of their multimodal nature.

Working towards an in-depth discursive account of EFL pedagogic materials, the research reported in this book is descriptive and qualitative in nature, though some statistical treatments will be employed to describe the status quo of the data as faithfully as possible. Owing to the limited amount of research on multimodal EFL textbooks in China, this study is exploratory in orientation. The major theoretical rationale informing the current research is SFL, and a Systemic Functional semiotic view is adopted when examining multimodal excerpts from EFL textbooks. The analysis will cover both interactive and personal dimensions of interpersonal meaning, encompassing three sub-studies that deal with engagement, attitude and modality respectively. The overall objective and specific research questions are provided in the ensuing section.

1.4 Aims and research questions of this study

The focus of this book is on the interpersonal meaning in EFL textbook discourse. The research findings will give rise to insights into both the interactive aspect like editor-reader alignment and the personal dimension such as the construal of evaluation. The research questions to be addressed in this book are as follows:

1. Reader-writer alignment and the graded engagement meanings: (1) How are linguistic and visual meaning-making resources deployed to mediate the heteroglossic space in the multi-voiced EFL textbook discourse?

(2) To what degree can the alignment of voices be graded by utilizing multimodal resources?
2. Attitudinal construction and intermodal relations: (1) How is the attitudinal stance in multimodal EFL textbook discourse construed through linguistic and visual semiotic resources? (2) What kinds of verbiage-image relations are there in the intermodal construal of attitudinal meanings?
3. Modality and pedagogical implications: (1) In what way are multimodal messages presented as real in the EFL textbooks targeting different groups readers? How is it conditioned by and construing the pedagogic context?

As implicated in the research questions, this study is intended to shed light on both theoretical and pedagogic issues. A close linguistic and semiotic analysis of EFL textbook discourse may facilitate the understanding of as well as provide solid evidence for some attention-engaging concerns like dialogic process and emotion and attitude goal in the given pedagogic context. An interrogation of the theoretical assumptions on which the current research is based will enrich the linguistic and semiotic studies of interpersonal meaning in multimodal discourse that involves more than one semiotic system.

1.5 Theoretical framework

As indicated earlier, the theoretical framework underpinning this study is SFL (Halliday 1994; Halliday and Matthiessen 1999, 2004; Martin 1992), specifically the APPRAISAL[2] system (Martin 1997, 2000a; Martin and White 2005) for modelling interpersonal semantics. A Systemic Functional semiotic approach (Hodge and Kress 1988; Kress and van Leeuwen 2006, 2020; van Leeuwen 2005) is drawn upon to analyse visual meaning-making resources. Two fundamental features of SFL, among many others, are used here to explore semiotic choices in EFL textbook discourse. In the first instance, SFL considers language as a social semiotic and defines 'a culture as a set of semiotic systems, as sets of systems of meaning, all of which interrelate' (Halliday 1985: 4). In other words, language together with other systems of meaning (e.g. visual, audio, gestural) constitute the human culture. Second, in SFL, language is theorized as conditioned by as well as construing social context. Meaning is construed in the immediate context of situation and the wider context of culture (Huang 2003; Huang and Ghadessy 2006). Recent advances in Systemic Functional semiotic theory recognize that the same meanings may often be encoded in different semiotic modes and common semiotic principles can operate in and across different modes (Kress and van Leeuwen 2001: 1–2). The functional-semantic orientation of SFL enables us to explore how semiotic systems within EFL textbooks both reflect and construct the language teaching and learning environment in which the textbook discourse is embedded.

In SFL, interpersonal meaning is one of the three metafunctions simultaneously construed whenever language is used. Situated within the broader model of SFL, the APPRAISAL system offers a functional model of interpersonal meaning at the level of discourse semantics, which may address the analysis demand arising from some current pedagogic concerns, including editor-reader alignment and construal of evaluative stance. The sub-systems and options within APPRAISAL are semantic categories, and as such the realizations of these categories may transcend monomodal verbal communication to include multimodal meaning-making resources. Together with Systemic Functional semiotic approach to images, the APPRAISAL network has the potential to bring together verbal and visual choices that might sometimes be omitted when considering values and voices in a text.

In addition to the application of linguistic and semiotic theory, the current research also aims to make a contribution to the functional theory it draws upon. The investigation into the resources realizing ENGAGEMENT, GRADUATION and ATTITUDE meanings in a multimodal context will lead to an expansion of the theoretical network of APPRAISAL. In addition, the degree of 'commitment' (Martin 2008b) and the ways in which choices from different systems may be 'coupled' (Martin 2008b) with one another in multimodal texts will also be considered. A detailed explanation of the theoretical foundations will be provided in Chapter 3, and further elaboration will be presented as the analyses unfold in Chapters 4 to 6.

1.6 Structure of the book

This book is divided into seven chapters. This introductory chapter has outlined the research background, design and objectives. Chapter 2 further clarifies the concepts of multimodality and multiliteracies, reviewing the existing body of work in the research area. Relevant textbook studies and major themes in *Curriculum Standards for English* in present-day China are outlined, with research gaps identified and the focus of this study framed. Chapter 3 introduces the theoretical rationale of SFL drawn upon in the ensuing analyses, particularly the semantic system of APPRAISAL and the Systemic Functional semiotic approach to visual analysis. The latter part of the chapter provides the theoretical justifications for the analyses to be conducted and serves as a transition to the three sub-studies in the subsequent chapters.

Detailed analyses and discussions of the different aspects of interpersonal meaning in EFL textbook discourse begin in Chapter 4 and continue through Chapter 6. Chapter 4 is devoted to the interactive dimension of interpersonal management, examining how linguistic and visual semiotic resources can be deployed to align the ideal reader with the propositions and values advanced in a text. Attempts will be made to explore and extend the semantic systems of ENGAGEMENT and GRADUATION by uncovering a range of ENGAGEMENT devices in multimodal communicative context, with a detailed description of the ways in which these multimodal resources mediate the heteroglossic space in EFL textbook discourse. The interplay between editor voice, reader voice and character voice will also be considered with reference to contact, social distance and point of view. Chapter 5 focuses on the intermodal construal of evaluative stance, investigating the ways in which verbiage and image either complement or co-articulate with each other in establishing the attitudinal orientation for different levels of education. A diversity of visual styles, ranging from cartoon to portrait and photograph, are investigated along with the corresponding verbal texts. With regard to the 'emotion and attitude' goal in curriculum standards, an ontogenetic view will be developed to discuss the attitudinal shift happening as students advance through the school years from primary to secondary education. Chapter 6 examines the concept of modality in multimodal discourse, which is concerned with how true a given representation is supposed to be taken. Multimodal texts from primary, junior and senior secondary textbooks will be compared, in order to provide an insight into the interdependent relationship between coding orientation and social solidarity. In relation to the educational theory on pedagogic discourse and nature of knowledge, a critical view on visual style in pedagogic context will be offered. The phenomenon of various visual styles adopted within a macrogenre[3] leads to a discussion of the influence of field on visual treatments.

Chapter 7 summarizes the major findings of the research and its contributions to both linguistic studies and pedagogic agenda. Suggestions for future research will also be indicated in the final section of the concluding chapter.

2

Research background
Multimodality, multiliteracies and EFL education in China

2.1 Introduction

This chapter focuses on both the linguistic and pedagogic landscape in which this study is positioned, aiming to offer a better understanding of the research background. The concepts of multimodality and multiliteracies will first be defined. Major literature representing different approaches to multimodality will be reviewed in detail and research gaps identified. Following the brief introduction of other approaches to multiliteracies research, a general account of the present-day scenario of multimodality research and textbook studies in China mainland will be provided, whose limitations partially explain the necessity of this study. The curriculum standards that exert influence on EFL textbook editing will then be discussed, with a particular focus on the interpersonal dimension.

2.2 Multimodality and multiliteracies

With the progress in modern communications technology, people's interaction and exchange inevitably draw upon channels and means that involve more than a single semiotic mode, and hence the notion of 'multimodality' emerges to cover the correlated changes in discourse studies. One of the theoretical advances conceptualizes multimodality as 'the combination of different semiotic modes ... in a communicative artefact or event' (van Leeuwen 2005: 281). The educational setting, which is the central concern of the current research, is one of the major contexts in which multimodal communication occurs. The influence of multimodality on pedagogic practices has captured scholarly attention.

2.2.1 Multimodality in education

In the exploration of multimodal discourse in relation to modern technology of printing, computing and multimedia, two influential trends are recognized. One of them takes a mediated discourse perspective, while the other draws on linguistic and social-semiotic theory. This section outlines the principles of the two approaches, with focus placed on their respective studies in educational contexts.

2.2.1.1 Mediated discourse analysis

Scholars in the field of mediated discourse analysis (Norris and Jones 2005; Scollon 2001; Scollon 2013) 'use discourse analysis to engage in social action' (Scollon and Scollon 2004: 7). The primary concern of mediated discourse analysis is not discourse per se but social action. This approach is often termed as 'nexus analysis', which is 'a form of ethnography that takes social action as the theoretical center of study' (Scollon and Scollon 2004: 13).

Setting out with an ethnographic position, mediated discourse analysts call for disciplinary diversity in studying social actions and believe that broader sociopolitical-cultural analysis can be grasped through micro-analysis of unfolding moments of social actions (Scollon and Scollon 2004: 8). As pointed out by Norris and Jones (2005: 9), mediated discourse analysis approaches the question of how discourse is a matter of social action through the action rather than through the discourse. In other words, it expresses the concern with social action before discourse and examines the role of discourse in action only after figuring out what the action is.

Mediated discourse analysts aim to understand and solve social problems by bringing together principles from diverse disciplines including ethnomethodology, conversation analysis, linguistic anthropology, psychology and sociolinguistics. Researchers in this field have covered topics including AIDS prevention (Jones 1999, 2002), immigrant's adaptation (Johnson 2002; Castillo-Ayometzi 2007), national identity (de Saint Georges and Norris 1999), news discourse (Scollon 1998), gender equality (Norris 2005), public policies (Scollon 2008), learning of traditional music (Jocuns 2009) and workplace practices (de Saint Georges 2014).

When it comes to the educational settings, mediated discourse analysts investigate the literacy technology that covers both traditional print literacy and the use of online communication (Scollon 2001: 10). Scollon and Scollon (2004), for instance, analyse the social actions of teachers and students involved in two university classes. The comparison of the traditional, face-to-face classroom teaching and the one mediated by technological means of email and audio conferencing illustrates the way in which technology as a mediational means redistributes the interaction order. Lewis et al. (2007) take the critical sociocultural perspective and mediated approach to investigate the issues of identity and power in literacy. Mosley (2010) and Rogers (2011) use the mediated discourse analysis to reconstruct the power relations in teacher education and graduate classes. Wohlwend (2009, 2014) and Wohlwend and Handsfield (2012) examine the mediated actions and non-verbal interactions in early childhood learning, including their handling of toys, literacy materials and digital technologies. Regarding writing as involving distributed, mediated and dialogic processes of invention, Rish (2015) deploys mediated analysis to investigate how three high school students wrote together for a collaborative project.

As for the methodological principles, mediated discourse analysis analyses discourse 'through a focus on social actions rather than language use' (Rish 2017: 476). By approaching discourse through actions, it shifts 'our attention away from discourse, and on to the actions people use discourse to take' (Jones 2014: 39). As Scollon and Scollon (2004: 9–13) articulate, nexus analysis could be interpreted as 'an extended study of action(s) undertaken by people in the course of living their lives' and stress the importance for an analyst 'to be identified within the nexus of practice under study'. Mediated discourse analysts treat nexus analysis as 'a set of heuristic tools' with which analysts can bring in various data collection and analytical tools as long as they are considered useful in dealing with social actions (Norris and Jones 2005: 201). In other words, what is relevant to mediated discourse analysts tends to be the action rather than the linguistic or semiotic features involved.

2.2.1.2 *Social-semiotic analysis*

Another approach that investigates multimodal meaning-making resources derives from Systemic Functional Linguistics and social-semiotic theory (Halliday 1973, 1978, 1994; Halliday and Matthiessen 2004; Hodge and Kress 1988; van Leeuwen 2005). The significance of research on multimodality has long been recognized by linguists and social semioticians. As pointed out by Hodge and Kress (1988: vii–viii), meaning resides so strongly and pervasively in semiotic systems other than language that a concentration solely on verbiage is insufficient. From the perspective of social semiotics, the order of the world 'is expressed semiotically through choices from a variety of sign systems including language, images, music, gesture, and three-dimensional objects' (O'Halloran 2005: 6). Beginning with the discussion of the grammar of images (Kress and van Leeuwen 2001, 2002, 2020; O'Toole 1990, 1994), linguists and social semioticians' exploration of the semiotic choices in multimodal texts has been extended to cover other semiotic systems such as sound and music (van Leeuwen 1999; Caldwell 2014), action (Martinec 1998, 2000), body language (Hood 2011; Hao and Hood 2018), spatial design and architecture (Martin and Stenglin 2007; Ravelli 2006; Ravelli and McMurtrie 2016; Stenglin 2004; O'Toole 2004), electronic media and film (Baldry 2004; Baldry and Thibault 2006; Bateman and Tseng 2013; Bateman et al. 2016; Thibault 2000; Tseng 2016, 2018; Zammit and Callow 1999), digital touch communication, Twitter and selfie (Jewitt, Xambó and Price 2016; Jewitt and Kerstin 2018; Zappavigna 2012; Zhao and Zappavigna 2017), online news galleries (Caple and Knox 2017) and software and PowerPoint (Djonov and van Leeuwen 2018; Zhao et al. 2014). Kress and van Leeuwen's analytical framework for images (2006, 2020) will be accounted for in detail in the ensuing chapter. The current review will focus on the foundational and recent research on multimodality conducted by systemicists and social semioticians, with particular focus on those studies concerning educational contexts.

When reflecting on the action research that has been carried out by the Sydney School[1] since the early 1980s, Martin (2000b) points out that the new millennium witnesses the fifth phase of the research in the context of education and workplace, which is characterized as multiliteracies. The SFL contributions to the study of multimodal teaching and learning resources cover various semiotic modes of communication ranging from print and electronic media to classroom interaction, and across a range of discipline areas. Given the pedagogical focus of this book, the following review mainly considers those seminal texts related to educational practices.

(i) Printed texts: There have been substantial studies on multimodal printed texts in educational contexts. The topics covered encompass modern science discourse (Lemke 1998a), mathematical discourse (O'Halloran 2005), multimodal documents (Bateman 2008), English-language learning texts (Weninger and Kiss 2013; Unsworth 2017), physics (Doran 2018, 2019) and the relations between different genres (Martin and Rose 2008). Lemke (1998a), for example, studied the meanings from the interaction between different semiotic systems in modern scientific texts. For Lemke, the metafunctional diversifications of presentational, orientational and organizational meanings provide the possibility of analysing co-existing semiotic systems (language, figures, tables, images, etc.) in scientific texts. These semiotic systems are incommensurable in the sense that the meaning constructed by one semiotic modality (e.g. image) cannot be constructed in exactly the same way by another semiotic modality (e.g. verbal text). He further points out that the interaction between different semiotic resources gives rise to a 'multiplying' effect (Lemke 1998a: 92). Mathematical discourse, as pointed out by O'Halloran (1999a, 2005), is multisemiotic in the sense that the three semiotic resources involved in mathematical discourse (i.e. mathematical symbolism, visual display and language) are functional sign systems that differentially construct reality. O'Halloran proposes a systemic framework to describe the meaning potential (i.e. experiential, logical, interpersonal and textual meanings) of mathematical symbolism and the role of visualization in mathematics. When examining the intersemiosis between various semiotic modes, O'Halloran introduces the notion of 'semiotic metaphor' to capture the phenomenon where an intersemiotic transition leads to a metaphorical expansion of meaning.

Bateman (2008) provides an empirical framework (i.e. the GeM model) for investigating the mechanisms of the multimodal interaction and multiplication of meanings in multimodal documents with texts, images and diagrams. This corpus-based model, with specification of the descriptive layers, is intended to support hypothesis building and analysis, and to construct multimodal document corpora. The primary layers in the GeM model that include content structure, genre structure, rhetorical structure, linguistic structure, layout structure and navigation structure (Bateman 2008: 19) enable the layered decomposition of a multimodal document for corpus annotation.

As for the studies on the multimodal texts for learning English, Unsworth (2017) investigates the image-language interaction in the comprehension of multimodal texts in Australia. He demonstrates the significance of multimodal reading comprehension in enabling the completion of national and international reading assessment, facilitating reading effectiveness and supporting new pedagogies of multiliteracies. In exploring the visual narratives in contemporary children's picture books, Painter et al. (2013) explicate the visual construction of narrative plots and characters, the visual choices of focalization and appraisal in positioning the reader, and the visual framing and composition. It further extends social-semiotic studies by concentrating on discursive level meaning and semantic relations of sequences of images, thus enhancing the literacy demands and apprenticing techniques of children's literature. Drawing on Unsworth's (2013) work on multimodal literacy pedagogy, Macken-Horarik et al. (2017) propose the functional grammatics which include the grammatical tools for teachers of English to better understand and interpret visual and multimodal literacies in the narrative and persuasive texts of school English. Weninger and Kiss (2013) propose a semiotic framework to examine texts, images and tasks in representing culture in EFL textbooks. Through excerpts from two EFL textbooks written by and for Hungarians, the authors show that learners' meaning making in the classroom tends to be heavily guided, and images and texts should be explicitly manipulated to develop a more critical understanding of culture.

Drawing on Legitimation Code Theory (Maton 2014) and Systemic Functional Linguistics (Halliday and Matthiessen 2014; Martin 2011), Doran (2018, 2019) investigates the multimodal features of the discourse of physics, examining the semiotic resources of language, image and mathematics. It explores the principles of how knowledge in physics is developed and valued, revealing that images play an important role in the development of technical physics knowledge through abstractions.

When it comes to the studies on images in science, Martin and Rose (2008: 167–77) show that the ideational meaning construed in technical images can be systematically investigated along the axes of phenomenon focus, category and representation. When relating this social-semiotic exploration to the socioeconomic structure in modern industrial society, Martin and Rose (2008: 224–6) point out that the written scientific discourse becomes more remote from the construal of everyday experience in spoken discourse along the industrial ladder and education sequence, and the unequal acquisition of the genres may exert great influence on the social structure as well as occupational options.

(ii) Electronic and digital media: With the advances in computer and multimedia technologies, new kinds of literacy practices – computer-based or digital literacies – have emerged. As Unsworth (2001: 12) puts it, multimodality is not an exclusive feature of electronic texts, but the range of modalities, the extent of their use and the nature and quality of their articulation have significantly increased in electronic formats. Baldry (2000) argues for an awareness of the multimodal organization of scientific texts in EAP/ESP classroom by developing a historical and comparative view on both static (i.e. printed media) and dynamic (i.e. film and computer media) multimodal texts. He describes the changes happening in the organization of the printed scientific page in biological science and economics over a hundred years of development, and explores the evolution of dynamic multimodal texts such as lectures and film media in medical science. In addition, he points out the necessity of specialized software tools (e.g. online multimodal corpus) in the development of multimodal syllabuses for EAP/ESP classroom.

Jewitt (2002) investigates the transformation of a novel to CD-ROM in school English, with emphasis on the multimodal reshaping of the entity 'character' in the shift of representational modes. Specifically, she examines the way in which multimodal resources of the CD-ROM provide students with different possibilities for engaging themselves with specific characters in the novel. It is found that character is presented as a fluid entity rather than a stable one, thus requiring students to read in a wider social-historical context beyond the text. Also placing the focus on CD-ROMs in educational setting, Zammit and Callow (1999) examine the reading of multimedia CD-ROMs through the analysis of two screens from factual programmes. They describe how users may be influenced by the programme design and need to shift their reading positions when moving between different texts on the screen. Through the comparison between the ways in which the two CD-ROM programmes construct information, Zammit and Callow argue for explicit, critical reading skills for multimedia texts, which may enhance students' interaction with CD-ROM programmes.

Addressing the issue of children's multimedia digital literacy involving internet, electronic game narratives and CD-ROM, Unsworth (2005) demonstrates the way in which digital technology enhances children's literary experience, offering practical suggestions to teachers on planning programmes with e-literature. Furthermore, Unsworth puts forward the interpretive, organizational and pedagogic frameworks to enable practising teachers to effectively manage classroom literacy programmes with digital resources. To be specific, the interpretive framework describes the integrative role of language and images in computer-based texts and printed books, while the organizational framework introduces the electronically re-contextualized articulation in e-literary texts. Along with the explication of different facets of children's e-literature, Unsworth also provides concrete examples of e-literary classroom programmes targeting children at different levels of primary schooling. Unsworth and Thomas (2014) showcase a range of studies on the integration of multimedia narratives into English teaching. The digital and multimedia resources under consideration include animated films, digital novels and virtual treatment of masterpieces. It offers teachers and students practical advice on the pedagogy of new literacies and authority of digital multimedia narratives.

As for digital literacy activities, Lim and Toh (2020) investigate children's out-of-school digital multimodal composing practices. By examining the YouTube video productions of three children, they show that that children's digital multimodal composing practices demonstrate creativity, critical thinking and a semiotic awareness. Mills et al. (2020) analyse how elementary school students use semiotic resources to communicate attitude multimodally in their digital composition. By adapting the APPRAISAL system to the multimodal communication of attitude in digital comic making in schooling, they demonstrate the potentials for augmenting students' linguistic and visual semiotic resources to convey multimodal attitudinal meanings. By integrating translanguaging and social semiotics frameworks, Smith et al. (2017) examine how three bilingual eighth grade students composed across multiple languages and modes (e.g. text, images, sound and movement) when creating a digital project that includes screen capture, video observations, student design interviews and multimodal products. It is found that students' 'codemeshing process' involves simultaneous iterative motion across modes, phases of the process and sections of their projects, which has exhibited a range of textually driven and visually driven processes for creating content and followed unique compositional paths.

(iii) Classroom practices: As pointed out by Jewitt (2017), the investigation of multimodal discourses across the classroom could enhance teachers and students' understanding of the relationship between semiotic resources deployed in classroom practices, and also shed light on the production of curriculum knowledge, student subjectivity and pedagogy. Science classrooms have gained much scholarly attention in social semiotics. Through the close observation of a student's multiliteracy practices in advanced chemistry and physics classes involving videotapes, student notes, teacher handouts, overhead transparencies and textbook selections, Lemke (2000) demonstrates the multiliteracy competence that students need to develop to integrate and coordinate the specialized verbal, visual and mathematical literacies. The multimedia literacy demands of scientific genres, as the study shows, also exert influence on curriculum design, pedagogy, assessment and research.

In the sphere of mathematics education, O'Halloran (2000) examines the multisemiotic nature of mathematics on classroom discourse from an SFL perspective, with the purpose of understanding the difficulties in mathematics teaching and learning. It is shown that the three semiotic resources involved in mathematical discourse – mathematical symbolism, visual display and language – have their own unique lexicogrammatical systems for encoding meanings, and these three types of resources interact with each other to shape the construction of the pedagogical discourse in classroom practices. Particularly in the case of mathematical symbolism, meaning is encoded 'unambiguously in the most economical manner possible' through the use of specific grammatical strategies such as multiple levels of rankshifted configurations of 'mathematical Operative processes and participants'. The reconfigurations of symbolic Operative processes and participants in oral discourse in mathematics classroom are also examined. O'Halloran's research also indicates that the dense texture of mathematics pedagogical discourse derives from the inclusion of the symbolic constructions in the linguistic metadiscourse, and 'semiotic metaphor' is helpful in explaining how shifts in meaning of functional element occur and how new entities are introduced with movements between semiotic codes.

Kress et al.'s (2001) research in science classrooms challenges the traditional view on language's central or dominant role in teaching and learning. It is argued that other modes of communication such as image, gesture, spatial and bodily codes also contribute to the multimodal ways of meaning-making and knowledge construction. Students' action in the science classroom is regarded as the active engagement with all the multimodal modes of communication, and all participants in communication are viewed as active transformers of the meaning-making resources around them. Overall, the multimodal approach to the science classroom practice offers a way of reconsidering the role of language in the changing reality of contemporary literacy due to multimedia and electronic technology, thus drawing attention to the new demands on the development of students' multiliteracy competence.

Also placing emphasis on 'multimodal communicative competence', Royce (2002) investigates the 'intersemiotic complementarity' (Royce 1998) between images and written language in the TESOL classroom. Through the analysis of a multimodal environmental text at high school level with particular focus on ideational meaning, Royce demonstrates that the visual and verbal semiotic modes complement each other to realize 'an intersemiotically coherent multimodal text' when they co-occur in a text. The intersemiotic resources for realizing this complementarity can serve pedagogical purposes in the activities of the TESOL classroom, namely reading, writing, speaking, listening and vocabulary learning.

As for the research on multimodal classroom practices in different school subjects, Unsworth (2001) suggests developing and teaching multiliteracies in early school years as well as in upper primary and junior secondary schooling. He outlines the distinctive textual forms and literacy practices of different school subject areas including science and humanities, and explores the verbal and visual meaning-making resources in children's literature. Unsworth draws on sample lesson materials to show how to address the three facets of critical literacy, that is, recognition, reproduction and reflection (Luke 2000), and explores the complementary use of printed and digital resources in primary and secondary schooling. Unsworth further shows that the knowledge dimension, pedagogic dimension and multiliteracies dimension of classroom learning contexts are significant in dealing with the practicalities of implementing multiliteracies in learning and teaching, which provides implications for literacy educators in the design and implementation of literate activities.

Fernández-Fontecha et al. (2020) investigate how multimodal scaffolding techniques, especially the semiotic features of visual thinking, could be a useful tool for mediating content and language integrated learning (CLIL) in the science classroom. It proposes some strategies to promote the acquisition of scientific language and to facilitate the development of content knowledge.

When it comes to the study on the semiotics of gestures and space in classrooms, Lim (2019) examines the relationship between language and gesture used by the teacher in interaction with the students. Extending the concepts developed for language-image relations, he proposes the emergent meaning of 'structured informality', which offers a way to consider how a teacher can design an effective learning experience for their students using multimodal resources.

To summarize, the approach informed by social semiotics (Halliday 1978; Hodge and Kress 1988; van Leeuwen 2005) to the literacy practices interprets 'literacy' in a broad sense as involving meaning-making or semiosis in general (Lemke 2002: 22). This study draws on social semiotics to examine the verbal and visual meaning-making resources in the EFL textbooks in China, whose multimodal nature is far less understood and investigated when compared to their Western counterparts. Following the discussion of the concept of multiliteracies in the following section, the remainder of this chapter will be devoted to multimodality research in China, as well as the textbook studies and the interpersonal dimension of curriculum standards in the given pedagogical context.

2.2.2 Towards an understanding of multiliteracies

Multiple modes of representation and communication as well as diversified cultural and linguistic features are commonplace in modern discourse. It is argued that the traditional language-centred literacy pedagogy needs to be reconsidered so as to provide students with the skills and knowledge needed in the multimodal and multicultural world (New London Group 1996; Cope and Kalantzis 2000; Kalantzis and Cope 2001). Since the mid-1990s when 'multiliteracies' was proposed, substantial studies have been carried out from the perspective of cultural and linguistic diversity as well as multimediated literacy.

As the New London Group[2] (1996) observe, in contemporary society, dramatic changes are taking place in people's working lives, public lives as citizens and private lives as community members. The productive diversity calls for a new literacy pedagogy that accounts for the cross-cultural communication and negotiation across linguistic and cultural differences, so as to prepare students for the new forms of working life. Due to the local diversity and global connectedness, variations in register, hybrid cross-cultural discourses and multisemiotic meanings have become important skills that students need to master.

In response to the increasingly divergent lifeworlds mentioned earlier, the notion of multiliteracies has been proposed to take cultural differences into account and view language and other modes of meaning as dynamic, constantly remade in the changing contexts (New London Group 1996). Viewing curriculum as 'a design for social futures', the New London Group outline the changing realities that a pedagogy of multiliteracies needs to take into account (see Table 2.1).

One important concept in multiliteracies is 'pedagogy as Design' (capitalization in the original), which holds that literacy educators and students are supposed to consider themselves as active designers of meanings and social futures (Cope and Kalantzis 2000: 19). The foundational work on multiliteracies (New London Group 1996) suggests treating any semiotic activity as a matter of 'Design' and conceptualizes Design as embracing Available Designs (i.e. the grammars of various semiotic systems, orders of discourse and the intertextual context), Designing (i.e. the semiotic activity of production), and the Redesigned (i.e. the transformed meaning-making resources, or a new Available Design). The three elements together stress the fact that meaning-making is an active and dynamic process instead of something governed by static rules.

As the New London Group (1996) state, one objective of the multiliteracies schema is to develop a metalanguage in functional terms to describe meaning in various realms, including the textual, visual and the relationship between different modes. Their emphasis on the metalanguage echoes what has been

Table 2.1 The World That a Pedagogy of Multiliteracies Needs to Address (New London Group 1996)

	Changing realities	Designing social futures
Working lives	Fast capitalism/post-Fordism	Productive diversity
Public lives	Decline of the civic	Civic pluralism
Personal lives	Invasion of private spaces	Multilayered lifeworlds

pointed out in social semiotics – that no single code can be successfully studied or fully understood in isolation, and therefore 'a theory of verbal language has to be seen in the context of a theory of all sign systems as socially constituted, and treated as social practices' (Hodge and Kress 1988: vii–viii). The metalanguage is an educationally accessible functional model of language for supporting a pedagogy of multiliteracies. According to New London Group (1996), the metalanguage of multiliteracies does not describe the elements of Design as rules but is a heuristic process that accounts for the infinite variability of different forms of meaning-making in relation to specific cultures and subcultures. As the New London Group state,

> The primary purpose of the metalanguage should be to identify and explain differences between texts, and relate these to the contexts of culture and situation in which they seem to work. . . . In trying to characterize game and genre, we should start from the social context, the institutional location, the social relations of texts and the social practices within which they are embedded. (New London Group 1996: 77–8)

The emphasis on the strong connection between the meaning-making resources of semiotic systems and their use in social contexts aligns with one of the basic tenets of SFL (Halliday 1978; Halliday and Matthiessen 2014), which accords great significance to the dialectical relationship between linguistic system and the context in which it is embedded (see further explanations in Chapter 3).

The issue of how to put the multiliteracies schema into pedagogy practices has been addressed in the multiliteracies manifesto (New London Group 1996) by describing the four-component pedagogy involving Situated Practice, Overt Instruction, Critical Framing and Transformed Practice (capitalization in the original). As stressed by the New London Group (1996), the four components of multiliteracies pedagogy do not constitute a linear hierarchy or represent stages. Instead, the elements of each component may occur simultaneously while at different times one of these elements may predominate, and all of them are repeatedly revisited at different levels.

Recognizing diversities and differences in contemporary life, the concept of multiliteracies is designed to supplement traditional literacy pedagogy 'by addressing two related aspects of textual multiplicity' (Cope and Kalantzis 2000: 5–6). On the one hand, while traditional practices mainly concentrate on language, the pedagogy of multiliteracies takes into account other channels of communication beyond language. On the other hand, traditional pedagogies usually focus on a singular standard form of language, whereas the multiliteracies pedagogy argues for the necessity of assisting language learners in describing linguistic and cultural diversity.

Further explorations on multiliteracies demonstrate two continuing trends: one is the cultural and linguistic diversity and multiple Englishes, and the other lies in the investigation into the multimodal meaning-making resources (e.g. linguistic, visual, audio, gestural and spatial patterns of meaning) (Kalantzis and Cope 2001: 9). These two trends align with the dual acknowledgement highlighted in the manifesto – namely that multiliteracies research considers not only diversity of cultures and plurality of texts but also the multimodal modes of meaning enabled by modern information and multimedia technologies. The subsequent section will be devoted to the review of multimodal research in China and the pedagogic practices in the current educational context.

2.3 Multimodality research and textbook studies in China

As a new research area in linguistics, multimodality has drawn considerable attention among Chinese scholars in recent decades. At the same time, textbook editing and design are closely related to the curriculum standards for school subjects in the current educational context. This section will review the relevant multimodality research and textbook studies in China.

2.3.1 Development of multimodality research in China

Multimodality research in China includes both the explication of theoretical principles and the analytical practices of multimodal texts in various registers. Li (2003) provides a survey of the analytical framework for analysing images from social semiotics (Kress and van Leeuwen 1996; van Leeuwen and Jewitt 2001). In addition, she also highlights the significance of multimodality research in English teaching, pointing out that it will deepen people's understanding of language as social semiotic. Hu (2007) explores the issue of multimodalization in social semiotics. Based on the distinction between multimodal semiotics and multimedia semiotics, he points out that multimodal semiotics is based on the view that all texts inherently possess the nature of multimodality. Furthermore, Hu investigates some key issues including computer semiotics, semiotic resources as semiotic systems, the replacement of books with screens and the coherence involving discourse participants. With reference to educational context, Hu emphasizes the significance of cultivating students' multiliteracy skills in the era of multimodality. Zhu (2007) points out that the restricted focus on language in discourse analysis has led to the negligence of other ways of meaning-making in actual and natural communication, and this problem can be solved by multimodality research. He explores four important issues in multimodal discourse analysis: namely where it comes from, how it is defined, its theoretical basis and its content, methodology and significance. Further development of multimodality research, as Zhu states, demands cross-disciplinary collaboration, and future research trends in this area include the study on the complementarity between different modes of communication, and the increasing complexity. Zhang (2009) proposes a synthetic theoretical framework for multimodal discourse analysis, which takes into account the context of culture, the context of situation, the semantic level, the level of form and the level of media. Furthermore, Zhang examines the relations between different modalities, including complementary and non-complementary relations. Based on an investigation into the ways in which grammatical structures of different modalities realize ideational, interpersonal and textual meanings, he explores how grammatical categories can be established for the analysis of non-linguistic modalities.

Besides theoretical explorations, multimodal research in China has also covered analytical practices of multimodal texts. Hu (2010) studies the semiotic features of 102 multimodal essays, pointing out that such essays are multimodal compositions of written language, music, image and action. Hu (2011) further demonstrates that the different modes of multimodal essays could be used separately or synchronically. Ding (2007) examines the modality of Western fairy-tale illustrations from a social-semiotic perspective, which shows that the visual modality of the illustrations is a kind of 'surrealist illusionism' characterized by entertaining style, simplified perspectives and colouration, condensation of details, absence of background and some slight anatomical distortions. Drawing on Halliday's (1978: 164) notion of 'antisociety', Ding proposes that through reading fairy-tale illustrations, children are led to an 'anti-world' of their own, which is illusionary and exists symbiotically with the reality. Zeng (2006) investigates the dynamic construal of multimodal semiotics in international academic communication. Based on the identification of the multilayered and overlapping features in the schematic structure of academic communication, Zeng examines the representational function and organizational function (Lemke 1998a) of verbal language, the orientational function of gestures, and the roles of images such as graphs, tables and pictures in academic conference presentations. Her findings indicate that the understanding of multiple semiotic systems is of great importance in learners' successful multimodal communication.

As for the studies on multimodal textbooks, Chen and Wang (2008) examine the text-image relations in Chinese geography textbooks for primary, secondary and university education. Drawing on Martin and Rose's (2008) conception of ideational meaning in technical images and the logical relations between verbiage and image in scientific text, Chen and Wang demonstrate that at the primary level, the 'iconic' colourful cartoons and photographs either specify or repeat the verbal report and explanation; as for the secondary textbook, the iconic images with 'insets' (Unsworth 2005) either specify or restate what is described in the verbiage on entities and activities; and in the undergraduate science textbook, black-and-white 'symbolic' and 'indexical' diagrams are adopted for summarizing what is verbally represented in longer texts. This research calls for educators' as well as students' conscious awareness of the deployment of various semiotic resources in textbook discourse. Continuing this line of semiotic analysis on textbook discourse, this book will investigate how the verbal texts and visual images combined to engage readers, indicate attitudinal stance and realize modality values.

As for the multimodal studies on English-language teaching in China mainland, Zhang (2009, 2010, 2012, 2018) and his colleagues (Zhang and Zhang 2010; Zhang and Li 2012; Zhang and Qu 2015) are the pioneering scholars who investigate multimodal resources in tertiary EFL contexts. Zhang (2009) provides guidance for choosing effective procedures and practices in foreign language teaching (college level) under the condition of modern media technology from three perspectives: new teaching environments, enabling conditions and multi-channels for meaning-making. Furthermore, Zhang (2010) investigates the concept of design in multimodal foreign language teaching and the selection of modes. Based on the study of the major constraining factors, that is the content, the characteristics of the teacher, the students and teaching conditions, he proposes choosing multiple modes based on the general principle of optimal result and three sub-principles of effect, match and economy. In investigating students' ability of multiliteracies, Zhang (2018) examines the affordance, process and outcome of selecting multimodal resources, and further proposes a framework for cultivating students' ability of multiliteracies. In the study of the multiple competences of college students majoring in foreign languages, Zhang (2018) introduces the cultivation models of three types of competences: knowledge competence, discourse practice competence and integrated competence. He also develops a macro and comprehensive teaching mode of multiple competence cultivation for foreign language majors. Zhang and Zhang (2010) explore the compilation principles of multimodal textbooks for foreign language teaching in college. Based on the analysis of the genre of textbooks and the constraining factors such as teaching conditions, they divide the multimodal textbooks into three types: printed, electronic and presentational textbooks. In addition, they elaborate on the macro and micro principles of compiling multimodal textbooks for college English teaching. Zhang and Li (2012) examine the synergy between different modes in foreign language classroom, investigating the relation between the oral mode and PowerPoint. They show that the same mode may have different functions at different stages of classroom teaching, and the choice of mode is largely determined by the teaching objectives at different stages. Zhang and Qu (2015) explore the multimodal translation from college English textbook to classroom teaching by analysing the impacting factors, the changes and effects caused by the multimodal translation in terms of mode, medium and meaning, which provides pedagogic implications for college English teaching in China.

As for the studies on the multimodal textbooks in Hong Kong SAR, Feng (2017) analyses the representation of social values and their ontogenetic development in English textbooks in Hong Kong. His study shows that the social values follow a pattern of development from the personal domain through the interpersonal domain to the altruistic concern for all humankind, indicating that the textbooks are more concerned with the didactic education of good citizens for the harmony of the society than with cultivating children's critical thinking. Guo and Feng (2015) examine the visual construction of knowledge in English textbooks in Hong Kong and develop a social-semiotic framework for infusing English-language curricula with multiliteracies. It demonstrates that the textbook illustrations change from narrative to conceptual representations, from specific to generic participants, and from local to global settings, which is consistent with the change of text type from narrating to expounding. It is also found that the ontogenetic change contributes to the change of knowledge domain from the concrete and commonsensical in early years, to the abstract in later years of schooling.

While scholarly attention has been paid to the multimodal resources in tertiary education in China mainland and early years of schooling in Hong Kong SAR, few studies, however, have addressed the issue of multimodality in EFL pedagogic materials for primary and secondary education in China mainland. The following section will review textbook studies and curriculum reform in China, by way of mapping out the educational landscape in which this study is located.

2.3.2 Other relevant textbook studies in China

Textbooks are considered as symbolizing 'the visible heart of any ELT program' with significant advantages for both students and teachers (Sheldon 1988: 237). Textbooks are one kind of teaching materials, which also include other printed documents such as exercise books, reference books, multimedia and electronic teaching materials. However, textbooks are frequently regarded as the most important teaching tool since they usually determine not only what will be taught but also how it will be taught. Thus, a textbook could sometimes be viewed as a teacher, a map, a resource, a trainer and an authority (Cortazzi and Jin 1999).

Textbook editing has always been an important topic in educational reform in China. For instance, the practices of textbook production for primary and secondary education have gone through three main developmental stages: from a unified compilation stage to a revision and approval stage, and then to the ministry-edited stage. At the first unified compilation stage (from the 1950s to the end of the 1980s), the Ministry of Education promulgated the teaching syllabus and assigned PEP to edit the textbooks. At the second revision and approval stage (from the 1990s to 2017), as textbook compilation meets the curriculum standards, authorized publishers could edit and publish different editions of textbooks. Various editions including the common edition, coastal edition and inland edition have coexisted, which has been referred to as 'one syllabus, multi-edition' (Wang 2000). The ministry-edited stage started in September 2017, and at its initial phase three school subjects (i.e. Chinese, moral education and history) have been edited by the Ministry of Education and published by PEP (Ethnic Education of China, 2017).

Research on textbooks for primary and secondary education in China has been carried out at both macro and micro levels (Zhang 2005: 9–11). Macro-studies include those on the positive and negative aspects of textbooks (Wang 2000; Yang 2002), textbook compilation and selection principles (Xie and Song 2003; Yuan and Chen 2007) and structure and evaluation of textbook (Ding 2001; Kuang 2002). Studies adopting the micro-approach explore the issues of linguistic sexism (Zhang and Yang 2003), illustration (Chen 2006; Chen and Qin 2007; Chen and Zhang 1997; Cui and Ren 2001; Shen and Tao 2001; Tao and Shen 2003; Wang et al. 2006), cultural implications (Wang 2000; Xiao 2004) and the representation of cultural values (Xiong and Peng 2020). In most pedagogic contexts, communication takes place through the complex interplay of a range of modes including language, images and other meaning-making resources (Jewitt

2002; see also Kress et al. 2001; Lemke 2000, 2002). Textbook discourse is no exception, and the role of images in school textbooks has also attracted scholarly attention. In China, the subjects covered in textbook illustration studies by school teachers and textbook reviewers include history (Du 1982; Wang and Lu 2006; Zhang 1993), biology (Cui and Ren 2001; Jiang 1984), physics (Tang 2007; Zhang 2005), chemistry (Wang et al. 2006; Zuo 1986), Chinese (Chen 2006; Yan et al. 2003), mathematics (Xu 1997), moral education (Huang 1999) and geography (Bo 2000). However, the existing studies are mainly concerned with the 'How' (e.g. 'How to use illustrations in classroom teaching?') but neglect the 'Why' (e.g. 'Why the illustration is needed in this context?', 'Has the illustration achieved what it is supposed to achieve, and why?') (Chen 2005: 94).

While most studies taking the cognitive and psychological stance have focused on the role of images in reading comprehension (Shen and Tao 2001; Song 2005), the semiotic resources in textbook discourse have not been fully examined and understood. In the eighth curriculum reform in China, the three-dimensional goal encompasses 'knowledge and skill, emotions and values, and process and methods' with moral education and values education highlighted (Zhong 2006; Zhu 2006). Nevertheless, how multimodal meaning-making resources in textbooks are co-deployed to realize the dimension of 'emotions and values' in the overall goal is still far less explored. As Zhang (2005: 11–12) states, there remain substantial gaps in the understanding of textbook discourse in China, which is evident in the following three aspects: first, few studies have been carried out at the micro-level as compared with those at the macro-level; secondly, how the goal of emotion and attitude education is incorporated in school textbooks remains a topic relatively unexplored; thirdly, the EFL textbooks for primary and secondary education are far less investigated as compared with the textbooks for other school subjects. This book contributes to the growing body of work in the aforementioned three areas.

2.4 Summary

This chapter has first provided a retrospective of studies on multimodality and multiliteracies, including the introduction of relevant definitions, technical terms and major research trends. In terms of the research on multimodality, emphasis has been placed on the social-semiotic approach. As for multiliteracies, the development of a metalanguage in functional terms for the description and explanation of multimodal meaning-making resources has been underlined, and the connection between meaning-making resources and their use in social contexts has been emphasized.

The remainder of the chapter has been devoted to the review of multimodality research and textbook studies in China, which has identified four research areas that demand further exploration. First, the multimodal features in China's primary and secondary pedagogic context are far less understood than those in the West. Second, though dialogic process is advocated for classroom teaching, the ways in which multimodal resources are deployed to manage heteroglossic space in textbooks have been underexamined. Third, while emotion and attitude education has been highlighted in the reformed curriculum standards, how linguistic and visual meaning-making resources in textbooks are deployed to realize the emotion and attitude goal has yet to be investigated. Fourth, image producers' assumptions about the viewers, as reflected in the choice of visual arrangement in textbooks, also call for further semiotic explorations.

In addressing these concerns, this book will investigate the verbal and visual realizations of interpersonal meaning in EFL textbooks. Three major gaps in the existing research will be further specified and suggestions will be put forward in Chapter 3 in relation to the theoretical foundations underpinning this book.

3

Theoretical foundations

3.1 Introduction

As mentioned in Chapter 1, the main theoretical foundation for this book is SFL, particularly the recent advances in interpersonal semantics and the Systemic Functional semiotic approach to images. By taking an inter-organism perspective and attaching great significance to language functions, SFL has found wide applications in both linguistic and semiotic fields of study. The purpose of this chapter is twofold: first, some of the major theoretical assumptions of SFL closely related to the current research will be introduced and explained; and secondly, the rationale of an SFL approach to the present multimodal pedagogic materials will be outlined before looking in detail at specific examples in the ensuing chapters. As for the explanation of the theoretical framework, this chapter will draw on the pioneering work of Halliday (1973, 1978, 1979/2002, 1994; Halliday and Matthiessen 1999, 2004) and the recent developments by other systemicists and social semioticians (e.g. Eggins 2004; Hu et al. 2005; Kress and van Leeuwen 2001, 2006, 2020; Lemke 2002; Martin 1985a, 1992, 1997, 1999a, 2000a, 2001, 2004; Martin and Rose 2007a; Martin and White 2005; Thompson 1996).

3.2 Some basic tenets of SFL

Taking an inter-organism perspective to study language in relation to its social context, SFL focuses on language function – oriented to both the functions of language and also an exploration of how language is structured according to its functions (Halliday 1973, 1978). This section is devoted to a brief introduction of the relevant theoretical preliminaries of SFL, which regards language use as 'functional, semantic, contextual and semiotic' (Eggins 2004: 3).

3.2.1 Language as social semiotic

SFL attaches great significance to the social context in which verbal or any other semiotic communication is embedded. 'Language as social semiotic' (Halliday 1978) explores the strong connection between meaning-making practices and the relevant social and cultural contexts. For Halliday, semiotic choices depend on the social context of use. As he points out,

> the formulation 'language as social semiotic' . . . means interpreting language within a sociocultural context, in which the culture itself is interpreted in semiotic terms – as an information system. (Halliday 1978: 2)

The conception of 'language as social semiotic' is often referred to as the interest common to all systemic linguists, despite their different research emphases or application contexts (Eggins 2004: 3). As interpreted by Lemke (2002), in social semiotics language use is considered as a semiotic practice that makes use of the language to make social meanings. Social semiotics broadens this perspective to show how social meanings and social relations are constructed by the deployment of semiotic meaning-making resources beyond language.

In explaining the 'natural dialectic' relation between language and social system, Halliday (1978: 183–92) distinguishes between 'language as system' and 'language as institution' when presenting the underlying conceptual framework. As Halliday (1978: 183) states,

> the salient facts about language as *system* are (a) that it is *stratified* (a three-level coding system consisting of semantics, lexicogrammar and phonology) and (b) that its semantic system is organized into *functional* components (ideational, interpersonal and textual). Language as *institution* indicates the fact that language is *variable*, and there are two kinds of variation: (a) *dialect* (variation according to the *user*), and (b) *register* (variation according to the *use*). (emphasis in the original)

The rest of this section will elaborate on these basic tenets. In terms of 'language as institution', focus will be placed on the registerial variation due to its high relevance to this study.

3.2.2 Stratification within and between semiotics

Developing Hjelmslev (1961), who makes a distinction between the linguistic planes of content and expression, SFL takes a step further and divides the content plane into the strata of semantics and lexicogrammar – with a natural rather than an arbitrary relation between these two meaning-making strata. This articulation of wording as naturally related to meaning reflects one of SFL's key assumptions; that is language is structured in light of its functions. In other words, language in the SFL model is theorized as a tri-stratal semiotic system (i.e. semantics, lexicogrammar and graphology/phonology), with a relationship of realization between strata. In SFL, semantics operates at the highest stratum within the linguistic system and thus serves as the interface with context. As Martin (1992:1) points out, discourse semantics 'focuses on text-size rather than clause-size meanings' (Martin 1992:1). Three strands of meanings (i.e. ideational, interpersonal and textual) are simultaneously construed at this stratum (see Section 3.2.4), and this functional diversification enables discourse analysts to coordinate language choices with diversified contextual demands, and at the same time to associate discourse semantic choices with their lexicogrammatical realizations. Lexicogrammatical descriptions take the clause as the basic unit of analysis. The systems of TRANSITIVITY, MOOD and THEME constitute three strands of simultaneously construed meanings (Halliday 1994; Halliday and Matthiessen 2004).

In SFL language and its functions are examined with regard to the social context in which language is embedded. According to Halliday (1978: 109–10, 122–3), social context is a semiotic structure – the semiotic environment in which communication takes place. The relation of language system to the higher-level social context is a 'more complex natural dialectic' one, in which 'language actively symbolizes the social system, thus creating as well as being created by it' (Halliday 1978:183).

In accounting for social context, this study draws on the stratified model developed by Martin (1985a, 1992, 1999a),[1] whose relevance to this book is evident on both theoretical and practical grounds (Hasan and Martin 1989; Painter and Martin 1986). In this multi-stratal model, context is interpreted as consisting of three communicative planes: register, genre and ideology (Martin 1986, 1992: 501–8). Drawing on Hjelmslev's (1961) work on connotative semiotic systems, Martin proposes (1992: 495–6) that language functions as the expression form of register (context of situation), which in turn functions as the expression form of genre (context of culture). This stratified model of context is represented in Figure 3.1.

In later work (e.g. Martin 1997, 1999a) Martin has primarily focused on the strata of register and genre. Register is used as a cover term for field, tenor and mode.[2] As explained by Martin,

> in the model developed here, register is the name of the metafunctionally organized connotative semiotic between language and genre. This means that instead of characterizing context of situation as potential and register as

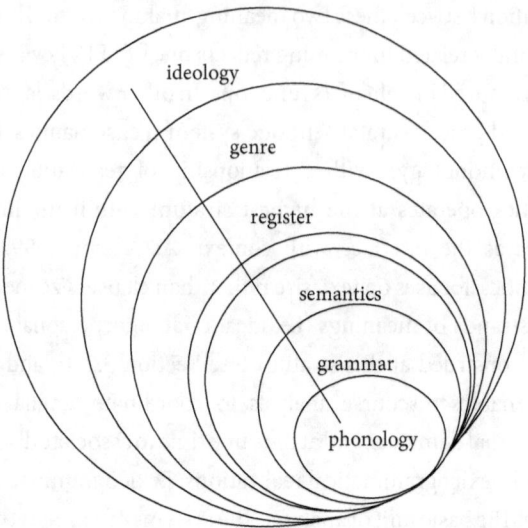

Figure 3.1 Language and its semiotic environment (Martin 1992: 496).

(context's) actual, . . . [register is treated] as a semiotic system in its own right, involving notions of both system and process. (Martin 1992: 502)

The stratified model considers genre as a stratum of higher-level abstraction, which is characterized for practical purposes as a 'staged, goal-oriented social process' (Martin 1986). Genre takes responsibility for the integration of the semantic diversification projected from the functionally organized language system onto the stratum of register (i.e. ideational meaning by and large construing field, interpersonal meaning by and large enacting tenor and textual meaning by and large composing mode). Accordingly, a metafunctionally diversified view on context is presented through register, whereas genre provides a standpoint from which analysts can transcend metafunctions to consider a text's global social purpose and the relations between genres. The concept of genre will be taken up in Chapter 6 when visual choices in macrogenre are analysed.

3.2.3 Realization and instantiation

A complementary relationship in the theoretical architecture of SFL is instantiation,[3] which theorizes the relationship of system to text as that of generalized potential to actual instances of language use. Along this 'cline of instantiation' (Halliday and Matthiessen 1999: 385), language can be viewed as

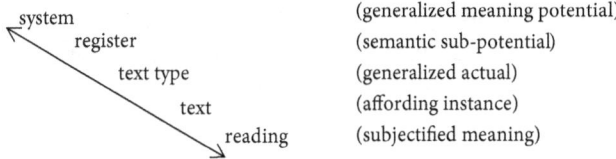

Figure 3.2 Cline of instantiation (Martin and White 2005: 25).

a generalized system of meaning-making potential at one end, and identify the actual reading, that is the 'act of reader/listener interpretation' at the other end of the cline (Martin and White 2005: 162–3). Figure 3.2 summarizes Martin and White's version of the scale – from the language system at one end to the ultimate reading made of individual texts at the other.

In exploring instantiation, Martin (2008b) proposes two dimensions of analysis that call for further investigation: coupling and commitment. Coupling refers to the ways in which meanings combine as a number of coordinated choices from system networks.[4] Some initial work in this area has been done by Nesbitt and Plum (1988) in their study of clause complexing. As pointed out by Martin (2008b), this orientation to instantiation needs to be further pursued – for instance, from the perspective of the discourse semantics of APPRAISAL (Martin and White 2005). Options from the simultaneous sub-systems within APPRAISAL (i.e. ATTITUDE, ENGAGEMENT and GRADUATION) can be coupled, and the logic of system networks enables discourse analysts to identify the relevant coupling at any point in delicacy. Furthermore, coupling can be across simultaneous systems not only within a metafunction but between metafunctions. In addition lexicogrammatical realizations are deployed across clause and group ranks and can be coupled there. In sum, coupling can be identified across strata and ranks. The crucial point is that 'what realization freely combines, instantiation specifically couples' (Martin 2008b). The hierarchy of instantiation constrains what can be combined so as to make it recognizable as belonging to a certain generalized, conventional combinations in a given culture. The concept of coupling brings out the importance of the combinations of meaning across systems.

Another orientation to instantiation drawn upon in the ensuing analysis is commitment, which is concerned with the amount of meaning potential activated in a particular process of instantiation. Commitment in other words, deals with the degree to which meanings are taken up and the degree of delicacy selected (Martin 2008b). In terms of ideational meanings, Hood (2008) documents that a great variety of relations (including de/classification, de/composition, role/incumbent identification, de/specification, metaphor/congruence and deffusion/infusion) make room for committing different degrees of meaning potential. As for the interpersonal semantics, particularly for the APPRAISAL system, the concept of commitment can be adopted to re-interpret the various degrees of explicitness in encoding attitudinal meanings – that is, the cline from overt inscription to the covert 'flagging' via non-core vocabulary and 'affording' via ideational selections (Martin 2000; Martin and White 2005: 61–7). As Martin (2008b) points out, in terms of commitment, direct inscription is more attitudinally committed than flagging, which in turn is more committed than affording. The concepts of coupling and commitment will be deployed in examining the different degrees of multimodal attitude in Chapter 5.

3.2.4 Metafunctional diversification

A further complementary theoretical dimension of SFL is metafunctions. The notion of function is accorded a special status in SFL, in that it is interpreted as 'a fundamental property of language itself, something that is basic to the evolution of the semantic system' (Halliday and Hasan 1985: 17). Due to the focus of this book, particular emphasis will be placed on the interpersonal metafunction.

As remarked by Halliday (1994: xiii), all languages are organized around the ideational and interpersonal meanings, which manifest 'the two very general purposes which underlie all uses of language: (i) to understand the environment (ideational), and (ii) to act on the others in it (interpersonal)'. The third dimension in this semantic complex is textual meaning, which is intrinsic to the language system and 'breathes relevance into' (Halliday 1994: xiii) the other two metafunctions. According to Halliday (1992), the concept of metafunction is a theoretical category,[5] which is general to all languages and has a fundamental place in the construction of a general linguistic theory.

The aforementioned three strands of meanings are simultaneously encoded in virtually every utterance of verbal communication. The ideational metafunction, which involves the speaker as 'observer' perspective (Halliday 1978: 112), construes not only the processes in the outside world and in individual consciousness but also the relations between these processes (Halliday and Matthiessen 1999: 511). They are accordingly categorized into the experiential metafunction and logical metafunction respectively. In lexicogrammar this perspective involves the TRANSITIVITY system in its lexicogrammatical construal of experiential meaning. It also implicates logico-semantic interdependency relations in the clause complex (Halliday 1994; Halliday and Matthiessen 2004). A more detailed description will be provided in the data analysis in the ensuing chapters.

The interpersonal metafunction 'represents the speaker's meaning potential as an intruder', and it is the 'participatory function of language' (Halliday 1978: 112). It deals with the enactment of social relationships, whereby language negotiates our social collective as well as personal being (Halliday and Matthiessen 1999: 511). In other words, interpersonal metafunction is concerned with how people use language to interact with each other, to enact and maintain social relations, to express one's own attitudes, and to influence others' opinions and behaviours. Systemicists have approached various kinds of interpersonal meaning under the headings of MOOD, MODALITY, ATTITUDE and NEGOTIATION (Thompson 1996: 39; see also Eggins 2004; Halliday 1994; Halliday and Matthiessen 2004; Martin 1992; Martin and Rose 2007a). The diverse aspects of interpersonal management may be summarized into two broad categories: the interactive and the personal (Thompson 1996: 69). The former deals with the interaction between communicating parties, and the latter is concerned with personal articulations of evaluation and modality judgements.

Recent developments in SFL have modelled interpersonal discourse semantics as a set of three broadly based systems: APPRAISAL, NEGOTIATION and INVOLVEMENT (Martin 1997; Martin and White 2005: 34–5). NEGOTIATION is concerned with interaction as an exchange between speakers, including the way speakers adopt and assign roles to one another in dialogue and the organization of moves. It involves mood-based resources for exchanging information and goods-and-services (Martin 1997; Martin and Rose 2007a: 219). INVOLVEMENT focuses on non-gradable resources for solidarity. It refers to meanings by which interlocutors code social alignment arising from intimacy or their shared membership in some distinct discourse community (Martin and White 2005: 33–4, White 1998). APPRAISAL is concerned with 'evaluation – the kinds of attitudes that are negotiated in a text, the strength of the feelings involved and the ways in which values are sourced and reader aligned' (Martin and Rose 2007a: 25). A detailed account of the APPRAISAL system (Martin 1997; Martin and White 2005) informing this study will be provided in Section 3.3. Considering the wide application of APPRAISAL to verbal texts in a great variety of registers (Coffin 2000; Eggins and Slade 1997; Iedema et al. 1994; Macken-Horarik 2003; Rothery and Stenglin 2000; White 2003), the analysis and discussion of the multiple semiotic resources encoding

APPRAISAL meanings remain relatively undeveloped within SFL, a point which gives impetus to the current study.

The textual metafunction is the 'relevance function' of language. It is the enabling functional component that allows the other two metafunctions to be composed as coherent text, and manages the relation of language to its verbal and non-verbal environment (Halliday 1978: 48, 112–13; Halliday and Matthiessen 1999: 512). According to Halliday and Matthiessen (2004: 579), there are two kinds of lexicogrammatical resources realizing the textual meanings in English: structural resources (including thematic structure and information structure operating at the level of clause) and cohesive resources (such as reference and conjunction) that make explicit the relations between clauses and clause complexes. These two types of resources work together in the marking of points of textual transition as well as textual status.

When considering the relationship of the three metafunctions to the types of structure at clause level, Halliday (1979/2002: 209) points out that experiential structures tend to be elemental, interpersonal structures tend to be prosodic and textual structures tend to be cumulative or periodic. In extending the discussion of the association between structural types and modes of meanings from clause to text, Martin (1997) explicates a complementarity of particulate, prosodic and periodic structure. As Halliday (1979/2002: 205) articulates, interpersonal meaning is 'strung throughout the clause as a continuous motif or colouring' and 'the effect is cumulative'. This type of realization is referred to as 'prosodic' in that 'the meaning is distributed like a prosody throughout a continuous stretch of discourse'.

In SFL, the intrinsic metafunctional diversification within language is projected upwards onto social context. In other words, the organization of language and social context are both treated as functionally diversified along similar lines – and accordingly there is a proportionality between the three metafunctions (i.e. ideational, interpersonal and textual) and the three register variables (i.e. field, tenor and mode). This hook-up is represented in Figure 3.3. Field refers to the social action in institutional practice; tenor focuses on the set of social relations among relevant participants; and mode is the effect of the communicative channel or medium on information flow. As explained in Section 3.2.2, the realization relationship between register and language is probabilistic and dialectic, in the sense that language construes, is construed by, reconstrues and is reconstrued by social context (Martin 1999a). The resonance of intrinsic with extrinsic functionality is explored in more detail by Halliday (1978), Halliday and Hasan (1985) and Martin (1991, 1992, 1999a).

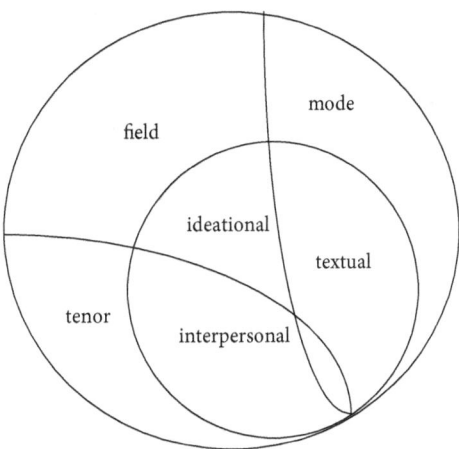

Figure 3.3 Functional diversification of language and social context (Martin 1997: 5).

3.3 The semantic system of APPRAISAL within SFL

As noted earlier, one of the underpinnings in this study is the APPRAISAL system (Martin 1997, 2000a; Martin and Rose 2007a; Martin and White 2005) developed within the broader theoretical framework of SFL (Halliday 1994; Martin 1992; Halliday and Matthiessen 1999, 2004). Adopting as it does a functional view on interpersonal meaning at the level of discourse semantics, the APPRAISAL system encompasses three sub-systems (i.e. ATTITUDE, ENGAGEMENT and GRADUATION) – to explore the attitudinal meanings encoded in a text, the ways in which dialogic space can be opened up or closed down for different voices, and the resources for adjusting the strength and categoricality of feelings. The APPRAISAL system is outlined in Figure 3.4, with square brackets representing either/or choices and curly brackets representing both/and choices. Each of these sub-systems has its own sub-categories or options, and all these choices within the APPRAISAL system are semantic ones that transcend diverse lexicogrammatical structures (Hood 2004: 13–14; see also Martin and Rose 2007a; Martin and White 2005). In fact a wide range of meaning-making resources, including the non-verbal ones, can be brought together and considered systematically as encoding common evaluative meanings and constructing a global rhetorical orientation (Martin and Zappvigna 2019, Ngo et al. in press). In what follows some basic concepts of the APPRAISAL system will be introduced, with necessary elaborations provided in Chapters 4 and 5 where detailed analyses of attitudes and voices are conducted.

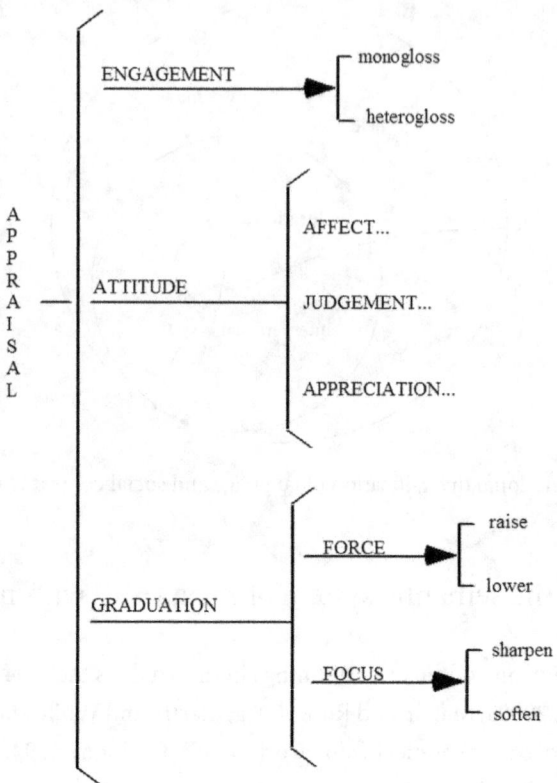

Figure 3.4 An overview of APPRAISAL resources (Martin and White 2005: 38).

3.3.1 ATTITUDE

As demonstrated in the overview of APPRAISAL system earlier (Figure 3.4), ATTITUDE is one of the three interacting dimensions. It is concerned with emotional responses, judgements of human behaviours and evaluations of products and processes. ATTITUDE can be subdivided into three semantic regions – AFFECT, JUDGEMENT and APPRECIATION (which might be referred to as emotions, ethics and aesthetics in traditional parlance). In terms of verbal communication, ATTITUDE is realized through attitudinal lexis (e.g. people are *grateful* because their food has been gathered for the winter, he said I was *hard-working*, my *favourite* subject is science) and mental process of reaction (e.g. we *love* animals, people *were shocked by that episode*). Along with overt realizations, ATTITUDE can also be indirectly invoked through various strategies. For instance, there is no explicit attitudinal meaning inscribed in the clause *everywhere they looked nearly everything was destroyed*. However, a sense of fear might well be invoked by the devastation described in the clause.

AFFECT is considered as situated at the heart of the semantic system of ATTITUDE, since it deals with meanings related to inborn feelings – from which the more institutionalized feelings of JUDGEMENT and APPRECIATION can be seen to develop (Martin 2000a; Martin and White 2005: 42; Painter 2003). Martin (2000a; see also Martin 2017; Martin and White 2005: 46–52) identifies the following six factors taken into account when classifying AFFECT:

- whether the emotions are construed as positive or negative (e.g. *satisfied* vs. *upset*);
- whether they are realized as an emotional surge or as an internal disposition (e.g. *attentive* vs. *satisfied*);
- whether the feelings are reactions to a certain emotional stimulus or as an undirected ongoing mood (e.g. she *disliked* swimming vs. she was *upset*);
- whether the emotions involve a reaction to an existing stimulus or an intention towards a prospective stimulus (e.g. she *liked* meeting new friends vs. she *looked forward to* meeting new friends);
- whether the emotions are concerned with un/happiness (e.g. *misery/cheer*), in/security (e.g. *nervous/confident*), or dis/satisfaction (e.g. *bored with/ satisfied*); and
- the degree of the intensity of emotions (e.g. from low through medium to high values: *dislike, hate, loathe*).

More specific information with respect to types of AFFECT will be provided in Section 5.3.1.1.

JUDGEMENT is concerned with the evaluative meanings, either positive or negative, that construe attitudes towards human characters and behaviours. According to Martin (1997: 23; see also Martin 2001, 2004), JUDGEMENT can be regarded as the institutionalization of feelings in the context of proposals. In other words, JUDGEMENT recontextualizes individual emotions in the realm of proposals about human behaviour; these proposals may be formalized ideationally as rules and regulations in a given culture and thus are institutionalized as part of a given field. The attitudinal sub-system of JUDGEMENT is generally divided five sub-types organized into two broad categories: 'social esteem' and 'social sanction'. JUDGEMENT of social esteem involves norms of behaviour; the sub-types included in this category are 'normality' (how usual someone is), 'capacity' (how capable someone is) and 'tenacity' (how resolute someone is). In contrast, JUDGEMENT of social sanction has ethical implications; this category deals with 'veracity' (how truthful someone is) and 'propriety' (how ethical someone is).

The attitudinal system of APPRECIATION encompasses evaluations of either man-made or natural, phenomena and processes – both abstract and concrete. These evaluative meanings are discussed under the headings of 'reaction' (the product or process is evaluated in terms of its impact or quality), 'composition' (the product or process is evaluated according to its complexity or conformity to organizational principles) and 'valuation' (the product or process is evaluated based on its institutional value). Like AFFECT and JUDGEMENT, positive as well as negative evaluations can be identified in APPRECIATION. All of AFFECT, JUDGEMENT and APPRECIATION can be directly inscribed in discourse through the use of attitudinal lexis, or realized through other indirect means such as the selection of ideational meanings to invoke evaluations of people and things (Martin 2000a; see also Martin and White 2005: 61–8, Martin 2019, 2020). In Chapter 5 we will elaborate on the issue of attitudinal inscription and invocation as verbal and visual attitudinal resources are investigated.

3.3.2 Engagement

The sub-system of ENGAGEMENT draws on notions of dialogism and heteroglossia generally attributed to Bakhtin[6] (1981, 1986) (see also Bota and Bronckart 2011). It comprises networks of options for opening up or closing down the play of voices in a text. ENGAGEMENT resources cover a wide range of devices that implicate a range of perspectives in a text, including alternative points of views and anticipatory responses from the audience.

The ENGAGEMENT network includes both monoglossic and heteroglossic options. The focus of this study is mainly on how multiple voices are mediated through multimodal meaning-making resources, and the discussion here is thus focused on the heteroglossic dimension. According to Martin and White (2005: 94), the ENGAGEMENT network covers 'all those locutions which provide the means for the authorial voice to position itself with respect to, and hence to "engage" with, the other voices and alternative positions construed as being in play in the current communicative context'. As Martin and White (2005) point out, the taxonomy of ENGAGEMENT meanings include four main categories:

[disclaim]: the textual voice positions itself as at odds with, or rejecting some contrary position;

[proclaim]: by representing the proposition as highly warrantable (compelling, valid, plausible, well-founded, generally agreed, reliable, etc.), the textual voice sets itself against, suppresses or rules out alternative positions;

[entertain]: by explicitly presenting the proposition as grounded in its own contingent, individual subjectivity, the authorial voice represents the proposition as but one of a range of possible positions – it thereby entertains or invokes these dialogic alternatives;

[attribute]: by representing proposition as grounded in the subjectivity of an external voice, the textual voice represents the proposition as but one of a range of possible positions – it thereby entertains or invokes these dialogic alternatives. (Martin and White 2005: 97–8)

More delicately, these ENGAGEMENT meanings can be divided into sub-categories (e.g. [disclaim] is subdivided into [deny] and [counter]) to specify dialogic positioning. Less delicately they are generalized as two broad categories – of 'dialogic expansion' and 'dialogic contraction' – with respect to whether they are opening up or closing down the heteroglossic space. Resources under the headings of [disclaim] and [proclaim] are dialogically contractive, while those under the categories of [entertain] and [attribute] are dialogically expansive. Figure 3.5 outlines the ENGAGEMENT system, specifying typical realizations at the level of lexicogrammar.

The following chapter will focus on the ENGAGEMENT system, with multimodal ENGAGEMENT resources identified and their contributions to the negotiation of the heteroglossic diversity explored.

3.3.3 Graduation

Another sub-system within APPRAISAL is GRADUATION, which provides meaning-making resources for scaling attitudinal and heteroglossic meanings. As pointed out by Martin and White (2005: 135–6), gradability is 'a defining property of all attitudinal meanings' in that all the values of AFFECT, JUDGEMENT and APPRECIATION construe higher or lower degrees of positivity or negativity, as demonstrated in Table 3.1 via lexicogrammatical realizations.

Gradability is also 'generally a feature of the ENGAGEMENT system' because ENGAGEMENT values are scaled in terms of the speaker/writer's investment in a given value position (as illustrated in Table 3.2). In other words, GRADUATION is central to the whole system of APPRAISAL, and ATTITUDE and ENGAGEMENT can

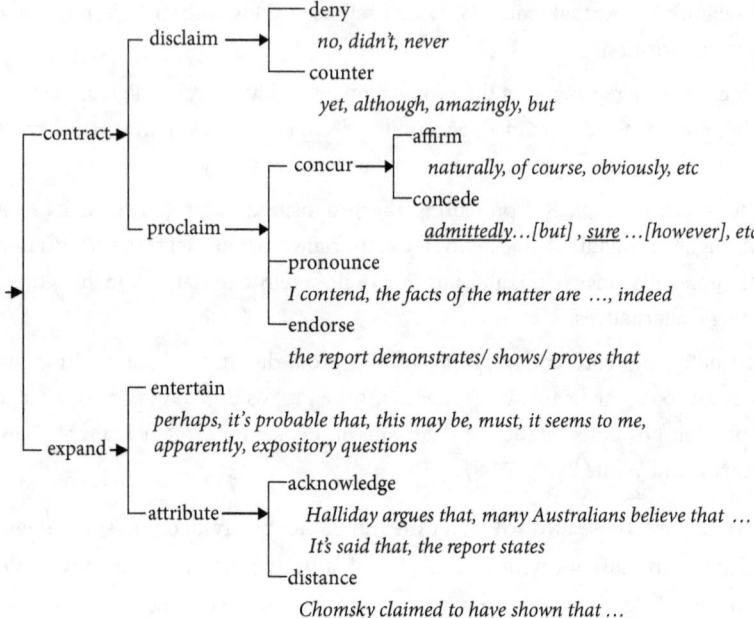

Figure 3.5 The ENGAGEMENT system (Martin and White 2005: 134).

Table 3.1 The Gradability of Attitudinal Meanings (Martin and White 2005: 136)

	Low degree			High degree
JUDGEMENT	competent player	good player		brilliant player
	reasonably good player	quite good player	very good player	extremely good player
AFFECT	contentedly	happily	joyously	ecstatically
	slightly upset	somewhat upset	very upset	extremely upset
APPRECIATION	a bit untidy	somewhat untidy	very untidy	completely untidy
	attractive	beautiful		exquisite

be regarded as domains of GRADUATION that differ in terms of the nature of the meanings being scaled (Martin and White 2005: 136).

As shown in Figure 3.4, there are two axes along which the semantic system of GRADUATION operates: FORCE and FOCUS. FORCE grades meanings in terms of the intensity or amount of a scalable value (e.g. she is *rather* upset, she has *many* regrets). FOCUS grades meanings according to the prototypicality and precision

Table 3.2 The Gradability of Engagement Values (Martin and White 2005: 136)

	Lower		Higher
	I suspect she betrayed us	I believe she betrayed us	I am convinced she betrayed us
[entertain]	possibly she betrayed us she just possibly betrayed us	probably she betrayed us she possibly betrayed us	definitely she betrayed us she very possibly betrayed us
[attribute]	she suggested that I had cheated	she stated that I had cheated	she insisted that I had cheated
[pronounce]	I'd say he's the man for the job	I contend he's the man for the job	I insist that he's the man for the job
Co[concur]	admittedly he's technically proficient (but he doesn't play with feeling)		certainly he's technically proficient (but ...)
[disclaim]	I didn't hurt him		I never hurt him

whereby a categorical boundary is drawn (e.g. she found *true* happiness, she felt *kind of* sad). More comprehensive accounts of the GRADUATION resources at the level of lexicogrammar are provided by Eggins and Slade (1997: 133–7), Martin (1997), Martin and Rose (2007a: 42–8) and Martin and White (2005: 135–60).[7] Hood and Martin (2007) further extend the GRADUATION network, specifying FORCE as embracing INTENSITY (of a quality), QUANTITY (of a thing) and ENHANCEMENT (of a process), and FOCUS as encompassing VALUE and FULFILMENT. At the level of lexicogrammar, a great variety of linguistic resources – including sub-modification (e.g. *most* important), processes infused with an attitudinal meaning (e.g. *explore* this area) and circumstances of manner (e.g. illustrate *convincingly*) – can be deployed to intensify an attitude. QUANTITY may construe the meanings of 'amount' (e.g. *considerable* study) and also 'extent' in time and space – either as scope (e.g. *for ten years, around the world*) or distance (e.g. *more recently, far away*). The scaling of a process in terms of ENHANCEMENT can be achieved through a circumstance of manner (e.g. understand *comprehensively*). GRADUATION as FOCUS scales meanings along the dimensions of authenticity (e.g. a *real* killer), specificity (e.g. no one *in particular*) and fulfilment (e.g. *fail to* finish). GRADUATION is an important resource for 'flagging' an invoked attitudinal reading by scaling ideational meanings (Hood and Martin 2007, Martin 2020). GRADUATION in multimodal texts will be investigated in relation to ENGAGEMENT values and attitudinal meanings in Chapters 4 and 5.

3.4 Systemic Functional semiotic approach to visual communication

Over the past decades, Halliday's social-semiotic approach to language has been extended to include other semiotic resources such as images (Kress and van Leeuwen 2001, 2002, 2006, 2020; O'Toole 1990, 1994), sound (van Leeuwen 1999), spatial design (Martin and Stenglin 2007). As Kress and van Leeuwen remark,

> we aimed at a common terminology for all semiotic modes, and stressed that, within a given social-cultural domain, the 'same' meanings can often be expressed in different semiotic modes . . . we move towards a view of multimodality in which common semiotic principles operate in and across different modes. (Kress and van Leeuwen 2001: 1–2)

Inspired by a metafunctionally diversified perspective on language systems, social semioticians have explored multifunctionality across different modes of communication. This multifunctional perspective on the modalities of verbiage and image is summarized in Table 3.3.

Here we focus on the analytical framework proposed by Kress and van Leeuwen (2006, 2020), which will be adopted for visual analysis in the following three chapters. As was outlined in Table 3.3, there are four major components in Kress and van Leeuwen's model – representational resources for visually representing the material world, including the participants, events and objects involved in it, interactive resources that visually construe the interaction between viewer and what is viewed, modality judgements that deal with the reality of visual messages and compositional arrangements that are concerned with information value and visual emphasis. Among the four components, interaction and modality are

Table 3.3 Multifunctionality for the Modalities of Verbiage and Image (Martin 2001: 311)

Metafunction modalities	Naturalizing reality	Enacting social relations	Organizing text
verbiage			
-8Halliday (1994)	Ideational	Interpersonal	Textual
Image			
-Kress and van Leeuwen (1996, 2006)	representation	Interaction Modality	Composition
-3O'Toole (1994)	Representational	Modal	Compositional
-Lemke (1998)	Presentational	Orientational	Organizational

particularly concerned with the interpersonal meaning. Some relevant concepts of the other two aspects of visual communication will also be reviewed here, since one of the important advantages of metafunctional perspective lies in the fact that it enables us to discuss interpersonal meaning in relation to ideational (representational in visual displays) and textual (compositional) choices in a multimodal text.

3.4.1 Representation

Unlike the time-based semiotic modes such as language in which structure is a matter of sequencing, the space-based semiotic modes such as image have 'syntactic patterns' that are encoded in spatial relationships (Jewitt and Oyama 2001). Kress and van Leeuwen (2006: 45–113) identify two types of structure in terms of representation: narrative structure and conceptual structure. What makes the difference between these two representational structures is the way the participants in the image are related to each other – that is, whether the relation is based on the 'unfolding of actions and events, processes of change', or based on their 'generalized', 'stable and timeless essence' (Kress and van Leeuwen 2006: 59). The presence of a vector (i.e. an oblique or diagonal line that connects participants) can be taken as a visual marker of narrative representation, while its absence indicates conceptual representation.

According to Kress and van Leeuwen (2006: 59–70), there are four types of process within the category of narrative representation, each of which has its own represented participants and circumstantial elements. An action process can be transactional – when both Actor (i.e. the active represented participants from which the vector emanates) and Goal (i.e. the passive represented participants at which the vector is directed) are present and connected by a vector. An action process may alternatively be non-transactional when the vector departing from the Actor does not point to any other participant. When the vector is formed by an eyeline of a represented participant, the process is a reactional one. The two represented participants involved in a reactional process are termed as Reacter and Phenomenon. When the eyeline vector emanates from the Reacter but does not point at another represented participant, the reactional process is non-transactional.

Narrative structure also includes speech processes and mental processes, which can be recognized by the presence of 'dialogue balloons' and 'thought bubbles' respectively. In these processes, the oblique protrusion of dialogue balloons and thought bubbles functions as the vector, connecting the represented participants to their speech or inner mental process. Accordingly, the content of speech or thought is mediated through a Sayer (in the case of speech process) or a Senser (in the case of mental process). Still another narrative structure is the conversion process, which involves a change of state in the represented participant. In this case, the 'goal' of one action process is at the same time the 'actor' of another action process, and this participant is referred to as Relay. Narrative representations also involve circumstantial elements such as setting, means and accompaniment.

Images that do not contain vectors are discussed under the heading of conceptual representation (Kress and van Leeuwen 2006, 2020). Unlike narrative structures that focus on dynamic 'doing' or 'happening', conceptual structures are concerned with static 'belonging', 'being' or 'meaning'. Three types of processes can be identified in terms of class, structure and symbolic meaning (Kress and van Leeuwen 2006: 79–109). A classificational process relates represented participants to each other in terms of a taxonomy, with a set of participants distributed symmetrically across the picture space to demonstrate that they have something in common and thus belong to the same class. These participants act as the Subordinates of another participant, which acts as their Superordinate. A classificational process may involve an overt or a covert taxonomy, depending on whether the Superordinate is present in the image. The second type of process within the conceptual category is analytical process, in which participants are related based on a part-whole structure. The two types of represented participants involved in an analytical process are Carrier (i.e. the whole) and Possessive Attribute (i.e. the parts that constitute the whole). If the Carrier as well as its Possessive Attributes can be easily identified in an image; when labels are attached to the Possessive Attributes, they are part of a structured analytical process. On the other hand, if the image shows us only the unordered set of Possessive Attributes but not the Carrier itself, the analytical process is considered to be unstructured. The third category, that is symbolic process, defines the meaning or identity of a represented participant, and can be further divided into symbolic attributive and symbolic suggestive. There are two participants in symbolic attributive, Carrier and Symbolic Attribute – with the Symbolic Attribute conferring meaning onto the Carrier. There one participant is involved in a symbolic suggestive process, the Carrier (with the symbolic meaning coming in some sense from 'within' the Carrier). Image process types will be analysed when the multimodal engagement and attitudinal resources are identified in Chapters 4 and 5.

3.4.2 Interaction

In visual communication, there are resources for creating and maintaining an interaction between the viewer and what is represented within the picture frame. At stake here is the way an image engages the viewer and implies the position he/she should take in viewing a visual display. Kress and van Leeuwen (2006: 129) identify three main factors in the visual realizations of interactive meanings: contact, social distance and point of view. Each of them encompasses options to specify the relationship between the viewer and the represented participants (as summarized in Figure 3.6).

In the visual system of 'contact' outlined here, a distinction is made between those images describing people or anthropomorphized things that directly gaze at the viewer and those images in which represented participants do not gaze at the viewer. Based on Halliday's (1994) work on speech functions, Kress and van Leeuwen (2006: 117–18) use the term 'demand' to refer to the images where an imaginary contact is established. They argue that the represented participants' gaze symbolically asks the viewer to 'enter some kind of imaginary relation' with them, and that the facial expressions and gestures of the represented participants further specify what is being demanded. Those images depicting represented participants as objects of the viewer's detached observation are 'offers' (Kress and van Leeuwen 2006: 119–20). They point out no contact is made in this type of image, and thus any anthropomorphized creatures or inanimate objects are offered as 'items of information' to be contemplated by the viewer. The choice

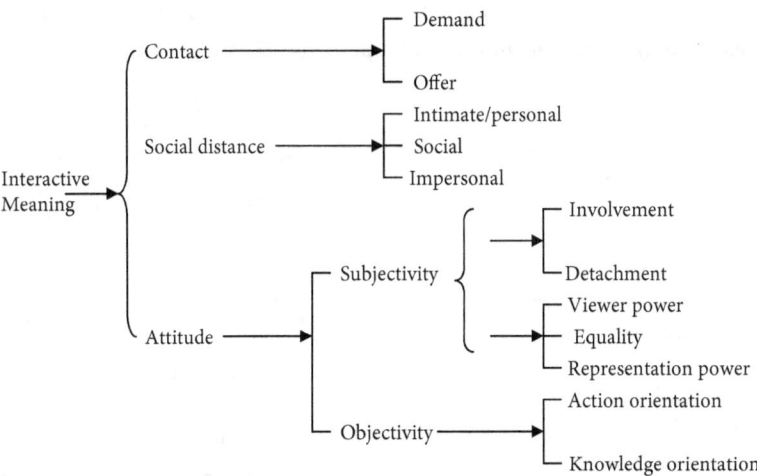

Figure 3.6 Interactive meaning in images (Kress and van Leeuwen 2006: 149).

between 'demand' and 'offer', as proposed by Kress and van Leeuwen (2006: 120), is one way of enacting different relations between the viewer and the represented, inviting viewer to engage with some representations and to remain detached from others.

The basic opposition in terms of 'contact' is further elaborated and developed by Painter (2007) and Painter et al. (2013) into a system network of visual focalization (see Figure 3.7), which the current research will draw upon. In this network, 'contact' and 'observe' are the technical terms for describing whether there is eye contact or not, indicating how the viewer is positioned to engage with the represented participants (termed 'character' in Figure 3.7), or merely to observe what happens within the picture frame. In addition, the viewer of an image can be positioned to view the visual world directly (on their own) or vicariously (through the eyes of a represented participant). Focalization may be structured across frames on adjacent pages in picture books or within a single frame. Within a picture frame, vicarious 'observe' can be achieved by viewing the world in the picture in terms of what the represented participant himself/herself sees, or alternatively by viewing the visual world along with the 'focalizing character' within the frame. The ways in which an eye contact is made will be considered in Section 4.4.1 of Chapter 4, while the way character focalization is managed will be addressed in Section 5.3.2.2 of Chapter 5.

The second dimension of visual interaction is social distance, which is concerned with how images depict represented participants (e.g. as close to or far away from the viewer). This in turn is interpreted through the 'size of frame' in photographic technology. For example, an extreme close-up shot that shows only the face or head indicates intimate distance, while a close-up shot including the head and the shoulders implies close personal distance. A medium close shot

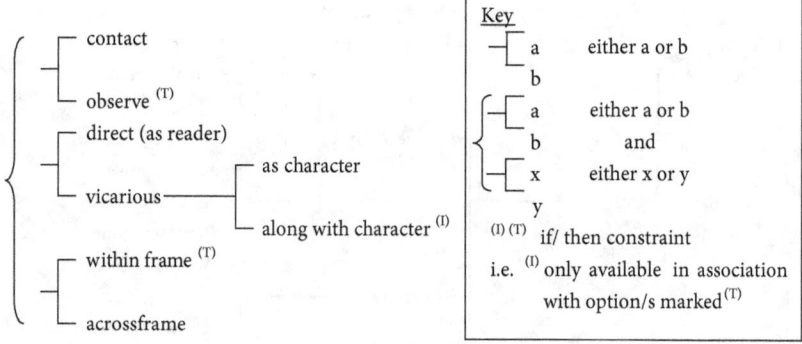

Figure 3.7 Visual focalization (Painter 2007: 47).

(that cuts off the participants approximately at the waist) suggests far personal distance, while a medium-long shot (that represents the whole figure) enacts close social distance. Finally, shots longer than the medium-long shot show the whole figure with space around it, or the torso of several people – corresponding to far social distance and public distance respectively (Hall 1964, 1966; Kress and van Leeuwen 2006: 124–5). The continuum of social distance reflects different social relation – ranging from intimate, through social, to impersonal. In other words, participants can be represented as intimate (whether friends or otherwise), or as distant (whether strangers or otherwise) which can construe people visually more like general types than individuals with personalities. The association between putative reading position and social distance will be discussed in Section 5.3.2.1 of Chapter 5.

Turning to attitude in visual interaction, our research primarily focuses on subjective, perspectival images and sets aside technical, objective drawings that 'disregard the viewer' (Kress and van Leeuwen 2006: 131). For the former, the system point of view enables the creation of the symbolic relations of involvement and detachment along the horizontal axis, alongside different power relations along the vertical axis. To be specific, the horizontal angle of frontality allows the viewer to be directly confronted, and thus maximally involved with what is represented; whereas those images with the oblique angle depict the participants from the side as 'others' or 'strangers', positioning the viewer as a detached onlooker.

In the case of the vertical angle, symbolic power is given to the viewer if low angle is taken, so that the viewer looks down on the represented participant. If the represented participants are depicted from a high angle from which the viewer looks up at them, the symbolic power is with the represented participants. Still another possibility is the eye-level angle, and in this case there is a relation of symbolic equality. As explained by Jewitt and Oyama (2001), the terms 'power', 'detachment' and 'involvement' are used in relation to the meaning potential of angles. The issue of point of view will be addressed as the analysis unfolds in the subsequent three chapters.

3.4.3 Modality

The concept of modality deals with the reliability or credibility of messages. In visual communication, photographs are generally taken to be faithful representations of phenomena – a 'seeing is believing' motif. The truth value of photographs is based on the dominant, conventional and most widely accepted perception of reality in contemporary times, which is referred to by Kress and van Leeuwen (2006: 165-6) as naturalistic coding orientation. This reality standard has been defined by modern 35 mm photographic technology, and any pictorial expression that exceeds or does not meet this standard is thought to be of low modality as far as a naturalistic coding orientation is concerned.

Scientific and technical graphs and diagrams however are held to a different standard. They are abstract, general and often colourless but can claim to be real in a scientific and technical context, owing to the fact that they reveal the essential qualities and look below and beyond the surface of things. They possess high modality value when viewed from this standard of reality, and involve an abstract coding orientation according to Kress and van Leeuwen (2006: 165).

Coding orientations other than these two standards can be identified in other communicative contexts. If an image displays a higher degree of colour saturation, a sharper contrast in terms of the play of light and shade, or a more detailed representation than the normal resolution of the 35mm colour photography, it may seem exaggerated – 'more than real' for a general viewing audience who adopt a naturalistic coding orientation as their standard of truth. This type of image is often found in advertising, surrealist art and horror films, where visual credibility is based on a 'pleasure principle'. What matters in this type of image is not being faithful to the appearance of phenomena or their hidden essence, but rather the exciting, stirring or soothing impact that the image designer aims to achieve. Kress and van Leeuwen (2006: 165) refer to this kind of visual reality as involving a sensory coding orientation.

Finally, when using assembly instructions or a route map, people attach great importance to the practical use of the image as a blueprint. Here the usefulness or effectiveness of the image plays the essential role, and this truth criterion is referred to as a technological coding orientation (Kress and van Leeuwen 2006: 165).

When analysing the different degrees of articulation in different aspects of a given coding orientation, Kress and van Leeuwen (2006: 160-3) identify eight modality markers for analysing the four coding orientations (naturalistic, abstract, sensory and technological): colour saturation, colour differentiation, colour modulation, contextualization, representation, depth, illumination and brightness. Chapter 6 will focus on the analysis of visual modality, adopting a multilevel view on the choice of different coding orientations in the primary and secondary EFL textbooks.

3.4.4 Composition

While representation deals with the way images construe phenomena within an image and interaction is concerned with the relations between images and their viewer, composition composes the representational and interactive meanings as a meaningful whole through three interrelated systems: information value, salience and framing (Kress and van Leeuwen 2006: 177).

Information value is realized through the placement of visual elements. Specifically, it is argued that different 'zones' of an image are endowed with different information values. For instance, it is suggested that the 'left-right' placement produces the 'Given-New' structure, reflecting the conventional direction of alphabetic written texts in Western culture.[8] The element located on the left is regarded as the familiar agreed-upon point of departure for the message, while the element on the right is considered to involve less expected, problematic or contestable information that is not yet known. Along the vertical axis from top to bottom within the picture space, what is placed in the upper part is presented as the 'ideal', generalized essence of the information that implies a promise of 'what it might be', whereas what is placed in the lower part is the 'real', practically oriented, down-to-earth information that indicates the actual situation of 'what it is'. In addition to the polarized compositions of Given-New and Ideal-Real, there is also a centred compositional principle whereby an opposition is established between Centre and Margin. The central element provides the nucleus of the information, while the marginal elements are subservient to and organized around it.

With its particular applicability in the multimodal advertisements and magazine texts as illustrated by Kress and van Leeuwen (2006), this framework of Given/New and Ideal/Real information value, nevertheless, remains a topic for scholarly contention. As Caple (2013: 86–7) points out, this analytical framework for compositional configurations seems problematic when examining newspapers and individual press photographs. Further discussion on its limitations in the application to the layout of different types of multimodal documents could be found in Bateman (2008: 40–52; 2014: 202) and Forceville (1999: 171).

Salience is the second dimension in composition analysis. It deals with how some elements can be more eye-catching than others. Kress and van Leeuwen (2006: 202) identify several factors that can make an element salient, including size, sharpness of focus, tonal contrast, colour contrast, foregrounding and some other specific cultural factors.

The third key parameter in visual composition, framing, is concerned with the separation and connection of visual elements. Disconnected elements can be separated through a wide range of devices, such as framelines, pictorial framing devices, empty space between elements, discontinuity or contrast in colour. Connection of visual elements, on the other hand, can be achieved through the absence of framing devices, vectors that connect elements, and similarity or continuity of colour.

Kress and van Leeuwen's (2006, 2020) analytical framework provides an applicable descriptive tool for visual analysis. They further distinguish options and sub-categories of the concepts reviewed earlier. The brief introduction here aims simple at outlining the key principles, while relevant illustrations and detailed explanations in relation to data analysis will be presented in Chapters 4 to 6.

3.5 Mapping interpersonal management in multimodal EFL textbook discourse

The previous sections have introduced the basic principles and key concepts of SFL, including the APPRAISAL system (Martin & White 2005) and the *Reading Images* (Kress & van Leeuwen 2006, 2020) model of visual analysis. We will now focus on why these models provide robust tools for the exploration of interpersonal meaning in textbooks involving both verbiage and image.

Adopting a social-semiotic perspective, our research views EFL textbooks as a set of predictable configurations of semiotic choices from both verbal and visual meaning-making systems. As mentioned in Section 3.2.4, studies of interpersonal meaning need to take into consideration both the interactive and the personal dimensions. This section will be devoted to the explanation of how to model the interaction between textbook editor and reader, how to analyse the intermodal construal of attitudinal meanings, and how to develop a multilevel view of visual modality.

3.5.1 Identifying multimodal ENGAGEMENT devices and play of voices

As mentioned in Section 3.4.1, we need to consider both the people and things within the picture frame and the image producer and viewer outside the picture frame. Accordingly, three kinds of relationships in visual communication can be identified: relations between represented participants, relations between interactive and represented participants, and relations between interactive participants (Kress and van Leeuwen 2006: 114). In previous studies, the first type of relation has been systematically approached under the heading of 'representation' (see Section 3.4.1 for further discussion), and the second type of relation has been comprehensively studied within the category of 'interaction' (see Section 3.4.2). However, the third type of relation in visual communication, that is how the image producer and receiver act on each other through images, has been relatively untouched.

For this reason we bring in the notion of ENGAGEMENT within the APPRAISAL system (Martin and White 2005, White 2003) to fill the gap. In doing so we focus on the fact that verbal communication is 'dialogic' – to speak or write involves acknowledgement of what has been said/written before, and simultaneously anticipation the intended reader/listeners' responses (Martin and White 2005: 92–3). If this view is extended to multimodal communication involving both language and images, a reader of verbal texts will at the same time be a viewer of images, and producers of the multimodal discourse will include both writers and image producers. This study will identify multimodal ENGAGEMENT devices and analyse the ways they are used to mediate heteroglossic space.

In EFL textbook discourse the voice of depicted characters deserves our attention. Chapter 4 will be devoted to the analysis of the interplay of multiple voices by drawing on the ENGAGEMENT and GRADUATION systems as well as analysis of visual interaction. The ways that the represented participants (i.e. characters) and the interactive participants (i.e. both textbook editors and the intended reader) engage with one another will also be explored.

3.5.2 Examining verbiage-image relations in attitudinal construal

As reviewed in Chapter 2, a concern with 'emotion and attitude' has been highlighted in the curriculum standards. However, few attempts have been made to consider how the multimodal meaning-making resources in textbooks can be deployed to realize the 'emotion and attitude' goal – something which has been recognized as a gap in the previous studies on textbooks in China (Zhang 2005). Although the significance of moral education and values education has been reflected upon by educationists (Zhong 2006; Zhu 2006), the discussions are seldom anchored in discourse analysis of pedagogic materials.

As introduced in Section 3.3.1, the system of ATTITUDE within APPRAISAL provides discourse analysts with an analytical framework for the description of verbal attitudinal meanings. Some studies of ATTITUDE have gone beyond language to include other semiotic resources including images (Economou 2006; Painter et al. (2013); Tian 2007; White 2006). The visual texts considered include lead pictures in newspapers, children's picture books and journalistic non-realistic visual displays. Chapter 5 of this book will further develop research on ATTITUDE in multimodal texts by examining the intermodal attitudinal inscriptions and invocations in EFL textbook discourse, including coverage of a range of visual styles from cartoons to photographs and portraits.

Taking into account both verbal and visual realizations of the three attitudinal regions (i.e. AFFECT, JUDGEMENT and APPRECIATION), this study pays particular attention to the verbiage-image relations in encoding the evaluative stance. Chapter 5 will be devoted to the cumulative effect of the intermodal construal of the 'emotion and attitude' goal in current pedagogy. Gradability, a central property of attitudinal meanings, will also be explored in Chapter 5.

3.5.3 Developing a multilevel view on visual modality

In addition to the evaluative positioning that the putative reader is assumed to take, another issue closely related to the various styles of images in EFL textbooks is how 'true' the message producer wants a receiver to perceive a representation to be. Chapter 6 explores this issue by drawing on the concept of modality in social semiotics (Hodge and Kress 1988; van Leeuwen 2005), adopting modality markers and coding orientations (Kress and van Leeuwen 2006, 2020) as analytical tools. It examines the 'interdependence' (Hodge and Kress 1988: 161) between modality and social relations – taking into account the influence of social relations (i.e. tenor) on the criteria for modality judgements. Analysis will be conducted for three teaching units on a similar topic but for different educational levels. Chapter 6 will also make some suggestions for ways in which the visual arrangements in textbooks may be improved.

Tenor is not the only factor affecting the choice of criteria for truth. Various degrees of deviation from the accepted truth criteria can be found in the multimodal texts targeting the same group of readers. Another register variable, that is field, will also need to be considered in the investigation of different choices of visual styles in teaching units conceived as a multimodal macrogenres.

3.6 Summary

This chapter has provided the theoretical underpinnings for this study and outlined the reasons for adopting an SFL approach to the interpersonal semantics of multimodal EFL textbook discourse. The following chapters engage with both interactive and personal dimensions of interpersonal management – including detailed analysis and discussion of relevant aspects of interpersonal semantics across visual and verbal modalities of communication.

4

Heteroglossic harmony

Multimodal ENGAGEMENT resources and voice interaction

4.1 Introduction

As explained earlier, interpersonal management includes both interactive and personal aspects. This chapter starts the exploration of interpersonal meaning in multimodal EFL textbooks with the interactive dimension, while the next chapter focuses on the attitudinal perspective. As one of the first endeavours to map multimodal choices onto the systems of ENGAGEMENT and ATTITUDE, Chapters 4 and 5 are intended to provide possibilities for further development of the dedicated linguistic systems in relation to images.

This chapter draws on the ENGAGEMENT system to analyse the alignment between the editor and reader, and/or image producer and viewer. It will first identify the multimodal ENGAGEMENT resources, and then investigate the ways they are employed to expand or contract the heteroglossic space, that is the room for mediating the multiple voices in the textbook discourse.

Specifically it will begin with the multiple voices in textbooks (i.e. editor voice, reader voice[1] and character voice), which is followed by the analysis of five types of multimodal resources as ENGAGEMENT devices in relation to the ways they function to mediate the interaction between multiple voices. It will then discuss the visual interaction in terms of contact/observe, social distance and point of view.

4.2 Identifying multiple voices in multimodal EFL textbook discourse

The notion 'voice' explored here needs to be clarified to avoid possible confusion with its grammatical usage. This study follows the fundamental works by

Bakhtin (1981, 1986) on heteroglossia – the dialogic and multi-voiced nature of all verbal communication, and draws on the semantic and rhetoric orientation that underpins the ENGAGEMENT network of resources for the management of heteroglossic space in a text (Fuller 1998; Martin 1997, 2000a; Martin and White 2005; White 2003). Recent studies have shown that ENGAGEMENT could be realized by multimodal resources (e.g. Fryer 2019). Before the identification and analysis of the dialogic interaction between multiple voices in multimodal EFL textbook discourse, this section will begin with a brief review of the previous studies on voice, with a particular focus on the efforts made by systemic linguists.

4.2.1 Previous studies on voice

According to Bakhtin (1981: 281), all spoken and written texts are intrinsically multi-voiced and should be understood 'against the background of other concrete utterances on the same theme'. As Bakhtin points out,

> Each utterance is filled with echoes and reverberations of other utterances. . . . Each utterance refutes, affirms, supplements, and relies on the others, presupposes them to be known, and somehow takes them into account . . . each utterance is filled with various kinds of responsive reactions to other utterances of the given sphere of speech communication. (Bakhtin 1986: 91)

The notion of heteroglossia was later developed by Kristeva (1986) into the concept of 'intertextuality'. Within SFL there are various perspectives on the issue of 'voice', which can be summarized as three main trends. Starting with the semiotic system of language, systemicists explore the heteroglossic nature of texts by analysing the resources of projection at the level of lexicogrammar (Halliday 1994; Halliday and Matthiessen 2004; Martin and Rose 2007a; Thompson 1996). The projection resources that introduce other voices into a text include the verbal and mental processes projecting locutions and ideas (e.g. I *think* . . ., He *doubts* . . .), and the embedded projections realized in nominal groups (e.g. *assertion, belief*). Along with projection, other linguistic resources such as those of modality (e.g. *probably, possibly*) and concession (e.g. *although*) also open space for other voices and enable negotiation between voices (Martin and Rose 2007a).

At the level of discourse semantics, a number of voice studies within SFL view voice in its abstract sense, modelling it as the recurrent configuration of evaluative resources, or a collection of recurrent 'syndromes of evaluation' (Martin 2003) in texts. This notion of voice has attracted substantial attention within SFL. Iedema et al. (1994) study multiple voicing in media discourse, identifying 'reporter voice', 'correspondent voice' and 'commentator voice' in different types of media genres. Coffin's (2000) work reveals the voice options of recorder, interpreter and adjudicator in history discourse. Macken-Horarik (2003) considers the writer/reader relations in students' responses to narratives in examination situations, and points out that the attributes of successful responses include a sensitivity to the hierarchy of voices and values. Hood (2004) examines 'voice' in academic writing from two perspectives: the actual source of a given evaluation, as well as the abstract evaluative syndromes technically named as 'voice roles' (i.e. 'observer', 'investigator' and 'critic'). It is noteworthy that voice in the abstract sense is distinct from the concept of 'voice' in heteroglossia studies. The former deals with the sub-potential of evaluative meanings that are characteristic of a specific register (e.g. 'reporter voice' in media discourse), which can be explicated as 'key' in the cline of instantiation concerning evaluation (Table 4.1); whereas the latter is concerned with the sources of propositions and evaluations heteroglossically present in texts (e.g. the 'voice' in Bakhtin's notion of dialogism).

The perspective on voice explored in the current research centres on voice in the sense of source, that is, whether a given proposition or evaluation is attributed to the author or to another source that is copresent in the text. In particular, this examination owes most to the taxonomy of ENGAGEMENT meanings and the ways in which ENGAGEMENT meanings can be graded (Martin 2000a; Martin and White 2005). Informed by Bakhtin's notion of heteroglossia, the ENGAGEMENT system (Martin and White 2005; see also White 2003) sets up networks of options for opening up or closing down heteroglossic space for multiple voices in a text. Given the large number of studies providing semantic

Table 4.1 Cline of Instantiation – Evaluation (Martin and White 2005: 164)

1. APPRAISAL (system) – the global potential of the language for making evaluative meanings, e.g. for activating positive/negative viewpoints.
2. Key (register) – situational variants or sub-selections of the global evaluative meaning-making potential – typically reconfiguration of the probabilities for the occurrence of particular evaluative meaning-making options or for the co-occurrence of options.
3. Stance (text type) – sub-selections of evaluative options within text; patterns of use of evaluative options within a given 'key' associated with particular rhetorical objectives and the construction of authorial personae.
4. Evaluation (instance) – instantiation of evaluative options in text.
5. Reaction (reading) – the take-up of evaluative meanings in a text according to the listener/reader's subjectively determined reading position; the attitudinal positions activated by the reader as a result of their interaction with the text.

and functional accounts of the linguistic resources that encode intersubjective positioning, few studies can be found that examine the ways in which multimodal meaning-making resources function to expand or contract the heteroglossic space. As mentioned in Chapters 1 and 2, modern communicative channels are far from being monomodal. The remainder of this chapter examines the role of multimodal ENGAGEMENT devices in mediating the play of multiple voices in the textbook discourse under the EFL teaching context in China. Before embarking on the detailed analysis and discussion, it will first identify the multiple voices existing in the multimodal EFL textbook discourse.

4.2.2 Multiple voices in EFL textbook discourse

In this section three voices that constitute the heteroglossic backdrop of EFL textbook discourse will be identified: editor voice, reader voice and character voice. First, editor voice can be easily observed in the use of imperative clauses as section titles, which has found wide application in EFL textbooks. These imperative clauses are either unmarked ones with no Mood such as *Read and write, Write and say, Match and say* and *Write and draw*, or the *let's* form where the understood Subject is 'you and I' (Halliday 1994: 87, Thompson 1996: 49) like *Let's start, Let's learn, Let's talk, Let's read, Let's play, Let's do, Let's make, Let's check, Let's find out, Let's draw, Let's sing* and *Let's chant*. As Martin and White (2005: 110–11) point out, in contrast with 'deontic' modality (e.g. *You* must *read the following paragraph*) that explicitly treats the demand as an assessment by the speaker of obligation instead of as a command, imperative is monoglossic in the sense that it does not refer to or allow for other possible alternative actions. Imperative is a monoglossic choice that includes the reader, and hence the speaker's (i.e. the editor's) role as a participant in the dialogic exchange is recognized. This type of section title encodes editor voice by way of giving general directions on what the reader is supposed to perform in certain tasks.

In addition to imperative clauses, section titles in EFL textbooks can also be nominal groups such as *Pair work, Group work, Story time, Pronunciation, Task time* and *Culture*. This type of section title encodes editor voice by clarifying the purposes or goals of teaching in the sections. Meanwhile, it implies the actions that the reader is assumed to take in the teaching section (e.g. *Group work* implies 'You *must* carry out the task in groups'). Through treating the proposal as an entity, this kind of section title backgrounds the proposer and conceals the 'must-ness' of the proposal, which tends to bear some resemblance to 'demodalization' in administrative discourse (Iedema 1995). Demodalization can be achieved in various ways, ranging from 'nominalization' (i.e. naming the commanding action) such as *Pronunciation*, 'demodulation' (i.e. masking the proposer and the controlling nature of the command) such as *Pair work* and *Story time*, to 'generalization' (i.e. generalizing the demodulations as members of a higher category) like *Culture*. Through ideationalizing the proposal, the process of control and demand is disguised as a natural and non-negotiable rule or institutional entity, and thus the institutional power of the editor is further enhanced.

Section titles are by no means the sole place where editor voice can be found. The practice of attaching labels to certain objects in an image, which is termed as 'labelling' in the current study, can equally convey editor voice. Take Figure 4.1 for instance. It is taken from an image in *Unit 1 My Classroom* in *PEP Primary Students' Book I for Year 4* (2003: 9). In this image, the unfinished words _ce-cream, _ish, _oose and _amburger are inserted as labels into an image depicting a chef holding a tray full of dishes, guiding the reader to complete the words and the drawings. Labelling is recognized as a kind of ENGAGEMENT device in multimodal EFL textbook discourse. Section 4.3.1 will explore this issue in detail. The labelling practice here is different from labelling in the general sense, in that it contains a missing letter that is intended to involve reader's participation. This type of intentionally unfinished text is classified into the category of 'jointly constructed text', which will be discussed in detail in Section 4.3.3.

The second voice of EFL textbook discourse is character voice. One of the distinctive features of the primary EFL textbooks under discussion is the extensive use of cartoon characters in creating the context of language in use. These characters either demonstrate how to play certain games that are considered to be conducive to language learning or guide the reader in performing certain

Figure 4.1 Multiple voices in multimodal EFL textbook discourse (adapted from *PEP Primary English Students' Book I for Year 4*, 2003: 9; Chen 2010a).

tasks. At the beginning of each primary EFL textbook there is a multimodal page introducing the major characters in the textbook (see for example Appendix I), presenting the names and images of fictional students and teachers (e.g. *Chen Jie*, *Mike* and *Miss White*) as well as the drawings of anthropomorphized animals (e.g. the bear *Zoom* and the fox *Zip*).

Character voice is often conveyed through a speech process (Kress and van Leeuwen 2006, 2020), which is visually realized by a dialogue balloon with an oblique line linking the Sayer (e.g. the character) to the content of the speech. Kress and van Leeuwen (2006: 68) describe this kind of structure as 'projective', as the utterance is not represented directly, but mediated through a Sayer. Take Figure 4.1 again for example. The dialogue balloon or speech balloon connects the character (i.e. *Mike* in the guise of a chef) with the utterance (i.e. *What are they? Do you know?*). Dialogue balloons are identified as one ENGAGEMENT device, which will be further analysed and discussed in Section 4.3.2.

The third kind of voice in EFL textbook discourse is reader voice. As Martin and White (2005: 162–4) point out, the subjectively determined reading position is the end point of instantiation. As observed in the data, the reader of an EFL textbook is not merely a passive addressee. Reader voice is explicitly articulated in jointly constructed text, which involves or requires reader's participation in its ultimate completion. Take Figure 4.1 for instance. The drawings of empty dishes and the blanks in the unfinished words _ce-cream, _ish, _oose and _amburger are left for the reader's completion. In SFL, language is regarded as a semiotic system of meaning potential, and language behaviour is interpreted as choice (Halliday 1978: 39; Eggins 2004: 20). Nevertheless, language is only 'one of the semiotic systems that constitute a culture' (Halliday 1978: 2). If this principle of potentiality is extended to include other semiotic systems, it can be argued that in making a choice from a semiotic system to finish a jointly constructed text, what the reader actually writes or draws (i.e. the actual semiotic choice) gets its meaning by being interpreted against the background of what he/she could have written or drawn (i.e. potential semiotic choices). Jointly constructed text, which is essential in engaging the reader in multimodal EFL textbook discourse, will be discussed in detail with examples in Section 4.3.3.

There are two additional resources for managing heteroglossic space in multimodal discourse: illustration and highlighting. The subsequent section will be devoted to the examination of the ways in which these five types of multimodal resources realize the ENGAGEMENT meanings of [disclaim], [proclaim], [entertain] and [attribute].

4.3 Multimodal resources as ENGAGEMENT devices

This section will identify multimodal ENGAGEMENT devices for managing heteroglossic space in multi-voiced EFL textbooks.

4.3.1 Labelling

As mentioned in Section 4.2.2, the term 'labelling' used in this study refers to the practice of inserting labels into an image to indicate some information concerning certain objects depicted. In primary and junior secondary EFL textbooks, labelling can be frequently observed in the images depicting the scene of a story which provides a context for language in use. See Figures 4.1 and 4.2 for instance.

Both Figures 4.2 and 4.3 include images of 'narrative representation' (Kress and van Leeuwen 2006: 45). Figure 4.2 is extracted from *Unit 3 Is This Your Skirt?* in *PEP Primary English Students' Book II for Year 4* (2003: 31), depicting the scene in which the character *Amy* is looking for her white socks in her bedroom. The image encompasses an action Process, with *Amy* being the Actor and clothes the Goal, while *Amy*'s arms serve as the two vectors. Watching the messy bedroom, *Amy*'s mother is anxious to help. Thus the image also includes a reactional process, with *Amy*'s mother as the Reactor and the scene in the bedroom as the Phenomenon. The vector in this reactional process is formed by the eyeline of

Figure 4.2 Labelling in multimodal textbook discourse [PEP Primary English Students' Book II for Year 4, 2003: 31].

Figure 4.3 Labelling in a junior secondary textbook [PEP Primary English Students' Book II for Year 4, 2003: 31].

Amy's mother. Speech processes are also involved. The two characters' voices are conveyed through dialogue balloons.

As shown in the image, editor voice contributes to negotiating meanings with character voice via labelling. By putting the labels of *jeans, pants, shorts, socks* and *shoes* onto the clothes scattered around the room, editor voice challenges or rules out alternative positions and thus limits the range of choices. For example, the label *shoes* closes down such alternatives as *sneakers* or *sports shoes*. If worded as a clause, the meaning of the visual practice of labelling could be presented as something like: '*I contend* that they are called shoes.' Therefore, it may be inferred that labelling functions to contract the heteroglossic space and can be identified as one of the resources that encode [proclaim], or [pronouncement] to be more precise. By overtly pronouncing the names of the items portrayed in the image, editor voice intervenes in the visual narrative representation. The multimodal resource of labelling can be viewed as 'an interpolation of the authorial presence so as to assert or insist upon the value or warrantability of the proposition' (Martin and White 2005: 128).

Figure 4.3 is taken from *Unit 7 How Do You Make a Banana Milk Shake?* in the junior secondary EFL textbook *Go for It Students' Book I for Year 8* (2005: 42). In Figure 4.3, through the use of labels indicating the names of the ingredients, editor voice interacts with the image depicting *Marie* and *Katie* making fruit salad. The reader of the textbook is required to fill in the table on the left of the image with the labels proclaimed by editor voice. The proclamations like *yogurt* and *apples* actually rule out other possibilities such as *milk* and *strawberries*, and such emphasis or insistence once again closes down any potential opposing viewpoint. Therefore, the formulation of labelling recognizes the heteroglossic diversity in the communicative context through presenting editor voice as challenging against any dialogic alternative. These labels function to close down the heteroglossic space in the text and help concentrate the reader's attention on the pronounced vocabulary items, which are supposed to be part of the prescribed language goals.

As analysed earlier, the ENGAGEMENT resource of labelling interpolates editor voice into the multimodal discourse of the textbooks, stresses the prescribed teaching goals, and confronts possible contrary positions. These instances of [pronouncement], according to Martin and White (2005: 129), are dialogic in the sense that they acknowledge the presence of counter viewpoints in the given communicative setting, and at the same time they are also contractive due to their challenge or resistance to possible dialogic alternatives. It is worth mentioning that this labelling practice cannot be found in the senior secondary EFL textbooks analysed for this project. In other words, editor voice chooses other means, that is verbal texts instead of images, to negotiate meanings with character voice in the senior secondary English-teaching context. I shall return to this issue in Section 4.3.5, where the ENGAGEMENT resource of highlighting is examined.

4.3.2 Dialogue balloons

Dialogue balloons, with their oblique protruding line connecting the Sayer with his/her utterance, are commonly found in the primary and junior secondary EFL textbooks. As discussed in Section 4.2, this type of visual structure is referred to as projection due to the indirect representation of the utterance. Dialogue balloons introduce character voice into a text, thus encoding the ENGAGEMENT meaning of [attribute]. In EFL textbook discourse three types of dialogue balloons are identified based on the different functions they perform: lending support to editor voice, explaining rules of games by demonstration and giving directions to the reader.

4.3.2.1 Lending support to editor voice

In bringing the external character voice into a text, certain dialogue balloons function to lend support to editor voice in the verbal text. See Figure 4.4 for instance, which is a teaching section entitled 'Good to know' taken from *Unit 2 My Favourite Season* in *PEP Primary English Students' Book II for Year 5* (2003: 24).

The upper part of Figure 4.4 verbally describes seasonal differences between Beijing and Sydney. The image underneath the verbal text demonstrates a

Figure 4.4 Dialogue balloons in lending support to editor voice [PEP Primary English Students' Book II for Year 5, 2003: 24].

dialogue between the two characters: *Chen Jie* and *John*. *John* asks *Chen Jie* what season it is in March in Beijing. She says it is Spring and asks him what season it is in Sydney. He then answers that it is Fall. The dialogue balloons bring in the external character voice, associating the proposition advanced by editor voice within the verbal text (i.e. *In Beijing, it's spring from March to May. Summer is from June to August. Fall is September to November. Winter is December to February the next year. But, in Sydney, it's spring from September to November. Summer is from December to February the next year. Fall is from March to May.*) with the external source of support from the characters who are assumed to be two students from China and Australia. Consequently, the dialogue balloons contribute to the heteroglossic alliance in the text, and therefore realize the ENGAGEMENT meaning of [attribute], or [acknowledging] to be more specific. By introducing character voice that supports the argument, editor voice presents the proposition as highly credible, hence aligning the reader into the position held by the editor.

4.3.2.2 Explaining rules of games by demonstration

In addition to giving support to editor voice, some dialogue balloons can also function to explain the rules of games by demonstration, as illustrated in Figures 4.5 and 4.6.

Figure 4.5 Dialogue balloons in explaining rules of games by demonstration in a primary textbook [PEP Primary English Students' Book I for Year 3, 2003: 53].

Figure 4.6 Dialogue balloons in explaining rules of games by demonstration in a junior secondary textbook [Go for It Students' Book I for Year 8, 2005: 5].

Figure 4.5 is an excerpt from *Unit 5 Let's Eat* in the *PEP Primary English Students' Book I for Year 3* (2003: 53). Through the use of cartoons, it shows the reader (i.e. a primary school student) how to practice the expressions of commanding and offering by playing a game with pictorial cards. In Figure 4.5 there is no verbal instruction telling the reader how to perform the activity, but a visual demonstration is given through the use of two images involving a dialogue between the characters *Sarah* and *Wu Yifan*. Their utterances are indicated in three dialogue balloons, and the two images as a whole demonstrate how to play the game multimodally, encouraging the reader to play a similar one. Therefore, it can be inferred that the dialogue balloons in the images function to introduce character voice, and thus contribute to the explanation of the rules of the game via a visual demonstration.

In Figure 4.6 two images lie beneath a verbal text that serves as an instruction given by the editor to show how to conduct an informal classroom survey concerning *Who is the healthiest*. Through the use of five imperative clauses (i.e. *add five questions to the survey on page 81, then ask three classmates the questions and take notes* and *discuss and decide*) and one WH-interrogative clause (i.e. *who is the healthiest student*), the editor demands action and information from the reader. The accompanying two images provide a visual demonstration to support the verbal text. The image on the left (henceforth Image I) takes a 'public distance' shot (Hall 1966: 110–20, cited in Kress and van Leeuwen 2006: 124), and includes within the picture frame the figures of eight students who are interviewing each other and taking notes. The other image on the right (henceforth Image II) portrays at the 'close personal distance' (ibid.) a student reporting his findings to the class. While the verbal text primarily conveys editor voice, the two images mainly express character voice. A corresponding relationship can be found between the two semiotic resources. Take speech function (Halliday 1994: 69) for instance. Table 4.2 summarizes the speech functions in the verbal text of Figure 4.6 and their corresponding visual patterns in Images I and II.

It can be inferred from Table 4.2 that the verbal instruction and visual demonstration in Figure 4.6 work in tandem to encourage the reader to carry

Table 4.2 Speech Functions and Their Corresponding Visual Patterns in Figure 4.6

Speech functions	Verbal instances (editor voice)	Corresponding visual patterns (character voice)
Command	Add five questions	In Image I, a demonstration of two of the questions is given, as presented in the dialogue balloons (i.e. *How often do you eat vegetables?* and *What sports do you play?*).
Command	Ask three classmates the questions, take notes, discuss	In Image I, students ask each other questions, taking notes and having free discussion in groups of four people.
Command	Decide	In Image II, a demonstration of a student reporting to the class on *Maria*'s healthy lifestyle is provided, as indicated in the dialogue balloon (i.e. *Maria exercises every day. She likes to play . . .*).
Question	Who is the healthiest student?	

out a similar survey about habits and health, with the visual demonstration providing an example for them to follow. Here character voice echoes editor voice in the way that the dialogue balloons demonstrate what kind of questions should be added to the survey and how a report should be made according to the findings of the survey. Therefore, it may be justified to say that the dialogue balloons in Figure 4.6 have the dual functions of explaining the rules of games by demonstration as well as lending support to editor voice. The images as a whole, on the one hand, can be read as an elaboration (Halliday 1994) of the verbiage, that is, as an example of how to conduct the survey, while on the other hand, they work together with the verbal texts in giving instructions to the reader, though in an implicit way.

It is noteworthy that the visual demonstration with dialogue balloons can be frequently observed in the task-oriented teaching sections such as *Let's play*, *Task time*, *Pair work* and *Group work*. In the teaching sections where interaction between readers is required in fulfilling the tasks, at least one way of accomplishing the tasks is exemplified by the characters in the images. Here the dialogue balloons actively make allowance for character voice, hence opening up the heteroglossic space and encoding the ENGAGEMENT meaning of [attribute].

4.3.2.3 *Giving directions to the reader*

In most images of the EFL textbooks, the represented participants (i.e. the characters) do not gaze out at the viewer (i.e. the reader of the textbook). As mentioned in Section 3.4.2 in Chapter 3, these images belong to the 'observe' type (Martin 2008a; Painter 2007), where the reader is positioned to simply observe what is represented within the picture frame. However, in the data there are a few images in which the characters look directly at the viewer and thus eye-to-eye engagement is created as far as focalization is concerned. As for this 'contact' type of image, directions are often given through character voice, which is indicated in the imperative or interrogative clauses in the dialogue balloons. The following example is taken from *Unit 1 How Do You Go There* in *PEP Primary English Students' Book I for Year 6* (2003: 12).

In Figure 4.7 the little policeman in the image looks at the viewer outside the picture frame, and therefore an eye contact is set up between the character and the viewer. The character's gaze symbolically invites the viewer to engage in an imaginary relation. The language in the dialogue balloon (i.e. *Look, read and match*) gives directions to the reader, clarifying what is required from the reader in completing the exercise. In the case of Figure 4.7, the reader is required to match the traffic signs with their corresponding meanings.

Figure 4.7 Dialogue balloons in giving directions to readers [PEP Primary English Students' Book I for Year 6, 2003: 12].

Figure 4.1 in Section 4.2.2 is another example that illustrates the function of dialogue balloons in giving directions to the reader. In Figure 4.1, the character *Mike* looks into the viewer's eyes. Through the gesture of holding the tray full of dishes and the use of a WH-interrogative clause and a yes-no interrogative clause in the dialogue balloon, the character encourages the viewer to draw the dishes and complete the words. Figures 4.1 and 4.7 belong to jointly constructed texts, in which the reader's contribution is essential in the completion of the texts.

4.3.3 Jointly constructed text

Another multimodal ENGAGEMENT resource encoding heteroglossia in EFL textbook discourse is the jointly constructed text. The term 'jointly constructed text' used in this book refers to any text that is intentionally unfinished and aims to involve reader's participation in its ultimate completion. Jointly constructed text, which is essential in aligning the reader, has found wide application in primary, junior and senior secondary EFL textbooks. Jointly constructed text takes a great diversity of forms, and the multimodal modes of communication expand the possibilities for expressing reader voice. This section will analyse and discuss the multimodal jointly constructed text as an ENGAGEMENT device in the EFL textbooks for different educational levels.

4.3.3.1 *Jointly constructed drawing exercises*

Figure 4.8 is an excerpt from *Unit 2 Look at Me* in *PEP Primary English Students' Book I for Year 3* (2003: 16). It is a multimodal exercise whose main body is an unfinished picture of a human face. The human face image is an analytical process (Kress and van Leeuwen 2006: 87) to be completed. As reviewed in Section 3.4.1 in Chapter 3, there is a part-whole relation between the participants (i.e. Carrier and Possessive Attributes) in an analytical Process. In Figure 4.8, the picture of human face is the Carrier, while the eyes, ears, nose and mouth to be drawn by the reader are the Possessive Attributes. The labels *eye, ear, nose* and *mouth* proclaimed by editor voice indicate what should be drawn. The reader is thus required to follow the labels to complete this structured analytical process.

The strong, diagonal line of the pencil at the top left corner of the human face image forms a vector, indicating the presence of a narrative representation. According to Kress and van Leeuwen (2006: 59–63), the vector links Actor and Goal in a transactional visual narrative Process, with the Actor being the participant from which the vector departs and Goal as the participant at which the vector is directed. In some circumstances, the Actor can be fused with a vector to different extents. In the case of Figure 4.8, the salient pencil, which is placed in the foreground with full colour saturation, plays the dual role of both the Actor and vector. The Goal in this transactional action Process is the unfinished drawing, and the vector formed by the oblique pencil encourages the reader to participate in co-constructing the multimodal text.

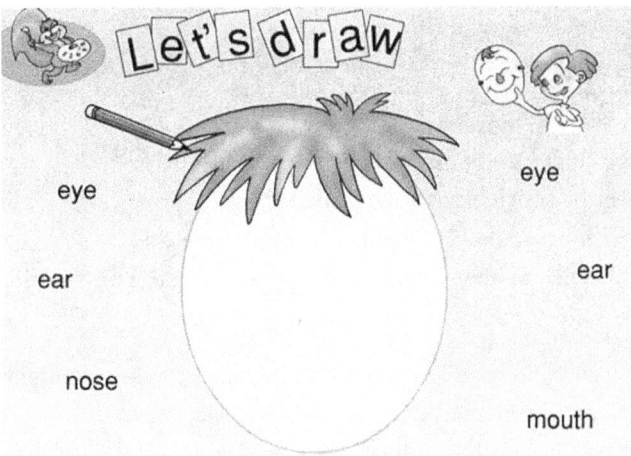

Figure 4.8 Jointly constructed drawing exercise [PEP Primary English Students' Book I for Year 3, 2003: 16].

In light of the labels that indicate the Possessive Attributes and the contour of human face, the reader is supposed to achieve the distant, Ideal goal as indicated in the upper smaller image. In this multimodal text the practice of labelling conveys editor voice, whereas the upper smaller image expresses character voice (which will be analysed as the ENGAGEMENT device of 'illustration' in Section 4.3.4). The lack of completion or fulfilment in this multimodal jointly constructed text in effect opens up space for other viewpoints or voices (in this case, reader voice) to join in. Reader voice engages with editor voice and character voice through co-constructing the text. Owing to the fact that the answer to this multimodal exercise comes from the external voice of the reader, the meaning of the unfinished jointly constructed text can be expressed in the clause '*According to* the reader, the picture will be . . .'. Therefore, it can be inferred that jointly constructed text functions to encode the ENGAGEMENT meaning of [attribute], expanding the heteroglossic space by bringing in reader voice.

4.3.3.2 *Multimodal jointly constructed herald page*

The multimodal jointly constructed texts commonly found in junior secondary EFL textbooks appear at the very beginning of each teaching unit. Consequently, this type of jointly constructed text is referred to as 'multimodal jointly constructed herald page'. Figure 4.9, which is taken from *Unit 10 Where Did You Go on Vacation* in the junior secondary textbook *Go for It Students' Book II for Year 7* (2005: 59), provides a good example.

The herald page in Figure 4.9 is part of *SECTION A* in the teaching unit, consisting of an image and three exercises (i.e. *1a, 1b* and *1c*). Editor voice is explicitly conveyed in the *Language Goal* on top of the image and in the instructions of the three exercises:

> Language Goal: Talk about past events.
> 1a. Match the activities with the pictures [a-g].
> 1b. Listen and number the people [1-5] in the picture.
> 1c. PAIRWORK Where did the people in activity 1a go on vocation? Make conversations.

Five imperative clauses and one WH-interrogative clause are employed in the *Language Goal* and in the three instructions. The imperative clauses all take the unmarked form without Mood. Here the discursive role of the editor can be easily perceived through the speech functions of command and question realized in the clauses in the *Language Goal* and instructions.

Figure 4.9 Multimodal jointly constructed herald page [Go for It Students' Book II for Year 7, 2005: 59].

The image underneath the *Language Goal* provides further specification and elaboration, and serves as a communicative setting for the newly learnt expressions that are used for talking about past events. In this image seven characters are portrayed as sitting or lying on the grass, recollecting and talking about past experiences and activities. Character voice is brought into the multimodal text via two dialogue balloons and seven thought balloons. The utterances in the dialogue balloons verbally demonstrate how to ask and tell other people about past events. The function of a thought balloon is quite similar to that of a dialogue balloon, in that the bubbled vector protruding from a thought balloon links the inner mental Process with the Senser, and hence the content of thoughts is mediated through the Senser instead of being represented directly. However, in Figure 4.9, unlike the dialogue balloons that draw upon verbal utterances, the thought balloons visualize the past activities that the characters recall to mind. Moreover, a letter label is attached to each of the images within the thought balloons, which indicates editor voice's interaction with character voice. Meanwhile, these letter labels also function to invite the reader's attention to the relation between the images and the corresponding verbal expressions in exercise *1a*. In addition to the seven-letter labels, five square boxes are also inserted and left blank for the reader to fill in according to the tape recording in exercise *1b*. By doing the matching exercises in *1a* and *1b*, reader voice is active in this multimodal herald page.

Figure 4.9, like any other multimodal herald page, is placed at the start of a new teaching unit. At that beginning stage of studying a teaching unit, there is an unequal possession of knowledge between the editor and the reader. This is consistent with the discursive relationship enacted between the communicative parties in the goal-setting part and instructions, as shown in the analysis earlier. In addition, solidarity is established and enhanced through the interpolation of character voice and reader voice into the multimodal text. Through the use of dialogue balloons and thought balloons, a variety of situations for practising talking about past events are provided and mediated by Sayers and Sensers. These Sayers and Sensers are the characters of the textbooks, represented in a comic style as the peers of the reader (i.e. junior secondary students) so as to enhance intimacy and cordiality. In other words, the interpolation of character voice sets up the multimodal text as not only pronounced by editor voice, and hence reduces the interpersonal distance between learners and the content of the teaching unit. Furthermore, the herald page is not yet completed until the reader's participation is taken into account, which contributes to the expansion of the heteroglossic space. To sum up, in Figure 4.9 the multimodal ENGAGEMENT devices of dialogue balloon, thought balloon and jointly constructed text work together to construe the communicative setting as heteroglossic rather than monoglossic.

4.3.3.3 *Jointly constructed verbal text with accompanying images*

This section will examine a third type of multimodal jointly constructed text, in which the reader participates in constructing the verbal text in light of the accompanying images. Figure 4.10, for instance, is taken from *Unit 4 Earthquakes* in the senior secondary EFL textbook *New Senior English for China Student's Book 1* (2004: 30).

In Figure 4.10 editor voice is explicitly conveyed in the instruction that lies above the picture of a speech draft with four stamps depicting the new *Tangshan*:

> Imagine that after your speech, Zhang Sha asks you to give a short talk about the new stamps to honour the city. You may use the model or write your own little talk.

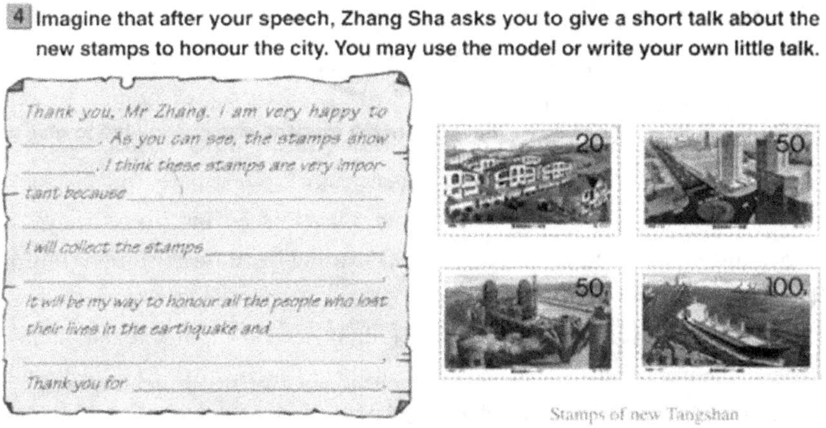

4 Imagine that after your speech, Zhang Sha asks you to give a short talk about the new stamps to honour the city. You may use the model or write your own little talk.

> Thank you, Mr Zhang. I am very happy to _____. As you can see, the stamps show _____. I think these stamps are very important because _____.
>
> I will collect the stamps _____.
>
> It will be my way to honour all the people who lost their lives in the earthquake and _____.
>
> Thank you for _____.

Stamps of new Tangshan

Figure 4.10 Jointly constructed verbal text with accompanying images [New Senior English for China Student's Book 1, 2004: 30].

By using an imperative clause, editor voice directs the reader to envisage preparing for a short talk about the four stamps designed to honour the *Tangshan* City. The use of a finite modal operator *may* in the second clause indicate the low degree of obligation. In other words, the reader is allowed to make use of the model provided in the draft, while the alternative choice of not using the draft is still valid. The character *Mr Zhang Sha* is verbally introduced into this text but not visually represented. His identity was indicated in the previous teaching sections as an officer from the government of *Tangshan* City. Through the introduction of this external character voice, the heteroglossic space of the text is expanded. Reader voice is invited to engage interactively with editor voice as well as character voice, in that the exophoric references of the second person *you* and the possessive deictic *your* associate the external reader voice with the proposal being advanced in the verbal instruction. Nevertheless, the jointly constructed speech draft will not be finalized until the reader's contribution is considered. Section 5.4.3 in Chapter 5 will return to this jointly constructed multimodal text, where emphasis will be placed on text-image relations in terms of the multimodal construal of attitudinal orientation in jointly constructed text.

To sum up, the multimodal resource of jointly constructed text brings in reader voice, and it is identified in the ENGAGEMENT network as encoding [attribute]. Character voice is often introduced into the jointly constructed text through a variety of semiotic modes, and relationships of power and solidarity in EFL textbook discourse can be negotiated through the play of the multiple voices.

4.3.3.4 Readership construal

As reviewed in Section 3.2.3 in Chapter 3, it is the act of reader interpretation that is at the end of the 'cline of instantiation' from system to reading (Martin and White 2005: 163; Martin and Rose 2007a: 312). In other words, the lowest level of instantiation is the meaning taken from the text based on the social subjectivity of a reader, rather than the text itself. The cline from the system of meaning-making potential to the final reading position is summarized in Figure 3.2.

This study follows Martin and White's (2005) view on alignment and putative reader, and jointly constructed texts are considered as construing for themselves an 'ideal', 'intended' or 'envisaged' reader,[2] with whom the textbook editor aims to align. As analysed earlier, jointly constructed texts open up space for dialogic alternatives for the reader, thus aligning the reader in the final completion of the texts.

A text construes or models its reader by presenting the writer as taking for granted that the reader shares with the writer a particular viewpoint, or as assuming that the proposition being advanced is problematic/unproblematic, or as supposing that the reader needs to be convinced of a particular viewpoint (Martin and White 2005: 95). In the case of jointly constructed texts, the editor assumes that the reader shares with him/her a certain amount of knowledge to understand the requirements of the texts. In Figure 4.8, for instance, the reader should have at least a general idea of the contour of human face, as well as the English vocabulary concerning the basic facial features. As for Figures 4.9 and 4.10, the English-language level of the intended reader is assumed to be advanced enough to comprehend and perform the tasks.

However, the issue of alignment or solidarity is by no means a matter of total agreement between the communicative parties. As Martin and White point out,

> solidarity can turn, not on questions of agreement/disagreement, but on tolerance for alternative viewpoints, and the communality into which the writer/speaker aligns the reader can be one in which diversity of viewpoint is recognized as natural and legitimate. (Martin and White 2005: 96)

While the blanks or gaps in the jointly constructed texts are left for the reader to complete, the reader still has certain degree of freedom, which depends largely on the context, to provide alternative answers other than those expected by the editor. For example, the reader of Figure 4.8 is allowed to draw the human face in ways other than the finished one held by the character *Mike*: the reader could depict the eyes with apparent pupils, or the mouth with teeth visible, or even a crying human face instead of a smiling one, as long as the depiction complies with the context of face-drawing. Similarly, in the *1c PAIRWORK* exercise of Figure 4.9, the reader is free to choose wording to make the conversations as long as it is concerned with the characters' activities on vacation and keeps to a dialogue pattern. And the reader of Figure 4.10 enjoys even more freedom in composing the speech draft, as long as the writing agrees with the communicative context of accepting the invitation from Mr *Zhangsha* to give a talk about the stamps to honour the city.

Turning to a more theory-based explanation of these examples, Martin and Rose (2007a: 312–13; see also Martin and White 2005:62) classify different types of reading into three categories: compliant reading, resistant reading and tactical reading. Compliant readings take up, or subscribe to the reading position which is naturalized by the general trajectory of meanings in a text; resistant readings positions work against the naturalized reading position; while tactical readings rework the reading position naturalized in a text for some specific interests or social purposes. It can be inferred from the analysis that the reading position construed in the jointly constructed texts in multimodal EFL textbooks is generally a compliant one, in that the completion of the texts requires a mostly cooperative performance of the ideal reader. This dialogic editor-reader alignment permits to some extent the possibility of answers other than those prescribed by the editor. Nevertheless, the construed putative reading position only allows for the possible alternatives that comply with the given communicative context.

4.3.4 Illustration

According to Barthes (1977: 38–41), text-image relations can be classified into three types: 'anchorage' (text 'elucidates' image), 'illustration' (image elucidates text) and 'relay' (text and image 'stand in a complementary relationship'). The major social purpose and function of EFL textbooks is for language teaching and learning, and there are quite a number of images clarifying or supporting the corresponding texts. This section will be devoted to the discussion of the ENGAGEMENT meanings encoded in the images of Barthes' illustration.

4.3.4.1 *Image as the link between verbal texts*

Take Figure 4.11 which exemplifies how an image illustrates verbal texts by serving as the link between them. Figure 4.11 is an excerpt from *Unit 3 How Many* in the *PEP Primary English Students' Book II for Year 3* (2003: 26). What

Figure 4.11 Image as the link between verbal texts [PEP Primary English Students' Book II for Year 3, 2003: 26].

is supposed to be learnt in this teaching section are the letters *j, k* as well as the words *jeep, jump, kangaroo* and *key*. Here two images in comic style play an essential role in associating these otherwise unrelated words with each other in a meaningful way. To be specific, the image on the left links *jeep* with *jump* by describing a *jeep* frightening a frog so it *jumped* away, whereas the one on the right associates *kangaroo* with *key* by depicting a big *key* in a *kangaroo*'s pouch. In doing so, the words to be learnt are meaningfully connected through the funny cartoons, which facilitates understanding and memorization. The editor associates the words by resorting to cartoon characters, and the characters on the other hand acknowledge and lend support to editor voice. The degree of openness in the multimodal text is therefore increased. In this sense, the illustration functions to realize the ENGAGEMENT meaning of [attribute].

4.3.4.2 *Illustration of improper behaviours*

The majority of the characters in the EFL textbooks exemplify proper behaviours. Nonetheless, illustrations of improper behaviours can still be found in these textbooks. For example, Figure 4.12 is taken from *Unit 1 Our School* in the *PEP Primary English Students' Book II for Year 4* (2003: 12).

In Figure 4.12 editor voice is explicit in the five imperative clauses, which advise the reader not to violate the regulations in school. Four of the five

Figure 4.12 Illustration of improper behaviours [PEP Primary English Students' Book II for Year 4, 2003: 12].

imperative clauses proscribe the violations by using negative polarity: *Don't drink or eat in the computer room*, *Don't walk on the grass in the garden*, *Don't push in the hallway* and *Don't waste food in the canteen*. As for the visual displays, five images are employed to illustrate the imperative clauses in the verbal texts by describing five instances of violation: playing noisily in the library, drinking and eating in the computer room, walking on the grass in the garden, pushing in the hallway and wasting food in the canteen. It can be inferred that in Figure 4.12 editor voice in the verbal texts and character voice in the five illustrative images go against each other. In between these five illustrations, there is another small image depicting an anthropomorphized fox holding a megaphone and shouting *NO*, which further strengthens the contrast in the voices. The illustrative images here function to contract or close down the heteroglossic space, and consequently the degree of openness to other voices is reduced. Therefore, it could be inferred that the five illustrative images in Figure 4.12 encode the ENGAGEMENT meaning of [disclaim].

4.3.4.3 *Backgrounded and foregrounded illustrations*

Another way of lending support to editor voice through the use of illustration is where the supportive image is backgrounded or foregrounded. A case in point is

Figure 4.13, which is taken from *Unit 1 Friendship* in the senior secondary EFL textbooks *New Senior English for China Student's Book 1* (2004: 2).

In Figure 4.13 the verbal text entitled *ANNE'S BEST FRIEND* tells the story about a Jewish girl named *Anne Frank*, who had to hide away from Nazis in the Second World War. She treated her diary as her best friend, and recorded her experiences and feelings in it. At the end of the verbal text an imperative clause is used (i.e. *Now read how she felt* . . .) to direct the reader to read an extract of *Anne*'s diary, which takes the form of a piece of torn paper from the diary. A monochromatic photograph of *Anne* is presented as the background of the first paragraph of the verbal text *ANNE'S BEST FRIEND*, where the character *Anne* is first introduced. *Anne*'s voice is further detected in the image of the extract of diary, at the foot of which the sepia-tone photograph of her diary is foregrounded. The photographs of *Anne* and her diary represent *Anne* as a real person and her diary as a tangible genuine document, which bears evidence of the factuality of the anecdote. Here the voice of the character *Anne* lends support to editor voice

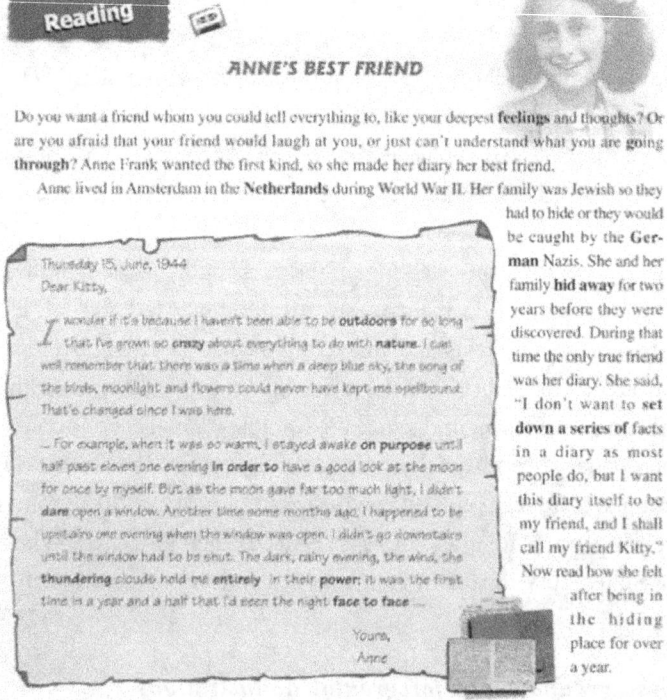

Figure 4.13 Background and foreground illustration [New Senior English for China Student's Book 1, 2004: 2].

in the verbal text via illustration, which functions to expand the heteroglossic space and can be identified as the ENGAGEMENT device that encodes [attribute]. Meanwhile, through supporting editor voice, this attribution further enhances the authenticity of what is described by the editor in the story, hence reinforcing the ENGAGEMENT meaning of [proclaim] in the text.

4.3.5 Highlighting

Certain elements in a visual display are more eye-catching than others, hence creating a hierarchy of visual importance. According to Kress and van Leeuwen (2006: 201–3), a high degree of visual importance is referred to as 'salience', which can be realized through relative size, colour contrast, tonal contrast, placement in the composition, sharpness of focus and all other means that attract the viewer's attention. This section will examine ways of prioritizing certain visual elements via the choice of colour or typeface: highlighting in image and verbal text, and examine the way it contributes to the construction of a heteroglossic setting.

4.3.5.1 *Highlighting text in image*

Take Figure 4.14 for instance to analyse highlighting in images, which is taken from *Unit 2 Where Is the Science Museum* in *PEP Primary English Students' Book I for Year 6* (2003: 16). The whole image includes two parts. The upper part depicts a girl asking a policeman about the location of the library. The word *library* is highlighted in the dialogue balloon that conveys the voice of the girl.

In the dialogue balloon, the word *library* is highlighted, which indicates that it is merely one of the many possible options that can be chosen from. Other alternatives can be found in the five smaller images in the lower part, which depict five buildings: *post office, hospital, cinema, bookstore* and *science museum*. Each of these five alternatives can be substituted for the word *library* which has already been chosen in the dialogue balloon. If put into words, the ENGAGEMENT meaning of the reason for highlighting the word *library* is that '*It is possible that you want to go to the library*' or '*You may want to go to the library*'. In addition, it is noteworthy that these alternatives all come from the multimodal discourse itself. In other words, the multimodal text has already determined the range of possible alternatives: the five locations presented in the five small images. Therefore, it can be inferred that the highlighted word in Figure 4.14 indicates the status of the highlighted word as one of the possible options against the wider backdrop that consists of alternatives from the multimodal text itself, hence functioning to realize the ENGAGEMENT meaning of [entertain]. The highlighted

Figure 4.14 Highlighting in visual image [PEP Primary English Students' Book I for Year 6, 2003: 16].

word *library* opens up the heteroglossic space to allow for other voices that come from the text itself instead of from somewhere outside the multimodal text.

4.3.5.2 Highlighting in verbal text

As mentioned in Section 4.3.1, it is mainly the verbal text rather than image that provides the context of language teaching in the senior secondary EFL textbooks. Accordingly, there must be other types of multimodal ENGAGEMENT devices besides the practice of labelling adopted in the senior secondary EFL textbooks to negotiate meanings with and around character voice. The current section will take the extract of *Anne*'s diary in Figure 4.13 for instance to describe how the highlighting in verbal text functions to mediate heteroglossic space.

The extract of *Anne*'s diary, as is represented in Figure 4.15 (bold-face in the original excerpt from the textbook), is written in the first person, as if *Anne* was sharing her experiences and feelings with her friend *Kitty* in a letter.

> Thursday 15, June, 1944
> Dear Kitty,
> I wonder if it's because I haven't been able to be **outdoors** for so long that I've grown so **crazy** about everything to do with **nature**. I can well remember that there was a time when a deep blue sky, the song of the birds, moonlight and flowers could never have kept me spellbound. That's changed since I was here.

... For example, when it was so warm, I stayed awake **on purpose** until half past eleven one evening **in order to** have a good look at the moon for once by myself. But as the moon gave far too much light, I didn't **dare** open a window. Another time some months ago, I happened to be upstairs one evening when the window was open. I didn't go downstairs until the window had to be shut. The dark, rainy evening, the wind, the **thundering** clouds held me **entirely** in their **power**; it was the first time in a year and a half that I'd seen the night **face to face**.

Yours,
Anne

The words and expressions highlighted in bold-face type signal textbook editor voice in this personal record of daily experiences/letter to a close friend. In other words, the highlighted verbal texts are the vocabulary and expressions selected by the editor for the students to learn. It could be inferred that the resource of highlighting here functions to expand the heteroglossic space and bring in editor voice, and hence can be identified in the ENGAGEMENT system as encoding [attribute].

4.3.6 Gradability of ENGAGEMENT values in multimodal discourse

As reviewed in Chapter 3, gradability is a general feature of the ENGAGEMENT system. This section focuses on how the aforementioned multimodal meaning-making resources up-scale and down-scale ENGAGEMENT values. As pointed out by Martin and White (2005: 135), the meanings scaled within the ENGAGEMENT system vary from sub-system to sub-system. Therefore, the current discussion concentrates on the same type of ENGAGEMENT device that encodes the same ENGAGEMENT meaning.

As analysed in Section 4.3.2, dialogue balloons can be categorized into three types according to their functions: (i) those that support editor voice (see Figure 4.4), (ii) those that explain rules of games by demonstration (see Figures 4.5 and 4.6), and (iii) those that give directions to the reader (Figure 4.7). In the case of Type (i), editor voice is present in the communicative context, which is represented in a separate paragraph above the image of the two characters whose conversation lends support to editor voice. The support from character voice further enhances editor voice by providing evidence for the editor's statement. The editor's 'proclamation' is accordingly strengthened, and hence the heteroglossic space is in a sense contracted as compared with the two other types of dialogue balloons. Editor voice in Type (ii), on the other hand, is absent from the demonstration of games (but sometimes appears in the instruction), while character voice is responsible for the verbal and visual demonstration. In Type (iii), the editor leaves it to character voice to be solely responsible for the exercise instruction. Therefore, it may be inferred that Type (iii) opens up more space for character voice than Type (ii), because the responsibility of giving instructions could have been undertaken by an editor, whereas demonstrations are not necessarily given by an editor. Type (ii) in turn creates more heteroglossic space than Type (i), in that editor voice is absent from Type (ii) but present in Type (i), and character voice in Type (i) actually enhances editor voice. In other words, within the ENGAGEMENT device of dialogue balloon, GRADUATION operates along the axis of FORCE, that is, the amount of responsibility that the characters undertake in instructing the reader or the amount of space opened up to engage character voice. In terms of the locations of these three types of dialogue balloon along the gradability cline of [attribute] value, it may be summarized that Type (iii) is scaled as occupying the point with the highest value among the three, Type (ii) is situated at the point with medium value, and Type (i) is the one with the lowest value among the three (Chen and Huang 2009), as is diagrammatically presented in Figure 4.15.

Based on the analysis in Section 4.3.3, jointly constructed texts in the EFL textbooks can be subdivided into three types: (i) jointly constructed drawing exercise (see Figure 4.8), (ii) multimodal jointly constructed herald page (see Figure 4.9), and (iii) jointly constructed verbal text with accompanying images (see Figure 4.10). The gradable [attribute] values encoded in jointly constructed text can be approached in light of the degree of their completion or 'fulfilment' (Hood and Martin 2007): that is, their prototypicality (i.e. FOCUS) as a co-construction that involves reader's participation. It may be argued that the higher degree of completeness a jointly constructed text possesses, the less heteroglossic space it opens up to alternative voices. This is because a jointly constructed text will not have much room for the external voices to participate in the co-construction if it is almost complete on its own. The image in Type (i) and the verbal text in Type (iii) are far from being finished. Moreover, the reader's participation in drawing facial features or filling in the gaps adds on new meanings to the original text. These two types of jointly constructed text invite,

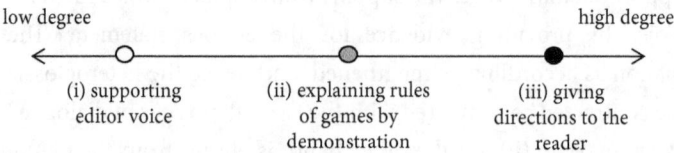

Figure 4.15 FORCE of three types of dialogue balloon in realizing [attribute] value.

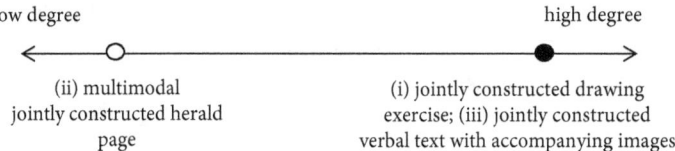

Figure 4.16 FOCUS of three types of jointly constructed text in realizing [attribute] value.

or even demand participation of the external reader voice, and therefore they may be scaled as possessing relatively high [attribute] value. Type (ii), on the contrary, is in itself a complete image as far as the drawing goes, and the square blanks that demand reader's participation are later added into the complete image. In other words, the incompleteness is not an inherent property but a later-added feature in Type (ii), and hence it encodes low [attribute] value (see Figure 4.16).

Of the three types of illustration identified in Section 4.3.4, two of them encode the same type of ENGAGEMENT meaning of [attribute]: (i) image as the link between verbal texts (see Figure 4.11), and (ii) background and foreground illustration (see Figure 4.13). The FORCE of [attribute] meaning realized in illustration can be investigated by looking at the indispensability of the image in linking different parts of a verbal text. As analysed in Section 4.3.4, Type (i) functions to associate the two semantically unrelated words with each other through the use of a meaningful and intriguing visual display. In other words, there would not be any semantic relevance between the two words with the same initial letter if the image were removed. As compared with Type (i), the de-focused, backgrounded photograph of *Anne* and the foregrounded photograph of *Anne*'s diary in Type (ii) is not so indispensable to the whole multimodal text. Even if the image were removed, the verbal text would still be coherent and consistent. Therefore, it may be concluded that Type (i) calls for the alternative voice of the characters to integrate different parts of the verbal text, hence opening up more heteroglossic space. Accordingly, Type (i) can be graded as encoding higher [attribute] value than Type (ii), which does not play an essential role in linking the verbal text, as is demonstrated in Figure 4.17.

As stated at the beginning of this section, the current discussion of the gradability of ENGAGEMENT values is mainly conducted within the same multimodal ENGAGEMENT devices encoding the same meaning in EFL textbook discourse. Further studies may be conducted to identify other multimodal

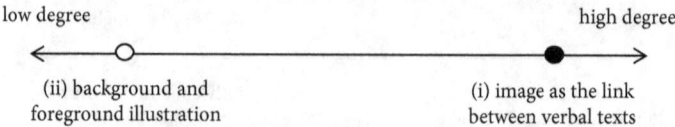

Figure 4.17 Force of two types of illustration in realizing [attribute] value.

ENGAGEMENT devices in various communicative contexts, and a GRADUATION continuum may be established within the same or across different semiotic resources encoding the same ENGAGEMENT meaning.

4.4 Voice interaction in multimodal EFL textbook discourse

The previous section has identified five types of multimodal ENGAGEMENT device in EFL textbook discourse (i.e. labelling, dialogue balloon, jointly constructed text, illustration and highlighting), and accounted for how these multimodal resources realize the ENGAGEMENT meanings of [disclaim], [proclaim], [entertain] and [attribute]. These multimodal ENGAGEMENT devices contribute to the expansion and contraction of the heteroglossic space in a text. This section is concerned with the interplay of the multiple voices, and will also explore the interactive meaning encoded in multimodal EFL textbook discourse in terms of contact/observe, social distance and point of view (for the theoretical account, see Section 3.4.2).

4.4.1 Focalization and eye contact

A large number of the images in the EFL textbooks depict people or human-like creatures with eyes and facial expressions, but the majority of these animate participants in the picture frame do not gaze at the viewer. In other words, they are 'observe' images (Painter 2007; see Section 3.4.2 for further discussion). Some of these represented participants in our data are characters in a story (e.g. Figures 4.2, 4.3 and 4.4); others provide demonstrations for the reader to follow (e.g. Figures 4.5 and 4.6). The text presents them relatively impersonally as items of information and objects of observation. This observation is mainly direct rather than vicarious. One notable exception is Figure 4.2, in which the observation is mediated through the eyes of the focalizing characters *Amy* and her mother. In this image, the viewer is visually placed behind *Amy*'s mother, observing her as well as what she sees in *Amy*'s bedroom. By the same token, the viewer is again observing the wardrobe 'along with' the character *Amy*.

Figures 4.1 and 4.7 are exceptions to the dominant 'observe' type of image. In these cases, the represented participants look directly at the viewer, and therefore the viewer is engaged in eye contact with the characters. These represented participants are requiring the reader to do the exercises or answer questions according to the requirements, and their gestures and/or the utterances in dialogue balloons further specify what is required. In other words, the represented participants are portrayed as people directly addressing the reader instead of passive phenomena merely for observation. These images belong to the 'contact' type, and more often than not they are also jointly constructed texts demanding reader's participation. Together with the imperatives and interrogatives in the dialogue balloons, the 'contact' images invite the reader to participate in the jointly constructed texts, and hence bring in reader voice and encode the ENGAGEMENT meaning of [attribute].

4.4.2 Reader involvement and social distance

The choice of social distance is another parameter that indicates various types of interaction between the viewer and the represented participants. In visual communication, the different degrees of social distance are interpreted as the continuum of the 'size of frame' of shots (Kress and van Leeuwen 2006: 124). In the present data of EFL textbooks, the images cover a wide range of shots from 'extreme close-up' to 'long shots', which suggests the degrees of distance vary from 'intimate distance' to 'public distance' with many intermediate degrees.

The social distance implied in the visual displays corresponds with the voice interaction. For instance, the image of Figure 4.14 shows the full figures of the represented participants and their surroundings, and thus the relationship between the viewer and the represented participants is that of 'public distance'. As revealed in the analysis in Section 4.3.5.1, the ENGAGEMENT meaning of [entertain] is encoded in this image through the use of highlighting, which indicates that alternative positions all come from the internal source within the multimodal discourse itself. In other words, the reader is not involved in determining the range of possible options, because they are already included in the five small images in the lower part of the multimodal text. Therefore, it may be justified to say that the distant, impersonal public distance complies with the ENGAGEMENT meaning of [entertain].

Public distance is also adopted in those images in which editor voice engages with character voice (such as Figures 4.2, 4.3 and 4.12). In these cases, the reader is addressed by the proclamation or disclamation from editor voice instead of actively engaging himself/herself with the voices within the discourse. This low degree of reader's involvement also echoes the choice of public distance. The high degree of reader's involvement can be found in jointly constructed texts (e.g. Figures 4.1, 4.7 and 4.8). The medium shots that show the figure from waist up in Figures 4.1 and 4.7 suggest the 'far personal distance', while the extreme close-up in Figure 4.8 implies 'intimate distance'. The represented participants in these images are presented within easy touching distance to the viewer. This agrees with the meaning of [attribute] encoded in these jointly constructed texts, in which the reader is invited to participate in the ultimate completion of the texts and thus has access to the field of heteroglossia.

Nevertheless, the discussion of the association of voice interaction and social distance here is by no means claiming that voice interaction plays a decisive role in choosing the patterns of social distance. The choice of shots that conveys the degree of social distance is a complex issue. Other factors such as the conventions in visual genres (Kress and van Leeuwen 2006: 126) need also to be taken into account before a comprehensive account of the social distance in images is achieved.

4.4.3 Character engagement and point of view

The third factor that should be considered in relation to voice interaction is point of view, which can be approached along the horizontal axis and vertical axis. As reviewed in Section 3.4.2, the horizontal angle conveys whether the interactive participant (i.e. image producer and viewer) is involved with (i.e. frontal angle) the represented participants or is detached from them (i.e. oblique angle); while the vertical angle implies whether it is the interactive participant has power over the represented participants (i.e. high angle) or vice versa (i.e. low angle) or their relation is an equal one (i.e. level angle) (Kress and van Leeuwen 2006: 133–43).

The majority of the images under examination adopt the frontal and level angle, and hence what is depicted in the image is presented as 'part of our world'. In other words, the relation between the represented participants and the viewer is one of relative equality. The frontal angle indicates a high degree of reader identification and involvement, which has a lot to do with the engagement of character voice. Although power differences do exist between the textbook editor and reader due to the unequal possession of knowledge, the interpolation of characters into the heteroglossic setting enables the reader to negotiate alignment with the characters on an equal footing. That partially explains why the represented participants are viewed from a level angle.

In closing, the interaction between editor voice, reader voice and character voice in the multimodal EFL textbook discourse could be summarized in

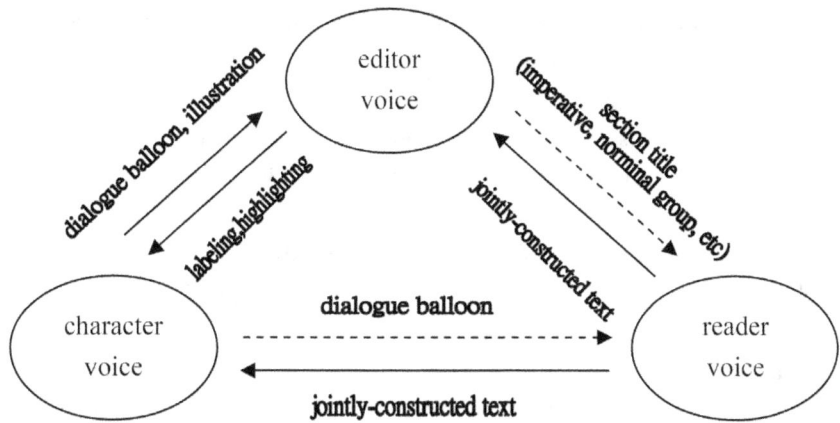

Figure 4.18 Voice interaction in multimodal EFL textbook discourse (Chen and Qin 2007).

Figure 4.18. The functions of the multimodal ENGAGEMENT devices (i.e. labelling, dialogue balloon, jointly constructed text, illustration and highlighting) are indicated above or underneath the arrows between the multiple voices to show how these voices interact with one another. To be specific, the broken-line arrow between editor voice and reader voice indicates that editor voice overtly instructs the reader through the use of section titles that may take the forms of imperatives or nominal groups, whereas the solid-line arrow represents the way in which reader voice interpolates editor voice through jointly constructed text. The arrows between editor voice and character voice show that dialogue balloon and illustration introduce character voice into the otherwise monoglossic texts, while editor voice intrudes itself into characters' visual stories or verbal recounts by attaching labels or highlighting words in verbal texts. As for the interaction between character voice and reader voice, a character may undertake the responsibility of instructing the reader via dialogue balloon, whereas reader voice is engaged in the co-construction of multimodal text in which character voice often provides the visual communicative setting. It may be inferred that the five types of multimodal ENGAGEMENT devices, along with other semiotic resources, work in concert to construe the heteroglossic harmony in EFL textbook discourse.

4.5 Summary

This chapter has first analysed and discussed the multimodal resources for the management of heteroglossic space in multimodal EFL textbook discourse. Five types of multimodal resources have been identified as the ENGAGEMENT devices that encode the ENGAGEMENT meanings of [disclaim], [proclaim], [entertain] and [attribute]. To be specific, the practice of labelling in multimodal texts signals the intrusion of editor voice, thus encoding the ENGAGEMENT meaning of [proclaim]. The use of dialogue balloons and illustration brings in character voice, and a given proposition or viewpoint is thus attributed to the character(s). Jointly constructed text opens up the space for dialogic alternatives involving the reader, and contributes to the construal of an ideal or putative readership. Highlighting functions to entertain other alternatives or possibilities grounded within the contingent subjectivity.

Acknowledging the fact that gradability is generally a property of the ENGAGEMENT system, I have also investigated how the multimodal devices scale up or down the ENGAGEMENT values encoded in the multimodal EFL textbook discourse. It is shown that three types of dialogue balloon can be located along the gradability continuum of [attribute] values based on how much responsibility the characters undertake in construing the heteroglossic setting. In light of the degree of completion, three types of jointly constructed text open up heteroglossic space to different extents for the external reader voice to participate in the construction of the text. As for the ENGAGEMENT device of illustration, the FORCE of the [attribute] meaning can be investigated from the perspective of the indispensability of the image in linking the different parts of the corresponding verbal text.

After the exploration of the heteroglossic nature of the multimodal EFL textbook discourse, a discussion concerning the voice interaction in relation to contact/observe, social distance and point of view has also been provided in this chapter. It is found that the characters' eye contact with the reader is only established in those images where the characters give directions and require actions from the reader. The different choices of social distance indicate various types of relationship between the characters inside the picture frame and the reader who observes them. Moreover, the interpolation of characters accounts for the adoption of the frontal and level angle in most of the images. Based on the investigations earlier, a triangle involving editor voice, reader voice and character voice is set up, which demonstrates the roles of the multimodal ENGAGEMENT devices in the play of multiple voices in multimodal EFL textbook discourse.

So far the focus of the discussion has been on the interactive aspect of the interpersonal management. As pointed out in Chapter 3, interpersonal semantics also includes the personal dimension. The ensuing two chapters will address this issue from two different perspectives respectively: the evaluative meanings and visual modality.

5

Attitudinal accumulation

Verbiage-image complementarity and co-instantiation

5.1 Introduction

The previous chapter has investigated the interactive dimension of interpersonal management in EFL textbooks. This chapter will be devoted to the personal aspect, to be precise, the evaluative meanings encoded. The intermodal relation between image and verbiage in realizing evaluative meanings has warranted scholarly attention. As pointed out by Martin (2001: 334): 'as far as interpersonal meaning is concerned, verbiage/image relations are more concerned with APPRAISAL than mood or modality'. This study aims at examining the ways in which verbal and visual resources are deployed to encode attitudinal meanings, with particular attention paid to the verbiage-image relations. The analytical frameworks drawn upon here are the semantic system of APPRAISAL (Martin 2000; Martin and White 2005), and Systemic Functional semiotic approach to multimodal texts (Kress and van Leeuwen 2006, 2020). Based on studies of the ontogenesis of the ATTITUDE system (Painter 2003), this study will also account for how attitudinal meanings are institutionalized and accumulated as students progress from primary to secondary education.

5.2 Attitudinal meanings in multimodal discourse

As reviewed in Chapter 3, the system of ATTITUDE covers three semantic dimensions: AFFECT, JUDGEMENT and APPRECIATION. In traditional, non-technical terms, they respectively refer to inborn human emotions or feelings, the ethical evaluation of people's behaviours, and the aesthetic awareness of man-made things or natural phenomena. This study endeavours to examine verbiage-image relations in encoding attitudinal meanings within multimodal EFL textbook discourse. Therefore, the social-semiotic approach to verbiage-image relations will be briefly reviewed, and the analytical tools for describing verbal and visual attitudinal meanings will be outlined.

5.2.1 Social-semiotic approach to verbiage-image relations

Verbiage-image relations have attracted scholarly attention from social semioticians over recent decades. Studies on verbiage-image relations include both the relations between different componential parts of a multimodal text and the relations between two or more whole multimodal texts (Martinec 2005: 166). This study focus on the verbal-visual construction of the interpersonal dimension within a multimodal text.

In light of the ideational dimension of verbiage-image relations, Lemke (1998a) investigates the interaction of different semiotic systems, such as in language, tables, graphs, images and diagrams, in modern science texts. He points out that the interplay of multiple semiotic systems creates new orders of meaning ('multiplying meaning' as he puts it), and thus recontextualizes the scientific knowledge. O'Halloran (1999a) studies the meaning arising from the interaction and interdependence between language, visual display and mathematical symbolism, with a particular focus on 'semiotic metaphor', which is referred to as the phenomenon of metaphorical representation across semiotic modes. O'Halloran (2015) further investigates how language, image and mathematical symbolism work in concert in the creation of meaning and effective communication of mathematical knowledge. The intersemiotic semantic relations between visual and verbal components of a text are approached by Royce (1998, 2002) through the concept of 'intersemiotic complementarity'. Drawing upon the study on lexical cohesion (Halliday and Hasan 1976), Royce identifies six ideational intersemiotic relations: repetition, synonymy, antonymy, hyponymy, meronymy and collocation. Still mainly concentrating on the ideational dimension, Martinec and Salway (2005) combine Halliday's (1994) logico-semantic relations (elaboration, extension, enhancement and projection) with Barthes' (1977) classification of image-text relations to build a generalized system of image-text relations. They also identify the units and realizations of both the logico-semantic and status relations, and try to specify some machine-recognizable realizations. O'Halloran (2008) proposes the development of new theoretical and practical approaches to multimodal discourse analysis by using digital technology in the form of image-editing software. Through the intersemiotic analysis as well as semantic and ideological interpretation, O'Halloran reveals how the metaphorical constructions of ideational meaning happen across linguistic and visual components in a print advertisement. Unsworth and Cleirigh (2009) propose and explain the synergistic modal of image-text relations in constructing the representational meaning in science textbooks, revealing the pedagogic implications of the intermodal identification including images identifying language elements and configurations as well as language glossing images. Wignell et al. (2018) compare the image-text relations in the Islamic extremist online magazines and Western online news which include recontextualizations of images found in the first data set. It is shown that the ISIS material tends to foreground the interpersonal and textual metafunctions, while the other data set tends to foreground the ideational metafunction.

Unsworth (2005) analyses the multimodal resources for the visual-verbal construction of ideational, interpersonal and textual meanings. Image/text relations including ideational concurrence, ideational complementarity, connection, interactive and evaluative meaning, and textual/compositional meanings in image/text relations are identified. It is shown that the understanding and explicit discussion of such meanings is crucial for teachers and students in comprehending and composing contemporary multimodal texts.

When it comes to the interpersonal aspect of verbiage-image relations, Martin (2001, 2004) points out that APPRAISAL can be considered as a resource for relating image to verbiage, in that images in multimodal texts provoke evaluation, hence functioning to co-articulate ATTITUDE with the verbiage. As for the textual aspect of verbiage-image relations with reference to the evaluative stance in a multimodal text, Martin (2001, 2004) points out that an image Theme can function as an interpersonal Theme (Halliday 1994), and hence can be deployed to naturalize the evaluation of the ensuing verbal Rheme. A more comprehensive critical review and explication of the linguistic and semiotic approaches to verbal-visual relations could be found in Bateman (2014).

Following this line of studies on verbal-visual relations,[1] this study takes the evaluative orientation as the point of departure and examines the co-instantiation and complementarity between the semiotic modes of images and verbal texts in encoding the attitudinal meanings in multimodal EFL textbook discourse. Before examining the verbiage-image relations from the attitudinal perspective, the following section will first outline the framework for analysing ATTITUDE in verbal text and images.

5.2.2 Inscribed and invoked ATTITUDE

In SFL, attitudinal meanings have first been explored in verbal texts before the discussion extends to attendant modes such as visual displays. The realizations of ATTITUDE cover the overtly construed attitudinal meanings, and the implicit meanings that arouse evaluation. These two types of resources are technically termed as inscribed ATTITUDE and invoked ATTITUDE'.

5.2.2.1 Verbal inscription and invocation

In the tri-stratal system of language, ATTITUDE is realized through explicit or implicit means at the level of lexicogrammar (Macken-Horarik 2003; Martin 2000a; Martin and White 2005; Page 2003). It can be directly inscribed in text through the use of evaluative lexis. For example, the attitudinal meanings can be encoded in epithet as in *a **magnificent** palace*, or in the attribute of a relational process such as *the servant is **honest***, or in the circumstantial elements like *the child went home **happily***.

In addition to the overt realizations, attitudinal meanings can also be indirectly invoked by using a range of strategies. Martin and White (2005: 61–8) explore the ways of invoking attitudinal meanings, including the use of lexical metaphor in provoking an attitudinal response from the reader, the use of non-core vocabulary infused with manner and counter-expectancy to flag or connote a positive or negative orientation to the proposition advanced in discourse, and the deliberate selection of ideational meanings in affording an ATTITUDE. Martin and White (2005) provide an outline of the strategies for inscribing and invoking ATTITUDE in verbal texts, as presented with examples in Figure 5.1. If the cline is read in a top-down manner, the increasing degrees of freedom that allow the reader to align with the naturalized value positions in the text can be perceived.

5.2.2.2 Visual inscription and invocation

Ongoing studies on the APPRAISAL system have been extended to cover the visual mode. The pioneering research in this area reveals the attitudinal repertoire in images, as well as the role of images in construing the global evaluative stance in a multimodal text.

The issue of invoked ATTITUDE in images has been approached by analysts who study media texts. Economou (2006) examines the verbiage-image unit of 'lead image-headline' in weekend news review feature stories from a Greek newspaper and an Australian newspaper. Drawing on Kress and van Leeuwen's (2006, 2020) framework for visual analysis and the APPRAISAL system (Martin

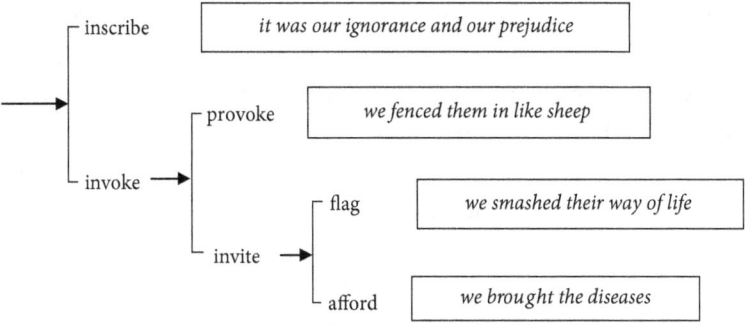

Figure 5.1 Verbal strategies for inscribing and evoking ATTITUDE (Martin and White 2005: 67).

2000a; Martin and White 2005), she shows that all three types of attitudinal meanings (i.e. AFFECT, JUDGEMENT and APPRECIATION) can be 'provoked by choices in content, composition, and interaction' in images. The choice of visual arrangements, as Economou (2006) explains, complies with the 'desired readership' and the 'known political position' of the particular newspaper.

As for attitudinal inscription in images, it is evident that AFFECT can be inscribed through the depictions of emotive facial expressions. Tian (2007) describes how the affectual meaning of worry is inscribed in the children's picture book *Silly Billy*. Her study demonstrates that the frequent use of 'worry' in verbal texts and its various realizations in images combine to produce evaluative meanings in multimodal texts. White (2006) points out that AFFECT is by no means the only attitudinal meaning that can be inscribed visually. Based on his observations on media images, White points out that both the presence of the image creator and the positioning of the viewer should be taken into consideration. If the image overtly signals either a JUDGEMENT or an APPRECIATION, it is categorized as inscribing JUDGEMENT or APPRECIATION. According to White (2006), in media discourse, inscribed visual ATTITUDE may involve distortions in cartoons and caricatures, as well as the deliberate selections of overtly positive or negative photographs or portraits in photojournalism.

Other explorations on the visual-verbal realization of evaluative meanings include Chen's (2017) analysis of the attitudinal variations in multimodal literary works by comparing the manuscript, the original and eight contemporary adapted versions of *Alice's Adventures in Wonderland*. It is shown that the verbal-visual relation in constructing the overall attitudinal stance shifts from complementarity in the manuscript to enhancement in the original published work and then to co-instantiation in the adaptations. Guijarro (2011) examines the verbal and visual semiotic choices in children's picture books to engage the young readers. It is found that images tend to contribute more than words in identifying the viewer with the main characters in the story. Myskow (2018) analyses the evaluative meaning in the verbal texts and visual images of a Canadian social studies textbook, with a special focus on how critical inquiry tasks facilitate readers' critical thinking. It shows a coexistence of the aims of critical engagement and the representation of the nation's collective experiences.

So far few attempts have been made to describe how the visual displays in pedagogic materials inscribe or invoke personal emotion, ethical judgement and aesthetic appreciation. Accordingly it is appropriate to further explore these three aspects of ATTITUDE in educational context where the cultivation of attitudes and values is an important function of the curriculum.

5.3 Co-instantiation and complementarity in encoding AFFECT and JUDGEMENT

This section is devoted to the analysis of attitudinal meanings encoded in multimodal texts describing people or anthropomorphized characters and their activities. The categories within the system of ATTITUDE drawn on are AFFECT and JUDGEMENT. These two semantic dimensions provide tools to describe the construal of emotions emanating from participants endowed with consciousness, and of evaluation of the ways they behave or the character they possess. According to the different drawing styles, the images under discussion are classified into the categories of cartoon, portrait and photograph. These three styles are unevenly distributed among the EFL textbooks for different levels of education. As indicated in Table 5.1, cartoon is the overwhelming style in primary EFL textbooks and junior secondary EFL textbooks, accounting for 97.9 per cent and 89.6 per cent respectively. On the contrary, in senior secondary EFL textbooks the numbers of portraits and photographs increase dramatically, with the proportion being 16.5 per cent (as compared with 1.9 per cent and 1.1 per cent in the primary and junior secondary EFL textbooks) and 53.8 per cent (in comparison with 0.2% and 9.3% in the primary and junior secondary ones). In this section portraits and photographs will be analysed under the same heading. This is motivated by the fact that the represented participants in cartoons are portrayed with a certain degree of deliberate distortion, whereas portraits and photographs belong to a more realistic style that aims at representing the participants as faithfully as possible (see Kress and van Leeuwen's (2006,

Table 5.1 The Distribution of Visual Styles in EFL Textbooks for Different Levels of Education (Chen 2010b)

	Cartoon (%)	Portrait (%)	Photograph (%)
primary textbooks	839 (97.9)	16 (1.9)	2 (0.2)
junior secondary textbooks	403 (89.6)	5 (1.1)	42 (9.3)
senior secondary textbooks	27 (29.7)	15 (16.5)	49 (53.8)

2020) 'modality' in images as discussed earlier). These human or personified participants can either overtly convey an evaluative position or indirectly invoke an attitudinal response in the reader.

5.3.1 Cartoon

Cartoon is a 'specific kind of semiotic domain' where meaning is produced either via verbal and visual modes or solely via visual mode. It is often considered to be 'a direct and easy to process means of communicating a message' (Tsakona 2009: 1171). In the primary and junior secondary EFL textbooks under discussion, the cartoon is the most frequently adopted style. In spite of the fact that differences do exist between the cartoons in primary and secondary EFL textbooks, which will later be examined in Chapter 6 from the perspective of visual modality, this chapter focuses on the attitudinal meanings encoded in this type of image with particular emphasis placed on the verbiage-image relations.

5.3.1.1 Inscribed happiness of English learning

As shown in Table 5.1, the cartoon is statistically dominant in the primary and junior secondary EFL textbooks. The majority of those cartoons in the EFL textbooks for primary education contain conscious participants covering a wide range of cartoon characters from primary school students, their teachers and family members, to the personified animals endowed with sense and sensibility. Those cartoon characters that have a high frequency of appearance are listed in a separate page at the start of the textbooks (see Appendix I). It is evident in Appendix I that most of the characters are primary school students with a similar age as the reader. Throughout the multimodal textbooks they are depicted as either learning English in class or involved in everyday activities.

Figure 5.2 is taken from *Unit 1 How Do You Go There* in the *PEP Primary English Students' Book I for Year 6* (2003: 5), which describes four school-age characters conducting a group discussion. Figure 5.2 contains two cartoons in a successive relation to one another, comprising two shots of the scene in which

Figure 5.2 Inscribed happiness of English-learning [PEP Primary English Students' Book I for Year 6, 2003: 5].

four primary students conduct a group discussion. Each of the characters in the cartoons demonstrates an expressive countenance indicative of delight, which can be observed from the characters' disproportionately large eyes with enlarged pupils that imply great interest, their facial expression of smiling broadly, as well as their demonstrative and enthusiastic gestures. Positive attitudinal meaning, AFFECT to be exact, is thus directly inscribed in the visual display, with the school-age cartoon characters as Emoters (i.e. the conscious participants experiencing the emotion) and the English-learning activities as the Trigger (i.e. the phenomenon responsible for that emotion) (Martin and White 2005: 46).

According to Martin and White (2005: 46–52), types of AFFECT can be categorized in light of the following six factors: (i) whether the emotions are construed as positive or negative in a given culture; (ii) whether they are realized as an emotional surge combined with behavioural manifestations, or as an internal mental process; (iii) whether the feelings are reactions to a certain emotional Trigger, or as an undirected ongoing mood; (iv) how the emotions are graded along a scale ranging from higher value to lower value; (v) whether the emotions involve a reaction to a present or past stimulus: realis values, or involve an intention with respect to some prospective stimulus, that is irrealis; (vi) whether they are concerned with 'affairs of the heart' (un/happiness), 'ecosocial well-being' (in/security) or the 'pursuit of goals' (dis/satisfaction). The types of AFFECT in Figure 5.1 and their corresponding visual patterns are presented in Table 5.2. It can be inferred from the analysis that the cartoons in Figure 5.2

Table 5.2 Types of AFFECT in the Cartoons of Figure 5.1

Types of AFFECT	Corresponding visual patterns
positive AFFECT	cheerful facial expressions showing great interest in the ongoing activities in class
behavioural surge	extralinguistic manifestation of exciting gestures indicative of active engagement
reaction to other	feelings directed at the ongoing English-learning activity
high value	overtly expressed emotions, high-spirited fun and great merriment
realis AFFECT	emotions involve a reaction to the present stimulus of group discussion
happiness,	appearance of comfort and enjoyment,
security,	confident when expressing themselves,
satisfaction	absorbed and satisfied in the group work

construe positive AFFECT through a series of overt, direct visual realizations (i.e. the depictions of facial expressions and behavioural manifestations).

As mentioned earlier, the two successive cartoons portray two moments when four primary students are practicing how to ask and answer questions concerning means of transport. The verbal texts in Figure 5.2 are framed in four dialogue balloons, which demonstrate two dialogues between the students.

(Cartoon on the left)
  Wu Yifan: How do you go to school?
  Sarah: Usually I go to school on foot, because my home is near.

(Cartoon on the right)
  Mike: How do you go to school?
  Zhang Peng: Usually I go to school by bus, because it's fast.

The verbiage is mainly concerned with the students' experiences: how they usually go to school and the reasons for choosing certain transportation means. As for the interactive aspect of interpersonal management, the speech roles of demanding and giving information are enacted, and the speech functions of question and statement are realized by the relevant Mood choices. However, when it comes to the personal aspect (Thompson 1996: 68–9), neither inscribed nor invoked attitudinal meanings are found in the verbal text. It is hard to tell simply by reading the verbal text whether the students who utter the words are happy or upset with the language learning activity. It is equally difficult to know whether they are confident or frustrated when giving the responses. In other words, the verbiage in Figure 5.2 commits no attitudinal meanings. As a matter of fact, it is through the images, in the case of Figure 5.2 the cartoons, that the affectual meanings are conveyed. The students feel excited, self-assured and engrossed, as represented in the images.

It is helpful to take into consideration the function of visual demonstration (see Section 4.3.2.2 for further discussion) so as to gain a better understanding of the verbiage-image relation in Figure 5.2. As shown in Figure 5.2, the title of the teaching section is *Group work*, while the images vividly describe the scene of a group of students working together in class, with a mood of happiness added via visual affectual inscriptions. The verbal texts within the dialogue balloons explain to the reader the way they are supposed to perform in the task by demonstrating two model dialogues, whereas the images indicate the attitude the reader is supposed to assume in undertaking that task, and perhaps in learning English in a broad sense. The atmosphere of happy English learning is thus created in Figure 5.2, and the verbiage-image relation in terms of attitudinal meanings is complementarity, in that the images commit positive affectual meanings inscribed in a range of visual resources which have no counterparts in the verbiage. As reviewed in Section 2.4.3, developing positive emotions and attitudes has been recognized as an essential part of the overall goal of primary and secondary EFL education. As the *Curriculum Standards for English* (Ministry of Education of the People's Republic of China 2001a: 1) mentions, it is a crucial task for EFL education to arouse and cultivate students' interest in English learning as well as to build up their confidence in the learning process. The analysis of Figure 5.2 demonstrates how the multimodal meaning-making resources in EFL textbook discourse, especially the visual patterns, are consistent with the focus on attitude in EFL education in China.

5.3.1.2 Gradability in affectual inscription

ATTITUDE involves gradable meanings, which means it has the potential to be intensified and compared (Martin and White 2005: 44). The gradability of attitudinal meanings in images can be investigated through a comparison of textbooks for different levels of education. Figure 5.3 is extracted from *Unit 7 How Do You Make a Banana Milk Shake* in the junior secondary EFL textbook *Go for It Students' Book1for Year 8* (2005: 43), which is an instance similar to Figure 5.2 in the sense that they both describe students' group work activity.

Figure 5.3 also involves two cartoons, portraying two teams of junior secondary students playing a *Recipe game*, with different background colours indicating the two different teams of students. Instruction on how to play the game is given in the verbal texts above the cartoons:

GAME Recipe game
Make two teams. Write a recipe. Then cut it up.
The other team has to put the recipe in order.

There are still two other verbal texts framed within oval bubbles, which demonstrate a sample recipe. The bubble on the left gives us a glimpse of the first part of the recipe written by the first team of students. The cartoon on the left correspondingly describes a team of three students busy writing the recipe.

First, cut up the tomatoes and beef. Next, boil the noodles.

The oval bubble on the right represents the remaining part of the recipe cut into pieces but in a correct order, while the corresponding cartoon beneath depicts another team of four junior secondary students working together to piece together the recipe.

| Then | add the ingredients to the noodles. |

| Add salt to the noodles. | Eat the noodles. |

The verbal texts give directions and provide a model demonstration, while the cartoons work in tandem with the verbiage to visually represent the scene of game-playing. More importantly, the attitudinal meanings that are not conveyed in the verbiage are realized visually. Figure 5.3 will be examined in comparison with Figure 5.2 in terms of the scaling of FORCE in affectual inscriptions. The similarity between the images in these two examples lies

Figure 5.3 Gradability in affectual inscription [Go for It Students' Book I for Year 8, 2005: 43].

in the attitudinally committed images. The affectual dispositions inscribed in both images are positive, directed at a specific phenomenon. They convey happiness, confidence and contentment, and hence the positive ATTITUDE towards English learning is promoted. However, the represented participants in Figure 5.3 are happy but less exuberant than those in Figure 5.2. The feelings of comfort and enjoyment can be detected in their smiling and attentive faces, and yet the smile is quite faint in comparison with that in Figure 5.2. Moreover, the gestures depicted in Figure 5.3 are merely those necessary in playing the recipe game, whereas other possible gestures that may indicate the represented participants' excitement and other joyful feelings are not found. In other words, a sense of seriousness is incorporated into the junior secondary textbook. When considering the point at which the affectual inscriptions in Figure 5.3 should be put along the scale of intensity, the cartoons in Figure 5.3 are less affectually committed than those in Figure 5.2 in terms of the degree of FORCE of the positive affectual meanings. The AFFECT encoded in the cartoons of Figure 5.2 is graded as high, whereas in comparison the AFFECT inscribed in the cartoons of Figure 5.3 is down-scaled towards the median value along the cline of affectual intensity.[2]

As explained earlier, the AFFECT encoded in images is gradable. In other words, the options from the sub-systems of AFFECT and FORCE within the APPRAISAL system are 'coupled' (Martin 2008b; see Section 3.2.3 for a more detailed discussion) to different degrees.[3] The gradual changes in the degree of happiness demonstrated in the images of primary and junior secondary EFL textbooks reflect the process of children's socialization, that is the transition from the playful and carefree childhood to adolescence, when a teenager has gone through puberty but not yet reached full maturity and thus a sense of responsibility should be cultivated. As will be shown in the analyses in Section 5.3.2, the earnest and non-jesting mood is more evident in the senior secondary EFL textbooks. The issue of emotion and attitude education in relation to socialization processes will be further discussed in Section 5.5, following the investigation into the invocations of JUDGEMENT and APPRECIATION in images and the verbiage-image relations in encoding attitudinal meanings within the senior secondary EFL textbook discourse.

5.3.1.3 *Logogenetic recontextualization*

As analysed in the previous section, the overwhelming majority of the images in primary EFL textbooks are inscribed with a high degree of positive affectual meanings. This section will examine the attitudinal response the images

Figure 5.4 Logogenetic recontextualization in multimodal textbook discourse [PEP Primary English Students' Book II for Year 3, 2003: 15].

invoke, and show how the deployment of multimodal resources accords with the cultivation of moral standards advocated in the curriculum standards in China.

Figure 5.4 is taken from *Unit 2 My Family* in *PEP Primary English Students' Book II for Year 3* (2003: 15), and its main body is a cartoon depicting a family of five members. In the cartoon of Figure 5.4, the feelings of the represented participants (i.e. the five cartoon characters) are made explicit via their emotive facial expressions, and hence the AFFECT value of happiness is inscribed directly in the visual display. Nevertheless, in addition to the explicitly inscribed affectual meanings, the cartoon also invokes attitudinal response from the viewer through the way it presents the represented participants. The five represented participants, that is the five members in a family, are connected with each other by the vectors of arms and/or eyelines. To be specific, the right arm of the grandfather forms an oblique line, and thereby generates a vector linking him with his granddaughter. On the other hand, the eyelines emanating from the granddaughter and the father relate them to the grandmother and the mother. This visual connection, together with the inscribed happiness, presents to the viewer the scene of a united, harmonious and happy family get-together. In doing so, the image 'invites', or 'affords' to be more precise (Martin and White 2005: 67), a favourable evaluation of the filial piety and parental responsibility from the putative viewer.

Thus, Figure 5.4 invokes positive APPRECIATION concerning the value of a family being united, through the JUDGEMENT of the ethical behaviour of filial piety and parental responsibility. In other words, the positive emotion is 'reworked' as ethics regarding propriety, which is in turn recontextualized as 'politicized aesthetics' (Martin 2002: 200) concerning the social value of a harmonious family. It conforms to the standard, conventional principle advocated in the given educational and social context. Adapted from Martin's (2002: 199) model of logogenetic recontextualization processes (cf. ontogenetic recontextualization to be discussed in Section 5.5.2 and mentioned earlier), the attitudinal recontextualization in the cartoon of Figure 5.4 can be diagrammatically represented in Figure 5.5. As Martin (2002) suggests, Lemke's (1995) notion of 'metaredundancy' can be adopted to explain this recontextualization movement. As for Figure 5.4, the APPRECIATION of family harmony is modelled as a pattern of the JUDGEMENT of filial piety and parental responsibility, which is in turn a pattern of the inscribed AFFECT (i.e. happiness).

As indicated in Section 2.4.3, the curriculum standards for each subject, including those for EFL education, attach great importance to emotion and attitude education. It may be justified to contend that the positive JUDGEMENT and APPRECIATION of value encoded in the cartoon complies with the goal of the cultivation of high moral standards stipulated in the *Curriculum Standards for English*. It can be inferred that the attitudinal meanings in the cartoon of Figure 5.4 include both inscribed AFFECT and invoked APPRECIATION, and the former is more committed than the latter in that it is overtly inscribed rather than indirectly invoked. Through the direct inscriptions as well as implicit invocations, a 'saturating' prosody (Martin and White 2005: 19) of positive attitudinal meanings that spreads across the image is established.

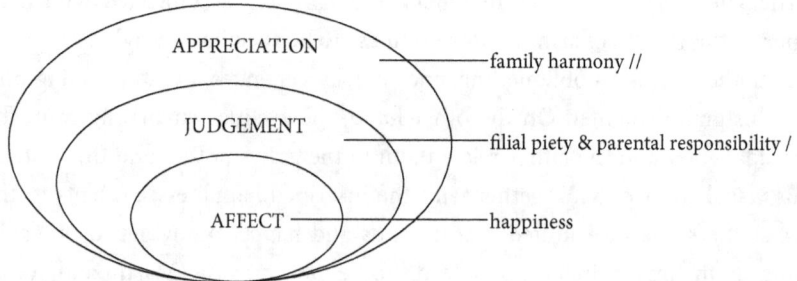

Figure 5.5 Recontextualizing feelings in a cartoon (Chen 2010b; adapted from Martin 2002: 199).

As for the verbiage-image relation in Figure 5.4, the verbal text in the image, that is labelling (for a detailed discussion on labelling, see Section 4.3.1), introduces the teaching content, that is the formal and informal forms of address for family members (i.e. *father (dad), mother (mom), grandfather (grandpa)* and *grandmother (grandma)*). These address forms are attached as labels for each of the four characters surrounding the little girl, who is supposed to use those address forms. The two other words, *man* and *woman*, are attached to the *father* and *mother*, who are the representatives of typical adult male and female humans. The verbiage is not attitudinally committed, whereas the image is inscribed with the emotion of happiness and invokes a positive APPRECIATION of family harmony. The whole cartoon integrates the family members into a harmonious whole by putting them in the context of outdoor activity. Contrasting this image with an example from another series of PEP primary EFL textbooks, we may gain a clearer understanding of the significance of such integrativeness in the invocation of positive JUDGEMENT and APPRECIATION.

Figure 5.6 is from Unit 2 in the *Super Kids Students' Book 4*, which illustrates four family members in four separate cartoons. In Figure 5.6, the four cartoon characters are independent of each other and spread across two pages. There is no connection between these represented participants, except for the captions underneath the cartoons indicating their family membership and the visual

Figure 5.6 A multimodal text without logogenetic recontextualization (a and b) [Super Kids Students' Book for Year 4, 2003: 7–8].

cohesion of consistent colour, size and spacing between the images. The four represented participants are depicted in four different contexts: *dad* is drinking a cup of tea/coffee, relaxing on the sofa; *mom* is carrying her handbag; *sister* is holding a lollipop; and *brother* is riding on a skateboard. In other words, the family members are not represented as a group involved in the same activity, but as individuals scattered in various situations. Happiness seems to be inscribed in the two cartoons describing *sister* and *brother*. However, the family members are not presented as a joyful, harmonious whole. Neither moral JUDGEMENT nor aesthetic APPRECIATION is invoked in these cartoons. It may be inferred that, from the perspective of emotion and attitude education that is highlighted in the *Curriculum Standards for English* in China, Figure 5.4 is more consistent with the emotion and attitude pedagogic aims than Figure 5.6 due to the fact that along with affectual inscriptions, Figure 5.4 is also attitudinally committed to some degree in terms of JUDGEMENT and APPRECIATION.

5.3.2 Portrait and photograph

Portraits and photographs are frequently adopted in senior secondary EFL textbooks in comparison with the primary and junior secondary textbooks, accounting for 16.5 per cent and 53.8 per cent of images respectively as shown in Table 5.1. The photographs in our data can be further divided into two subcategories: those close-up shots similar to the portraits usually for depicting famous or significant people, and those photographs describing a specific moment of events or activities. This section will cover both sub-categories, and the portraits whose function is similar to the first type of the photographs will be discussed together with those photographs.

5.3.2.1 *Co-instantiation and putative reading*

Figure 5.7 provides a good example of the serious portraits and the close-up photographs of a single person, which is taken from *Unit 5 Nelson Mandela – A Modern Hero* in *New Senior English for China Student's Book 1* (2004: 33–4).

It is a warming-up exercise entitled *Pre-reading* that precedes a passage for reading comprehension. It verbally and visually presents information about six important people, which includes six passages illustrated by three portraits (i.e. the upper three images) and three photographs (i.e. the lower three images). The caption underneath each image indicates the name, nationality and years of birth and death of the represented participant. The readers – the senior secondary students – are required to work in pairs and decide upon who are great among these six people, and what makes the difference between great men

Attitudinal Accumulation 107

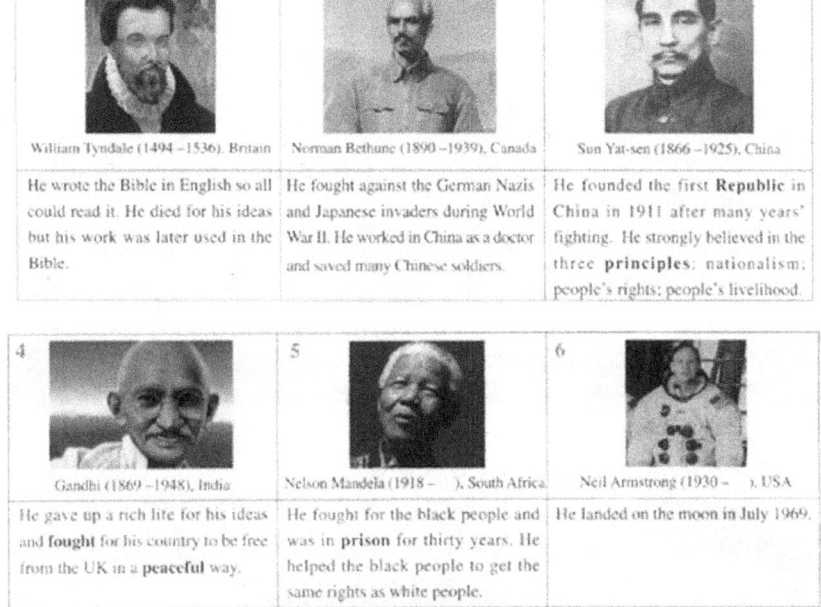

Figure 5.7 Co-instantiation and putative reading (a and b) [New Senior English for China Student's Book 1, 2004: 33–34].

and important men. According to the *New Senior English for China Teacher's Book 1* (2006: 86), five of them (i.e. *William Tyndale, Norman Bethune, Sun Yat-sen, Gandhi* and *Nelson Mandela*) are regarded as great people due to the assumption that they have 'gone through struggles and difficulties for their noble cause'; while *Neil Armstrong* is not considered to be great because he 'worked hard to be the first man on the moon but he did not sacrifice anything to do this so he should not be viewed as a great man'. Leaving aside the question of whether the opinion given in the teacher's book is justifiable, the discussion here focuses on how the verbal texts and images in Figure 5.7 work in tandem to attitudinally hint at the intended or putative reading.

What follows is the verbiage of Figure 5.7 , which is numbered by paragraph for ease of analysis. The systems of JUDGEMENT and APPRECIATION will be drawn upon to analyse the attitudinal meanings encoded.

① William Tyndale (1494–1536), Britain
   He wrote the Bible in English so all could read it. He died for his ideas but his work was later used in the Bible.
② Norman Bethune (1890–1939), Canada
   He fought against the German Nazis and Japanese invaders during the Second World War. He worked in China as a doctor and saved many Chinese soldiers.
③ Sun Yat-sen (1866–1925), China
   He founded the first Republic in China in 1911 after many years' fighting. He strongly believed in the three principles: nationalism, people's rights and people's livelihood.
④ Gandhi (1869–1948), India
   He gave up a rich life for his ideas and fought for his country to be free from the UK in a peaceful way.
⑤ Nelson Mandela (1918–2003), South Africa
   He fought for the Black people and was in prison for thirty years. He helped the Black people to get the same rights as white people.
⑥ Neil Armstrong (1930–), the United States
   He landed on the moon in July 1969.

As reviewed in Section 3.3.1, JUDGEMENT is concerned with the ATTITUDE towards people's behaviours, whether we admire or criticize them, or praise or condemn them. Those judgements dealing with 'normality' (how typical someone is), 'capacity' (how capable someone is) and 'tenacity' (how resolute someone is) are grouped under the heading of social esteem, whereas those judgements concerning 'veracity' (how truthful someone is) and 'propriety' (how ethical someone is) are studied under the category of social sanction. APPRECIATION on the other hand deals with the evaluations of inanimate phenomena and processes, which encompass 'reaction' (to the impact or quality of the thing that is under evaluation), 'composition' (of its complexity or conformity to formal organizational principles) and 'valuation' (based on its social value) (Martin and White 2005: 52–6). The attitudinal meanings encoded in the verbal texts are analysed in Table 5.3.

It can be inferred from Table 5.3 that in each of the first five verbal texts the appraiser is the textbook editor, and what is appraised is the represented participant portrayed in each of the five images or what he has done. As mentioned before, these five people are considered to be great in the putative reading. As Martin (2000a: 155) points out, APPRAISAL systems can be directly construed in the text via attitudinal lexis, or covertly implicated through the

Table 5.3 ATTITUDE Analysis of the Verbal Texts in Figure 5.5

Appraising items	Appraiser	Appraised	ATTITUDE
① all could read	Textbook editor	William Tyndale's work	APPRECIATION
② saved (many)	Textbook editor	Norman Bethune	JUDGEMENT
③ strongly believed	Textbook editor	Sun Yat-sen	JUDGEMENT
④ free	Textbook editor	his (Gandhi's) country	APPRECIATION
④ peaceful	Textbook editor	Gandhi's way of liberation	APPRECIATION
⑤ helped (get the same rights)	Textbook editor	Nelson Mandela	JUDGEMENT

selection of ideational meanings that redound with attitudinal meanings. Positive JUDGEMENT and APPRECIATION are encoded in the first five verbal texts of Figure 5.7. For example, *peaceful* and *free* in ④ inscribe APPRECIATION of the manner in which *Gandhi* fought for the freedom of his nation. Hood and Martin's (2007) further exploration of the GRADUATION system shows that the scaling of non-attitudinal experiential meanings can invoke ATTITUDE, or more exactly, 'flag' ATTITUDE. For instance, *all* in *all could read it* in ① flags a positive APPRECIATION of the valuation of *William Tyndale's* enduring work through 'quantifying' a Process (i.e. *could read it*). *All* quantifies the Process as 'extent', or to be more precise, as 'scope in space', which belongs to the category of FORCE in the GRADUATION system. Another example is *for thirty years* in ⑤, which quantifies the Process (i.e. *was in prison*) in terms of 'scope in time'. As Hood and Martin remark, one needs to read the prosody to nail down the value assigned to the attitudinal meanings. 'Intensification' is another category of FORCE along with quantification. It can be infused into the Process itself (Hood and Martin 2007: 748). Cases in point are *saved* in ②, *believe* in ③ and *helped* in ⑤. They intensify the manner as 'vigour', thus flagging the positive JUDGEMENT of *Norman Bethune's* capacity for surgery, *Sun Yat-sen's* tenacity of faithfulness and *Nelson Mandela's* propriety of generosity. The intensification infused in a Process can be further graded attitudinally with a Circumstance of manner, such as *strongly believe* in ③. Moreover, intensification can also work together with quantification, as in *saved many Chinese soldiers* in ② and *after many years fighting* in ③, where *many* quantifies the entity *soldiers* and *years* respectively.

The verbal text concerning *Neil Armstrong* is exceptional. Evaluative meanings are not inscribed in the comparatively much shorter text, *He landed on the moon in July 1969*; nor does it employ any options from the GRADUATION system to flag attitudinal meanings. There are no comments for evaluating the moon-landing action or its significance in human history, though it might otherwise be considered as quite an achievement and a variety of linguistic resources could have been drawn upon to inscribe or flag ATTITUDE.

I now look at the images to see how verbal and visual meaning-making resources work in tandem in the construal of the putative reading. The six images in Figure 5.7 include two portraits (those depicting *William Tyndale* and *Norman Bethune*), one black-and-white portrait (the one that depicts *Sun Yat-sen*) and three chromophotographs (those describing *Gandhi*, *Nelson Mandela* and *Neil Armstrong*). The first five images are similar in the sense that they all take close-up shots, ranging from the extreme close-ups that mainly show the head (i.e. those of *Gandhi* and *Nelson Mandela*) to the big close-ups that display the head and the shoulders (i.e. those of *William Tyndale*, *Norman Bethune* and *Sun Yat-sen*). These five people who are considered to be great men are represented at the close personal distance or even intimate distance (Hall 1964, cited in Kress and van Leeuwen 2006: 125) from the viewer. A human face is commonly accepted as a major means of recognition that best distinguishes a person. The five images under discussion bring the five great men within arm's length of the viewers, and thus their facial features are represented in a clear, easily recognized way. The background patterns of these five images are simple or even monochrome (e.g. those of *Sun Yat-sen* and *Nelson Mandela*), and hence the foregrounded represented participants are brought into focus. They are portrayed as typically dressed, with familiar dispositions that add to the ease of recognition. All the efforts mentioned earlier aim at making these important people's identities as distinct as possible, with the implication that they are worth remembering. Also, as indicated earlier, these five images are mainly serious with no inscribed AFFECT.[4] The style of the portraiture or photography (i.e. realistic images where the participant has a relatively natural expression, with no suggestion of a caricature or mocking depiction) also conveys a seriousness and solemnity which is conducive to the invocation of positive JUDGEMENT. In this multimodal text, the images and verbiage work in concert to construe a positive reading position for the reader.

I now turn to the treatment given to the photograph of *Neil Armstrong*, which is different from the five 'great people' images. In terms of 'size of frame', this photograph is a medium close shot, showing *Neil Armstrong* from the waist up and at a far personal distance. This makes his face quite fuzzy in such a small image. In this photograph *Neil Armstrong* is dressed in a space suit indicating his identity as an astronaut. Nevertheless, it is hard to distinguish *Neil Armstrong* from any other astronaut who may be dressed similarly, which would make it difficult to recognize him on the basis of this image. Together with the much shorter, and less value-laden verbal text as analysed earlier, this multimodal text represents *Neil Armstrong* as an important astronaut, but it does not distinguish him from other astronauts as an influential individual in human history.

Based on the foregoing analysis it can be inferred that the images and verbiage in Figure 5.7 resonate interpersonally with one another. Consequently, the relation between language and images in Figure 5.7 is a 'co-instantiation' of ATTITUDE choices (Martin 2008b). To be specific, positive JUDGEMENT of the people's great deeds and positive APPRECIATION of their noble causes are inscribed in the verbal texts, which are further reinforced by positive JUDGEMENT invocations through the corresponding portraits or photographs. The meanings made with one semiotic mode are thus 'multiplied' (Lemke 1998a: 92) by those that are made with the other. The verbal and visual APPRAISAL resources work in tandem throughout the whole multimodal text, contributing to the construction of the evaluative stance of the appraiser (i.e. the textbook editor). This stance construes the shared values of the putative community (cf. Martin and Rose 2007a: 59), thus aligning the reader with and directing them rhetorically to the intended reading position.

5.3.2.2 *Co-instantiation in JUDGEMENT invocation*

This section will examine the ATTITUDE encoded in the multimodal texts with photographs capturing a specific moment of human activity. The example for analysis is an excerpt from a historical recount entitled *A Night the Earth Didn't Sleep* (see Figure 5.8), which is one of the reading comprehension materials in *Unit 4 Earthquakes* in *New Senior English for China Student's Book 1* (2004: 26). What is recorded in this historical recount is the well-known big earthquake that happened in *Tangshan* in 1976. Several paragraphs precede the excerpted multimodal text, describing some strange signs before the earthquake, the horrible scenes when the earthquake happened, as well as its disastrous consequences. The verbal text in the multimodal excerpt is the final paragraph concerning the rescue and recovery work, which is accompanied by a photograph that depicts one of the rescue scenes.

The focus of the analysis here is still on the attitudinal meanings, and the verbal text is as follows.

> All hope was not lost. The army sent 150,000 soldiers to Tangshan to help the rescue workers. Hundreds of thousands of people were helped. The army organized teams to dig out those who were trapped and to bury the dead. To the north of the city, most of the 10,000 miners were rescued from the coal mines. Workers built shelters for survivors whose homes had been destroyed. Fresh water was taken to the city by train, truck and plane. Slowly, the city began to breathe again.

The opening clause, *all hope was not lost*, functions as the hyper-Theme of the paragraph. On the one hand, it serves as a turning point in the whole essay, shifting the account from the description of the huge damage caused by the earthquake to the timely rescue work that brought hope to the earthquake-stricken people. On the other hand, it functions to colour a larger segment of the text 'as a token of evoked APPRAISAL of some kind' (Page 2003: 216). *All hope was not lost* itself is inscribed with positive AFFECT, while at the same time it invokes APPRECIATION concerned with the quality of the situation. This in turn elicits a positive prosody of JUDGEMENT that deals with what the army and rescue workers do to help with the salvation. The ATTITUDE analysis of the verbal text in Figure 5.8 is demonstrated in Table 5.4, in which the sub-categories of JUDGEMENT and APPRECIATION are identified. In this historical recount it is the author who evaluates people and things and tells the reader how to feel, and therefore the author is the source of the APPRAISAL, that is the Appraiser.

The foregoing analysis shows that, after the positive APPRECIATION in the opening clause, the evaluation of the army and the rescue workers' actions

Figure 5.8 Co-instantiation in JUDGEMENT invocation [New Senior English for China Student's Book 1, 2004: 26].

Table 5.4 Inscribed and Invoked ATTITUDE in the Verbiage of Figure 5.6

Appraising items	AFFECT	JUDGEMENT	APPRECIATION	Appraised
all hope was not lost	Des		+reaction	the situation
to help the rescue workers		+propriety		the army
hundreds of thousands of people were helped		+capacity		the army
most of the 10,000 miners were rescued		+capacity		the army
built shelters for survivors		+propriety		(the rescue) workers
began to breathe again			+composition	the city

is implied through the invocations of JUDGEMENT, which spread across the whole verbal text and explain where that *hope* comes from. Some options from the category of quantification under FORCE are employed to invoke positive ATTITUDE. For instance, *150,000, hundreds of thousands of,* and *most of the 10,000* quantify the entities *soldiers* (who were sent to *help the rescue workers*), people (who *were helped*) and miners (who *were rescued*). This reinforces the efforts made to rescue the victims and the satisfactory outcome, hence flagging the positive JUDGEMENT (both propriety and capacity) of the soldiers and rescue workers. The prosody of the implied JUDGEMENT is further confirmed by the concluding positive APPRECIATION of the city that regains its balance after the rescue work. The prosodic realization in the verbal text of Figure 5.8 is *all hope was not lost* colours and thus tokenizes the attitudinal meanings in the rest of the text. Overall, the verbal text in Figure 5.8 is highly attitudinally committed through the use of both inscribed and invoked ATTITUDE.

The photograph illustrating the verbal text captures the scene in which the army and rescue workers are digging out the people trapped in the rubble. In terms of social distance, the photograph is taken at the public distance (Hall 1966: 110–20, cited in Kress and van Leeuwen 2006: 124) from which the viewer can see at least four or five figures with their surrounding environment. Although it is difficult to identify the represented participants individually, the viewer may recognize from the army uniforms that some of them are soldiers. The verbal text states that there are 150,000 rescuers like those in this photograph. The image is consistent with the verbal text in which all the positive JUDGEMENT is ascribed to the collective of the army and rescue workers rather than any individual. As for the point of view, the photograph adopts a level, frontal angle, which implies a high level of involvement and presents the represented participants as part of the viewer's world. Finally from the perspective of focalization, the back view allows the viewer to have a viewer perspective and a character focalized perspective simultaneously (see Section 3.4.2 for review of the conception of focalization). Visually positioned behind the rescue workers and soldiers, the viewer contemplates the disastrous scene along with the rescue team. In other words, the viewer shares a perspective with the represented participants in observing the horrifying aftermath and facing the strenuous and urgent task. Overall, in this photograph the represented participants are portrayed as an altruistic group of rescuers who devote themselves wholeheartedly to the urgent operation at the time of disaster and in the harsh environment. They are part of a far larger rescue team and remain unknown to the public. It can thus be argued that a positive JUDGEMENT of social sanction is invoked in the viewer, or at least in the construed intended viewer, because of the way they are positioned in relation to the photograph. This attitudinal invocation commits a positive evaluative meaning concerning the represented participants.

Taking into account both the verbal text and image in Figure 5.8, it can be inferred that a strong attitudinally cohesive bond is construed between these two semiotic modes. The positive APPRECIATION at the beginning of the verbal text provides colouration and confirmation for the ensuing invoked JUDGEMENT encoded in the selection of ideational meanings. The image on the other hand visually illustrates those ideational meanings while reinforcing the positive evaluation in the verbal text through invoking JUDGEMENT of social sanction in the viewer. The positive attitudinal meanings co-instantiated in the verbiage and image develop prosodically throughout the multimodal text, and peak at another positive APPRECIATION at the end of the verbal text that appraises the achievements of the rescue work and confirms the implicit evaluation established by the preceding verbiage and image. This serves as an example of how multimodal resources amplify one another (Martin 2004: 298) or in Lemke's (1998a) term, how 'multiplying meaning' happens.

5.4 Co-instantiation and complementarity in encoding APPRECIATION

This section will be devoted to the analysis of verbiage-image relations in appraising multimodal texts that describe places and civic landscapes. I shall position the analysis of language and visual displays within the framework of the APPRAISAL system. As stated in Chapter 3, among the three categories in the system of ATTITUDE, the dimension of APPRECIATION is an effective tool for analysing the evaluation of inanimate things, including man-made objects and natural phenomena, concrete entities and abstract concepts.

5.4.1 Invoked APPRECIATION of reaction

Figure 5.9 is extracted from *Unit 6 The Story of Rain* in *PEP Primary English Students' Book I for Year 6* (2003: 70). The image in Figure 5.9 chiefly depicts natural scenery. It is a cartoon with such features as birds with exaggerated eyes, over-simplified depiction of cloud patterns, ripples on a river, and mountains and trees with texture. This image adopts a 'sensory coding orientation' (Kress and van Leeuwen 2006: 165; see Section 6.3.2.2 in Chapter 6 for further discussion). One of the most important features of the 'sensory coding orientation' is that it is assumed to activate some feelings (e.g. excitement, horror, relief). In the case

Figure 5.9 Invoked APPRECIATION of reaction [PEP Primary English Students' Book I for Year 6, 2003: 70].

of Figure 5.9, the emotions to be stirred up in the viewer are evidently pleasure and excitement. Both the landscape and the creatures are portrayed in a way that it is pleasant to the eye, and the brilliant colouration adds to this pleasure principle. The verbiage in this multimodal text comes from the character voice outside of the image of the landscape. It is represented as a question uttered by the character *Wu Yifan* and enclosed in a dialogue balloon. The function of the dialogue balloon here is to instruct the reader to identify what they see in the landscape picture and to state it in English. The small image of *Wu Yifan* with the dialogue balloon is an indicator that encourages engagement with the landscape picture, and this engagement includes the positive reactions that the picture is supposed to invoke. Overall, the cartoon in Figure 5.9 invokes the response of positive APPRECIATION in the viewer, to be exact, a positive reaction to the arresting, interesting image.

When it comes to the verbiage of Figure 5.9, there are no attitudinal meanings encoded in the WH-interrogative clause *What can you see in the picture*, without any explicitly evaluative lexis or selected ideational tokens to 'invite' or 'provoke' an attitudinal response in the reader. On the other hand, as the explanation of the image has demonstrated, the cartoon image is attitudinally committed, which is evident in the pleasing style of the landscape image as well as in the small interactive image of the character *Wu Yifan*. Therefore, it is justified to say that the image and verbiage in Figure 5.9 are complementary in terms of ATTITUDE, since the image is attitudinally committed through the use of invoked APPRECIATION of reaction, whereas in the verbiage there is hardly any attitudinal commitment.

5.4.2 Co-instantiation in encoding Appreciation

The multimodal text drawn on to exemplify the verbiage-image co-instantiation of APPRECIATION is a reading exercise in the teaching section *Using Language* from *Unit 2 The United Kingdom* in *New Senior English for China Student's Book 5* (2004: 13–14). It is composed of a personal recount entitled *SIGHTSEEING IN LONDON*, narrating the protagonist *Zhang Pingyu*'s three-day tour in London, and a list-making exercise that is based on her tour and the comments on each place she has visited. The *Comments* columns that the reader is required to complete in the table involve the protagonist's evaluation of the places, which is encoded in the language and enhanced by the images. For ease of analysis the verbal texts and their corresponding visual displays are listed side by side in Figure 5.10. For those who are interested in the exact layout, please see Appendix II for the whole extract.

Worried about the time available, Zhang Pingyu had made a list of the sites she wanted to see in London. Her first delight was going to the Tower. It was built long ago by the Norman invaders of AD 1066. Fancy! This solid, stone, square tower had remained standing for one thousand years. Although the buildings had expanded around it, it remained part of a royal palace and prison combined. To her great surprise, Zhang Pingyu found the Queen's jewels guarded by special royal soldiers who, on special occasions, still wore the four-hundred-year-old uniform of the time of Queen Elizabeth I.

The Tower of London

There followed St Paul's Cathedral built after the

St Paul's Cathedral

Westminster Abbey

terrible fire of London in 1666. It looked splendid when first built! Westminster Abbey, too, was very interesting. It contained statues in memory of dead poets and writers, such as Shakespeare. Then just as she came out of the abbey, Pingyu heard the famous sound of the clock, Big Ben, ringing out the hour. She finished the day by looking at the outside of Buckingham Palace, the Queen's house in London. Oh, she had so much to tell her friends!

The second day the girl visited Greenwich and saw its old ships and famous clock that sets the world time. What interested her most was the longitude line. It is an imaginary line dividing the eastern and western halves of the world and is very useful for navigation. It passes through Greenwich, so Pingyu had a photo taken standing on either side of the line.

Royal Observatory in Greenwich

The last day she visited Karl Marx's statue in Highgate Cemetery. It seemed strange that the man who had developed communism should have lived and died in London. Not only that, but he had worked in the famous reading room of the Library of the British Museum. Sadly the library had moved from its original place into another building and the old reading room was gone. But she was thrilled by so many wonderful treasures from different cultures displayed in the museum.

Karl Marx

When she saw many visitors enjoying looking at the beautiful old Chinese pots and other objects on show, she felt very proud of her country.

The next day Pingyu was leaving London for Windsor Castle. 'Perhaps I will see the Queen?' she wondered as she fell asleep.

Make a list of Zhang Pingyu's tour of London and a comment on each place she visited.

Day 1	Comments	Day 2 and comment	Day 3 and comment
1	1		
2	2		
3	3		
4	4		

Figure 5.10 Co-instantiation in encoding APPRECIATION [New Senior English for China Student's Book 5, 2004: 13–14].

The verbiage of Figure 5.10 is value-loaded and the ATTITUDE analysis is presented in Table 5.5. Generally speaking, the author of the passage is considered to be the ultimate source of APPRAISAL. Nevertheless, when the attitudinal meanings are specifically ascribed to a certain participant, I shall analyse the participant as the Appraiser.

As shown in Table 5.5, the attitudinal meanings are either overtly inscribed or implicitly encoded through the selection of ideational tokens. Among the twelve overt inscriptions of APPRECIATION (i.e. *fancy, solid, splendid, interesting, famous, famous, what interested her most, very useful, strange, famous, wonderful* and *beautiful*) eleven of them are positive evaluations, which accounts for nearly 92 per cent of the total APPRECIATION. These include the reactions to the captivating nature of the places of interest, the evaluations of the durable and substantial quality of the *Tower of London*, and the recognition of the high value of the longitude line in navigation. The one and only lexical item with negative notation is the word *strange*, which indicates a sense of counter-expectancy during the protagonist's visit to *Highgate Cemetery*. Along with the explicit inscriptions of APPRECIATION, there are selections of ideational meanings (i.e. *had so much to tell, sets the world time* and *dividing the eastern and western halves of the world*) to invoke evaluations of the scenic spots that are described. Moreover, quantification is adopted to invoke ATTITUDE. For example, in *standing for one thousand years* the entity *years* is quantified as the Circumstance of manner *standing*, which aims at flagging a positive APPRECIATION of the long history and solid composition of the *Tower of London*. For instance, the expression of *so much to tell* implies the fruitfulness of *Zhang Pingyu's* first day's tour. *Standing for one thousand years* provides convincing evidence for the evaluation of the solidness of the *Tower of London*, while *sets the world time* and *dividing the eastern and western halves of the world* confirm the assessment of the great value of the clock and longitude line in *Greenwich*. In short, the selections of ideational tokens reinforce the explicit attitudinal lexis, while the overt attitudinal inscriptions confirm the implicit invocations.

In terms of the nine attitudinal lexical items inscribing AFFECT meanings (i.e. *worried, wanted, delight, great surprise, sadly, thrilled, enjoying, very proud* and *wondered*), six of them are positive. They encode *Zhang Pingyu's* as well as other visitors' great delight during the tour and their strong interest in the sightseeing. *Great surprise* is considered to be a neutral feeling that can be approached 'as a separate type of AFFECT' (Bednarek 2008: 161). Based on the studies on corpus data, Bednarek (2008: 161–5) articulates that surprise is not construed culturally as a negative or positive emotion. Rather, it is 'relatively neutral', and the

Table 5.5 Inscribed and Invoked ATTITUDE in the Verbiage of Figure 5.8

Appraising items	Appraiser	AFFECT	APPRECIATION	Appraised
worried	Zhang Pingyu	-security		time
wanted	Zhang Pingyu	+desire		sites
delight	Zhang Pingyu	+happiness		going to the Tower
fancy	Zhang Pingyu		+reaction	the Tower
solid	Zhang Pingyu		+composition	the Tower
standing for one thousand years	author		+composition	the Tower
great surprise	Zhang Pingyu	neutral		royal soldiers' uniform
splendid	Zhang Pingyu		+reaction	St Paul's Cathedral
interesting	Zhang Pingyu		+reaction	Westminster Abbey
famous	Author		+reaction	sound of Big Ben
had so much to tell	Zhang Pingyu		+reaction	the first day's tour
famous	Author		+reaction	the clock in Greenwich
sets the world time	Author		+valuation	the clock in Greenwich
what interested her most	Zhang Pingyu		+reaction	the longitude line
very useful	Author		+valuation	the longitude line
dividing the eastern and western halves of the world	Author		+valuation	the longitude line
strange	Zhang Pingyu		-reaction	Marx lived and died in London
famous	Author		+reaction	reading room
sadly	Zhang Pingyu	-happiness		library had moved
thrilled	Zhang Pingyu	+desire		Treasures
wonderful	Zhang Pingyu		+reaction	treasures
enjoying	Visitors	+happiness		old Chinese pots and other objects
beautiful	Visitors		+reaction	old Chinese pots
very proud	Zhang Pingyu	+security		her country
wondered	Zhang Pingyu	+desire		the next day's tour

positivity or negativity of this emotion 'can be contextually implied with the help of other evaluations preceding or following the emotion term'. In Figure 5.10, the protagonist indicated surprised at the fact that the present-day royal soldiers still wore the 400-year-old uniform on special occasions, which highlights what is unusual or interesting and thus implies a positive reaction. Retrospectively, the positive AFFECT *delight* at the beginning of the paragraph confirms the positive attitudinal orientation of the term 'great surprise'. The remaining two negative inscriptions are designed to invoke positive APPRECIATION. To be specific, at the beginning of the recount *Zhang Pingyu* was *worried* about the limit of time so she had made a list to organize the three days' tour before the sightseeing, which foretells the value and fruitfulness of the tour to be described later in the recount. Towards the end of her London tour, *Zhang Pingyu* felt sad because the *Library of the British Museum* had moved and the old reading room where *Karl Marx* had worked was gone. Nevertheless, the adversative conjunction *but* and the positively inscribed affectual lexis *thrilled* immediately after the negative emotion indicates that the tour is still highly rewarding. Overall, through the overt demonstration of how the protagonist feels, the inscribed AFFECT first initiates and then reinforces the prosody of the positive ATTITUDE throughout the verbal text.

Owing to the fact that there are no human participants depicted in the four accompanying photographs of selected buildings or statues, the visual analysis here mainly focuses on angle. Along the vertical axis, all five photographs are taken from a low angle, that is, the photographer and the viewer look at those buildings depicted in the photographs from below. As Kress and van Leeuwen (2006: 140) point out, in this kind of image construes the represented participants visually as having greater power than the interactive participants. The low angle in the five photographs endows the places of interest with symbolic power and authority, though a matter of degree of the power is involved. The *St Paul's Cathedral*, *Westminster Abbey* and *Royal Observatory in Greenwich* are presented in the photographs as steep tower above the viewer, whereas in the photographs of *Royal Observatory in Greenwich* and the *Karl Marx's statue* they show relatively gradual incline. In terms of the horizontal angle, the scenes are mainly photographed from an oblique point of view and thus indicate a sense of detachment from the viewer, which is consistent with the verbal expression of awe and magnificence in the written text. The *Karl Marx's statue* is represented in a different way from the buildings, in that this photograph is taken from a frontal angle so as to make the statue identifiable to the viewer. To sum up, the interplay of the vertical and horizontal angles encodes the ATTITUDE of reverence towards the civic landscapes in London, which co-articulates the APPRECIATION and AFFECT encoded in the verbal text. In other words, both the verbiage and the images commit positive attitudinal meanings, which together contribute to the positive prosody of evaluation of the landscapes in the multimodal text.

5.4.3 Co-instantiation in jointly constructed text

This section concentrates on the distribution of attitudinal meanings in multimodal jointly constructed text. The example drawn on here is the one used in Section 4.3.3.3 (see Figure 5.11), which is taken from *Unit 4 Earthquakes* in the senior secondary EFL textbook *New Senior English for China Student's Book 1* (2004: 30). In this multimodal jointly constructed text, the reader is required to participate in the construction of verbiage in light of the accompanying images. The focus of this discussion will be shifted from the management of heteroglossic space as analysed in Chapter 4, to the examination of the verbiage-image relation in encoding attitudinal meanings.

The images of Figure 5.11 are a set of four stamps entitled *The New Tangshan after the Earthquake*, which was issued in 1996 to honour the city twenty years after the *Tangshan* earthquake. The stamps adopt the commonsense naturalistic coding orientation (Kress and van Leeuwen 2006: 165–6) to depict the civic landscapes of *Tangshan* after the city reconstruction, portraying *Farmhouses*, *Factories*, a *Street Vista* and the *Harbour* respectively. The scenes are represented from a high angle, putting the viewer at the position of overlooking the whole picture. On the left of the stamps there is a speech draft to be completed by the reader. As indicated in the exercise instruction, the reader is required to give a short talk about the new stamps by using the model provided in the draft.

> Thank you, Mr Zhang. I am happy to_____. As you can see, the stamps show_____. I think these stamps are very important

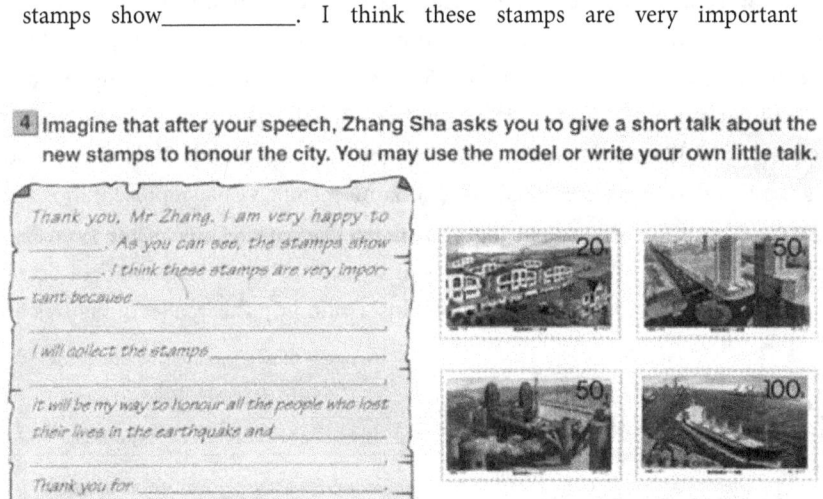

Figure 5.11 Co-instantiation in jointly constructed text [New Senior English for China Student's Book 1, 2004: 30].

because_____. I will collect the stamps_____. It will be my way to honour all the people who lost their lives in the earthquake and_____.
Thank you for_____.

The ATTITUDE encoded in this short speech draft covers all three dimensions: AFFECT, JUDGEMENT and APPRECIATION, as shown in Table 5.6. The ellipsis notation '...' in the table indicates what is to be filled up by the reader.

As indicated in Table 5.6, the target of AFFECT is to be completed by the reader, while the stamps are evaluated as *very important*. The reader is supposed to supply another target of the positive JUDGEMENT indicated by the verb 'honour', in addition to the victims of the earthquake already provided in the text.

As mentioned in Section 3.2.3 of Chapter 3, the concept of commitment, that is the amount of meaning potential instantiated in a given text, can be employed to capture how explicitly or implicitly a certain instance encodes attitudinal meanings. Based on a comparative study of three verbal accounts (one biographical and two auto-biographical), Martin (2008b) points out that direct inscription commits more attitudinal meaning potential than invocation does; while between the sub-categories of invocation, flagging is more attitudinally committed than affording. If this discussion is extended to include visual meaning-making resources encoding attitudinal meanings, Figures 5.2, 5.3, 5.4 and 5.9 employ depiction techniques that explicitly show the viewer how the represented participants feel (e.g. happy in these cases) and thus overtly tell the viewer about their emotions. There is no verbal commitment in terms of ATTITUDE in these four examples, and it is the images that are responsible for the attitudinal meanings. In Figures 5.7), 5.8, 5.10 and 5.11, language encodes attitudinal meanings, either through the use of evaluative lexis or via the selections of ideational tokens. The images in these examples do not encode AFFECT, and yet the ideational selections of certain visual representations do invoke an attitudinal response (i.e. JUDGEMENT or APPRECIATION) in the viewer. The indirect invocations in the images of Figures 5.7 , 5.8, 5.10 and 5.11 do not commit as much ATTITUDE as the direct inscriptions in the images of Figures 5.2,

Table 5.6 Inscribed and Invoked ATTITUDE in the Verbiage of Figure 5.9

Appraising items	Appraiser	AFFECT	JUDGEMENT	APPRECIATION	Appraised
Happy	I	+happiness			...
very important	I			+valuation	stamps
Honour	I		+propriety		people who lost their lives in the earthquake and ...

5.3, 5.4 and 5.9, in that the viewer needs to 'take a crooked path' to grasp the attitudinal meanings encoded in the images.

In those cases in which only visual patterns commit attitudinal meanings, the verbiage-image relation is that of complementarity rather than co-instantiation. The images complement the corresponding verbal texts in the sense that they are where the attitudinal meanings come from, whereas the verbal texts complement the images by providing the materials that are designed to meet certain teaching goals.

5.5 The accumulation of institutionalized feelings in EFL education

The preceding two sections have examined what sorts of attitudinal meanings are encoded in the various types of visual displays in the multimodal EFL textbook discourse, and analysed the ways in which image and verbiage co-articulate or complement each other in construing evaluation. Now I am in a better position to discuss the encoding of attitudinal meanings in the primary and secondary EFL textbooks in relation to the emotional and attitudinal goals in the curriculum standards, by drawing on the notion that JUDGEMENT and APPRECIATION are institutionalized feelings (Martin 2000a; Martin and White 2005). Before doing so, I shall first briefly mention what is emphasized in the curriculum standards as emotion and attitude education.

5.5.1 Emotion and attitude goal in the curriculum standards

In the educational context in China, perhaps the best-known aspect of emotion and attitude education is moral and values education. As has been observed by Zhu (2006), moral and values education in Chinese primary and secondary schools had for a long time been conducted mainly through the organizations including Youth League and Young Pioneer, and 'a special subject for moral education' in schools. But 2001 was the first time that emotion and attitude education, including moral and values education, was defined from the angle of 'the integrity and conformity of curriculum functions' in the curriculum standards published by the Ministry of Education of the People's Republic of China.

Emotion and attitude education is seen as indispensable to subject teaching in the reformed curriculum. These curriculum standards for each subject had a clear statement on the attitudinal goal of developing students' active emotion (Zhu 2006). Section 2.4.3 in Chapter 2 has provided examples and explanations concerning the right orientation of emotions, attitudes and values in the *Curriculum Standards for English*. It can be inferred that emotion and attitude education in the curriculum standards in China embraces having a positive attitude, confidence, a desire to learn and an ability to evaluate people's behaviours as well as things and phenomena. Language learning is regarded as 'far more closely related to emotion and attitude education than other school subjects' (Cheng 2002). As indicated in Chapter 2, the *Curriculum Standards for English* adopts a nine-grade system for stipulating the specific goals in EFL teaching and learning at each educational level. In terms of emotion and attitude education, the attitudinal outcomes assumed to be achieved by the students of Grades 2, 5 and 8 (i.e. primary, junior and senior secondary school graduates) are summarized in Table 5.7.

As demonstrated in Table 5.7, the emotion and attitude goals for Grade 2 are mainly about AFFECT (e.g. *interested, happy*) towards English learning, along with some indications of 'tenacity' from the system of JUDGEMENT required in the learning process (e.g. *dare to open one's mouth, take the initiative*). As for Grade 5, while positive emotions like happiness, security and satisfaction (e.g. *interested, happy, willing* and *confident*) are retained, more requirements are made in terms of 'capacity' from the system of JUDGEMENT (e.g. *clear, aware* and *able to actively cooperate.../to pay regard and understand...*), and 'tenacity' (e.g. *take the initiative*) from the system of JUDGEMENT, as well as the evaluation of Chinese and foreign cultures. When it comes to Grade 8, except for Items 1 and 3 that mainly deal with emotions, the goals primarily centre around 'capacity' (e.g. *clear, able to overcome difficulties.../to understand and respect.../to learn about and respect...*) and 'propriety' (e.g. *teamwork spirit, willing to share*) from the system of JUDGEMENT. Based on the description in the previous sections of the ways in which image and verbiage work in tandem to set up a positive evaluative orientation, the ensuing section will focus on the relationship between the three dimensions within ATTITUDE, and the implications of this relationship for the emotion and attitude education.

5.5.2 JUDGEMENt and APPRECIATION as institutionalized AFFECT

As indicated in Section 3.3.1, among the three attitudinal sub-systems AFFECT can be taken as the core system because it is concerned with the embodied feelings we are born with, which is later developed into culturally

Table 5.7 Emotion and Attitude Goals for Grades 2, 5 and 8 in *Curriculum Standards for English* (Ministry of Education of the People's Republic of China 2001a: 22)

Grade	Description of goal
2	1. Interested in listening to and speaking English, as well as other activities like reciting chants, singing songs, telling stories and playing games;
	2. Happy to follow good models; dare to open one's mouth and speak English; actively engage oneself and take the initiative to consult others.
5	1. Clear about the purpose for learning English; aware of the fact that learning English is for communication;
	2. Interested in learning English and willing to do so, happily engaged in a variety of English-learning activities and practices;
	3. Confident about mastering English; dare to express oneself in English;
	4. Able to actively cooperate with others, help one another and accomplish tasks together;
	5. Happy in learning English and willing to learn English songs as well as reading materials in English;
	6. Able to pay regard and understand others' feelings while communicating in English;
	7. Able to take the initiative to consult teachers or peer students and ask them for help when encountering problems;
	8. Happy to explore English and follow good models in everyday life;
	9. Have a deeper understanding of Chinese culture;
	10. Happy to learn about foreign culture.
8	1. Maintain interest in learning English as well as the desire to learn, and actively engage with those activities that are conducive to improving one's English;
	2. Have a proper motivation for learning English; clear about the fact that learning English is for communication and expression;
	3. Have relatively strong confidence in learning English, dare to communicate with others and express oneself in English;
	4. Able to overcome difficulties in learning English, and willing to consult others;
	5. Able to understand and respect others' feelings while communicating in English;
	6. Have relatively strong teamwork spirit in learning; willing to share learning materials with others;
	7. Able to introduce Chinese culture in English;
	8. Able to learn about and respect foreign culture, as well as demonstrate the spirit of international cooperation.

specific emotional repertoires (Martin 2000a, 2004; Painter 2003). AFFECT is recontextualized, or institutionalized into the realms of shared values in two directions: in relation to the evaluation of human behaviours that need to be controlled under social norms, AFFECT is recontextualized as JUDGEMENT; and with respect to the evaluation of things that need to be valued with reference to

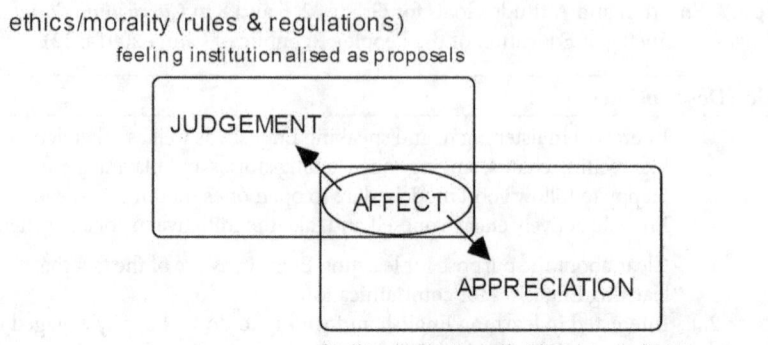

Figure 5.12 JUDGEMENT and APPRECIATION as institutionalized AFFECT (Martin and White 2005: 45).

their social significance, AFFECT is recontextualized as APPRECIATION. In other words, JUDGEMENT and APPRECIATION can be regarded as institutionalized AFFECT. Based on Halliday's (1994) concepts of proposition and proposal, Martin (2000a: 147) suggests that JUDGEMENT institutionalizes feelings as proposals (about behaviour), whereas APPRECIATION institutionalizes feelings as proposition (about things). Figure 5.12 shows diagrammatically these two recontextualizations or institutionalizations.

In developing an ontogenetic view on attitude in language development, Painter (2003) studies the ontogenesis of the ATTITUDE system and points out that a child's initial semiotic system is essentially one for sharing emotion or AFFECT. The institutionalizations of AFFECT, that is JUDGEMENT and APPRECIATION, occur 'only later with new semiotic steps on the child's part – either the adoption of mother tongue lexical words in lieu of protolinguistic symbols or a "meta" awareness of the sign itself' (Painter 2003: 189). In other words, the growing capability of symbolizing enables the evaluations in terms of JUDGEMENT and APPRECIATION to emerge along with the direct expressions of emotions.

The discussion here is extended beyond the early pre-school period to include primary and secondary education, which may account for the construal of evaluation in the given educational context. There is a wide range of semiotic resources, both visual and verbal, available to construe evaluative stance in EFL textbooks. As analysed earlier, the images in the textbooks for primary students mainly adopt cartoons to describe animate represented participants with explicit affectual inscriptions. This tendency gradually diminishes and images of serious style (i.e. portraits and photographs) emerge in the textbooks for secondary education. Combined with the ideational tokens that are designed to invoke APPRAISAL as well as the explicit JUDGEMENT in the verbal texts, the serious portraits and photographs encode JUDGEMENT invocations and colour the whole multimodal text. As for those multimodal texts depicting inanimate buildings and landscapes, images invoke APPRECIATION where the verbal texts are not responsible for the ATTITUDE encoding. In those multimodal texts in which verbal texts and images are both attitudinally committed, images enhance the verbally inscribed or invoked attitudinal meanings. This co-instantiation contributes to the establishment of the intended evaluative stance. To sum up, in examining the visual and verbal attitudinal inscriptions and invocations in EFL textbooks as the students advance through school years from primary to secondary education, an attitudinal shift from a more personal way of expressing individual emotions to a more institutionalized way of evaluating people's behaviours, abstract concepts and concrete objects can be identified. This change of preference both reflects and contributes to the gradual increase of institutionalized feelings that are supposed to be achieved, as indicated in the pedagogic context.

5.6 Summary

In sum, this chapter is concerned with the evaluative orientation construed in multimodal EFL textbook discourse, with emphasis placed on verbiage-image relations. To be specific, I have analysed the attitudinal meanings encoded in various styles of images widely employed in the textbooks under discussion, namely cartoons, portraits and photographs, and their correlated verbal texts. The research findings indicate that the frequently adopted cartoon style in the primary textbooks is often indicative of positive affectual meanings, and thus the emotion of happiness in English learning is directly inscribed. Some of the cartoons can also function to invoke APPRECIATION through logogenetic recontextualization. In short, the images of cartoons bear much of the responsibility for encoding attitudinal meanings in the textbooks for primary and junior secondary education, with the verbiage-image relation being a complementary one.

The trend for explicit affectual inscriptions gradually declines in the textbooks for secondary education. The emerging serious images signal a transition from the playful childhood to adolescence, when a sense of social responsibility is to be cultivated. The serious portraits and photographs with implicit JUDGEMENT or APPRECIATION invocations work in concert with the explicit attitudinal inscriptions and the ideational tokens designed to invoke APPRAISAL in the verbal texts. In other words, both language and images commit attitudinal meanings in these multimodal texts. The two semiotic modes co-articulate each other in leading the reader to the putative reading and guiding him/her in the completion of jointly constructed texts.

In the curriculum standards, emotion and attitude education has gained unprecedented attention. Taking a multilevel view on the attitudinal meanings inscribed in or invoked by multimodal EFL textbook discourse, this chapter has identified the gradual shift in ATTITUDE encoding, that is from personal emotion to an institutionalized way of evaluation, which both reflects and contributes to the orientations of emotion and attitude education stipulated in the curriculum standards.

6

Contestable reality

A multilevel perspective on modality in visual communication

6.1 Introduction

This chapter will explore the issue of 'what counts as real' in multimodal communicative contexts. The social-semiotic approach to modality holds that the reliability of a message is socially defined, based on the accepted criteria for truth in the intended social or institutional group, which in turn both reflects and constructs social relations (Hodge and Kress 1988; Kress and van Leeuwen 2006, 2020; van Leeuwen 2005). Before embarking on the detailed analysis and discussion, I will first briefly review the linguistic and social-semiotic underpinnings relevant to the present study, and then introduce several theoretical concepts that are crucial to understanding visual semiotics. The ensuing analysis is a multilevel, comparative investigation into the truth criteria in the primary, junior and senior secondary EFL textbooks, whose purpose is to clarify the connection between modality judgements and social relations in different EFL educational contexts. This will be followed by a discussion on visual style in relation to certain educational theories. Attention will also be paid to the possibility of choosing different visual styles in genres within a macrogenre.

6.2 Modality in multimodal discourse

The study of modality began with the 'absolute, context-independent truth of assertions' orientation in the philosophy of language before it moved to linguistics (van Leeuwen 2005: 165). This section aims at providing a general account of some previous studies on modality in language and other modes of communication relevant to the focus of this research.

6.2.1 Linguistic modality

Traditionally, the term 'modality' is generally defined as 'the manner in which the meaning of a clause is qualified so as to reflect the speakers' judgement of the likelihood of the proposition it expresses being true' (Quirk et al. 1985: 219). Studies of modality have tended to be confined to the discussion of modal auxiliary verbs such as *can, could, must, may, might, will* and *would*. In traditional grammar, the meanings of modality are divided into two categories: intrinsic modality and extrinsic modality. The former covers the meanings of permission, obligation and volition, whereas the latter includes possibility, ability, necessity and prediction. Each of the modal auxiliary verbs is believed to have both intrinsic and extrinsic uses (Quirk et al. 1985: 219–21). The distinction between epistemic modality and deontic modality (Coates 1983; Palmer 1990) again reflects these two different uses of the modals. Most of the modals are used in both senses, and modal verbs can be approached in terms of kinds of modality (e.g. epistemic, deontic and dynamic) and degrees of modality (e.g. possibility and necessity) (Palmer 1990: 8, 36).

As explained in Chapter 3, the theoretical rationale that underpins this study owes most to Halliday (1976, 1994). According to Halliday (1994: 88, 356), modality refers to the intermediate degrees of meaning between positive polarity and negative polarity. In English the choices of 'yes' and 'no' are expressed in the Finite element of the mood structure or Mood Adjuncts like *not*, while the various kinds of indeterminacy in between are conveyed through MODALITY – which is categorized into MODALIZATION and MODULATION based on whether it is concerned with a proposition or proposal respectively. MODALIZATION is subdivided into probability to express different degrees of likelihood (e.g. *possibly, certainly*) and usuality to express degrees of occurrence (e.g. *sometimes, always*). MODULATION, on the other hand, consists of the sub-categories of obligation (e.g. *supposed to, required to*) and inclination (e.g. *willing to, determined to*) (Halliday 1994: 88–9, 356–7).[1] The inclusion of MODULATION in the MODALITY system, as van Leeuwen (2005: 165) points out, has moved the traditional focus on the modality of representations a step further on by pointing out the fact that the same modal auxiliary verb (e.g. *may*) can express either a degree of social obligation (e.g. You *may* go home now) and a degree of representational truth (e.g. It *may* rain today).

Halliday (1994: 355–63) further identifies three variables in the MODALITY system: TYPE, ORIENTATION and VALUE. Types of MODALITY include probability, usuality, obligation and inclination, which represent different ways of construing the semantic space between the positive and negative poles. The second variable, ORIENTATION, is used to discuss how each type of modality can be realized. To be specific, there are distinctions between subjective modality and objective modality, and between explicit and implicit variants. It should be noted that the explicitly subjective (e.g. *I think* Alice likes it) and explicitly objective (e.g. *It is likely that* Alice likes it) forms of modality are metaphorical variants, in that they both represent the speaker's point of view through a projecting clause rather than an adjunct to a proposition. In the explicitly subjective modality, the speaker chooses to highlight his/her own position in assessing the validity of the proposition or the appropriateness of the proposal. On the contrary, in the explicitly objective modality the speaker dresses up his/her angle as objective, hence backgrounding the source of the attitude being expressed. The third variable is the value that is attached to modality. Take probability for instance. The value can be high (e.g. It is *certainly* that Tom knows the truth) or median (e.g. It is *probably* that Tom knows the truth) or low (e.g. It is *possibly* that Tom knows the truth).

As pointed out by Hodge and Kress (1988: 124), one of Halliday's fundamental contributions to the studies of modality lies in his extension of the use of modality beyond auxiliary verbs to cover all the elements with the same function, including nouns (e.g. *It is a matter of fact that . . .*), verbs (e.g. *I doubt that . . .*), adjectives (e.g. *It is foolish to deny that . . .*) and other expressions such as *kind of, hardly* and *the like*. Furthermore, Halliday points out that MODALITY is part of the interpersonal component of his functional grammar, rather than placing it in the ideational component as most logicians have assumed. To quote Hodge and Kress,

> Halliday's theory recognizes that modality is a matter of the relation of the participants in a verbal interaction, hence squarely in the domain of the social, and that modal forms are the traces of the activity of speakers acting in a social context. (Hodge and Kress 1988: 124)

Instead of considering modality as expressing the actual objective truth that exists between propositions and the real world, social semioticians examine it in relation to the semiotic resources employed to express 'as *how true* or as *how real* a given representation should be taken' (van Leeuwen 2005: 281; emphasis in the original). The social-semiotic approach to modality in visual communication will be explicated later, before developing a multilevel perspective on modality in texts in different educational contexts.

6.2.2 Social-semiotic approach to modality

Social semioticians (Hodge and Kress 1988; Hodge and Tripp 1986; Kress and Hodge 1979; van Leeuwen 1999, 2005) adapt the term 'modality' to the studies of other semiotic phenomena. In the eyes of social semioticians, modality is used to describe 'the stance of participants in the semiotic process towards the state and the status of the system of classification of the mimetic plane' (Hodge and Kress 1988: 122). Therefore, when exploring modality analysts need to examine the semiotic resources available to a speaker or writer in negotiating how true a given representation should be taken.

Drawing on this social-semiotic approach to modality, this research treats 'truth' as the shared truth produced by members of a group with the same values – enacted as an 'affirmation of solidarity' and an 'assertion of power' (Hodge and Kress 1988). Modality always involves at least two parties, and the degree of affinity expressed in modality posits the social relationship on a continuum from affirmation (i.e. high affinity/modality) to negation (i.e. weak or zero affinity/modality) (Hodge and Kress 1988: 122–3, 164). In social semiotics, all semiotic processes are treated as social processes, and thus all semiotic phenomena bear signs of modality. To take linguistic phenomena for example, some genres (e.g. encyclopaedia) are regarded as more factual than others (e.g. fiction). What is regarded to be credible for a certain social group may not be reliable in the eyes of another social group (Hodge and Kress 1988: 121; Kress and van Leeuwen 2006: 171). Whoever controls modality can control which version of reality is treated as valid, and the accepted representation of reality will serve as 'the basis of judgement and action' (Hodge and Kress 1988: 147). In sum, truth can be constantly challenged and tested in every social or semiotic exchange, and modality is a social or interpersonal concept, not an ideational one.

As indicated earlier, for social semioticians modality is a multimodal concept that goes beyond language and is extended to the non-verbal modes of communication. Research on modality in other semiotic modes will be briefly reviewed in the next section, for the purpose of gaining a better understanding of the social-semiotic principles informing studies of multimodal discourse.

6.2.3 Modality in modes other than language

As mentioned earlier, modality resources are involved in all modes of communication. If we take a step further beyond language, modality in other modes (such as images, three-dimensional objects and sound) can be examined through the lens of social semiotics. This section will provide a general delineation of the modality in those three modes of communication. Detailed elaborations of visual modality, which is the focus of the current research, will be presented in the following section.

Modality in visual media has been theorized with the advance of social semiotics. Hodge and Kress (1988: 128, 264) point out that modality judgements are conveyed through what they call modality markers but interpreted through what they call modality cues – by which they mean a more general category including both specialized modality markers and all the other bases for modality judgements in verbal as well as visual codes. The co-authors further summarize four general principles for analysing visual modality: (i) Modality cues in visual texts are signifiers of semiotic activity, signifying the status of the text or parts of the text as enacting high or low affinity; (ii) the modality value of a visual text is not fixed, but depends on receiver position and orientation – owing to the fact that receivers can be positioned in different ways in relation to mimetic content and to texts and producers; (iii) there is interaction between modality and ideology, with ideology assigning modality values and modality legitimating ideological values; and (iv) different genres establish sets of specific modality markers, and an overall modality value acts as the base-line for a specific genre with variations due to viewer/reader differences and other factors (Hodge and Kress 1988: 142).

Kress and van Leeuwen (2006, 2020) provide a more detailed analytical framework for analysing visual modality. They have identified eight modality markers, which are means of visual expression involved in the judgement of visual modality: colour saturation, colour differentiation, colour modulation, contextualization, representation, depth, illumination and brightness (Kress and van Leeuwen 2006: 160–3, see also van Leeuwen 2005: 167). Each of the eight aspects is regarded as a continuum that ranges from the maximal articulation to the minimum or absence of articulation. Explanations of these modality markers with instances from our data will be given in the following section. It should be noted that modality value does not always increase with the amplification of articulation. In a naturalistic coding orientation, there is a certain point on each of the continuums that represents the highest modality value: namely, a 'commonsense', 'everyday' representation based on the resolution of the standard 35mm photographic technology. Nevertheless, alongside this 'naturalistic coding orientation' (Kress and van Leeuwen 2006: 165) there are other contexts in which different kinds of truth are favoured. As reviewed in Chapter 3, scientific visuals aim at representing the essence of phenomena, and thus diagrams and figures with low articulations in colour, perspective, light and shadow are regarded as images with high modality value. They are viewed in terms of an 'abstract coding orientation'.

Taking a further step from two-dimensional images to three-dimensional visual displays, social semioticians investigate the modality of toys, sculptures, buildings and everyday design objects. It is found that some of the aforementioned principles work well in three-dimensional representations. For example, the modality of the toys for young children tends to be abstract and sensory in terms of detail and colour, whereas the modality of toys for older children is more naturalistic, bearing resemblance to the adult world. Three-dimensional modality differs from two-dimensional modality in the sense that there is no need to represent depth or the play of light and shade – since objects can be viewed from different perspectives (Kress and van Leeuwen 2006: 252–5).

Moving from visual perception to aural perception, van Leeuwen (1999: 170–87) proposes that the modality of sound can be approached along the same lines as visual modality. Eight parameters are used to study the articulation of sound-pitch range, durational variation, dynamic range, perspectival depth, degree of fluctuation, degree of friction, absorption range and degree of directionality. These eight dimensions are also seen as scales running from the maximal degree to the minimal degree. In addition, the coding orientation adopted in a given communicative context determines the modality value of a particular sound. Abstract-sensory, naturalistic and sensory are the three types of coding orientations identified in people's judgements of sound modality. The most abstract form of sound is music. Musical abstraction makes it possible for music to be both abstract and sensory.

6.3 Visual modality

I now narrow down the discussion to visual modality, with relevant examples from the data to account for the modality markers: that is the various parameters whose configurations express the modality of a given visual event, and the coding orientations, which provide criteria for modality judgements in different contexts.

6.3.1 Modality markers in naturalistic standard

This study concentrates on the modality markers from the perspective of a naturalistic coding orientation.

6.3.1.1 Colouration

As mentioned earlier, along each of the continua there is one point representing the highest modality. In terms of the photographic naturalism the point of highest value is not situated on either extreme of the continuum but on a certain point in between. Take the use of colour for instance. There are three dimensions of colouration to be considered: colour saturation, differentiation and modulation. The continuum of colour saturation ranges from the use of maximally saturated colour to the absence of saturation: black and white. The naturalistic modality scale for colour saturation is represented in Figure 6.1.

Figure 6.2 is taken from *Unit 1 Women of Achievement* in the senior secondary EFL textbook *New Senior English for China Student's Book 4* (2004: 1), which provides concrete exempla for the explanation of modality markers. In terms of

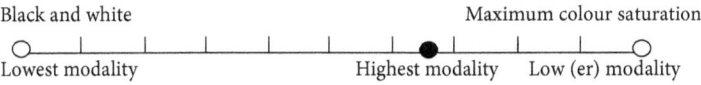

Figure 6.1 Modality scale for colour saturation (Kress and van Leeuwen 2006: 160).

Figure 6.2 Articulation of detail [New Senior English for China Student's Book 4, 2004: 1].

colour saturation, Image 1 has the lowest modality due to its absence of colour saturation, whereas all the other five images have the highest modality value since they represent naturalistic colour.

The second dimension is colour differentiation, which refers to the scale running from a maximally diversified range of colours to monochrome. In Figure 6.2, Images 3, 4 and 5 possess a greater diversity of colours than Images 2 and 6, while Image 1 has the lowest diversity among the six. The third aspect of colour that needs to be taken into account is colour modulation, ranging from the representation of all shades a given colour (e.g. the uses of different shades of green) to the use of plain, unmodulated colour. Take the skin colour of the represented participants in Figure 6.2 for instance. Images 2, 3 and 6 represent the fine nuances as well as the effect of shading on the face complexion and arm skin, whereas Images 1, 4 and 5 use relatively flat and less modulated colour for the depiction of skin.

6.3.1.2 Articulation of detail

When it comes to the articulation of details in an image, both background and foreground are taken into consideration. Kress and van Leeuwen (2006, 2020) use the term 'contextualization' to describe the scale running from the most fully articulated and detailed background to the absence of background. In Figure 6.2, the represented participants in Images 1, 5 and 6 are shown against the plain background of a single colour, which is almost equal to the zero articulation of background without any detail. The absence of setting, according to Kress and van Leeuwen (2006: 161), lowers modality in that this kind of decontextualization represents the people within the picture frame as 'generic' and 'typical' rather than specific figures who are associated with a particular point in time and space.

Images 2 and 3 are photographs with out-of-focus backgrounds, which is the intermediate degree between full contextualization and decontextualization. This meets with the naturalistic standard in which the combined effects of the 35mm photographic emulsion and the depth of field of standard lenses normally result in a less articulated background in comparison with what is represented in the foreground. If the background is represented as sharper and more defined, the impression of 'artificial' and 'more than real' will be produced (Kress and van Leeuwen 2006: 161). The background in Image 4 is considered as situated somewhere between the naturalistic contextualization and absence of background, in that the represented participants (i.e. *Jody Williams* and a dog) are represented as being involved in an activity at a specific moment and in a particular location; its pure black background, on the other hand, makes the whole image generic and thus seem unreal. Although this photograph might have been taken on pitch-dark night, it is noteworthy that the depiction of the background in this image causes it to deviate from the naturalistic standard.

As for the depiction of detail in the foreground, the term 'representation' is used to describe the pictorial details of represented participants (Kress and van Leeuwen 2006: 161). The scale of representation runs from maximum depiction of detail to maximum abstraction. It is evident that all the six images in Figure 6.2 are of similar modality value in terms of detail articulation in the foreground. In these six images, the represented participants' hair and facial features, as well as the creases in their clothes are depicted with the amount of detail that meets with the naturalistic standard.

6.3.1.3 *Depth, illumination and brightness*

'Depth' is concerned with perspective, and the scale of depth articulation ranges from maximally deep perspective to the absence of depth. Along this scale the highest modality value rests on the point that represents the central perspective. This is commonly found in naturalistic photographs, in which the objects far from the lens tend to reduce in size and the real-life parallel lines converge at a vanishing point within or outside the picture frame. Accordingly, central perspective is also termed as 'one-point perspective'. The six images in Figure 6.2 all belong to this category and meet the naturalistic standard. Kress and van Leeuwen (2006: 162) also consider different degrees of depth articulation such as the angular-isometric perspective and the frontal-isometric perspective. The modality value of these perspectives is lower than that of the central perspective. They are named 'isometric' due to the fact that the measurements of an object, no matter how far it is from the lens, are represented with a three-dimensional view while the value of object scaling is retained, and thus parallel lines remain parallel and there is no vanishing point. Towards the other extreme of the scale, the 'more than real' perspective, such as the 'fish eye' perspective that swells in the centre of a sphere with converging lines at its sides, is also of low modality.

Another modality marker that can be scaled is 'illumination', which refers to the play of light and shade. The various degrees on this continuum range from the fullest representation of light and shade to its absence. As Kress and van Leeuwen (2006: 162) state, naturalistic depictions normally choose to represent participants as they are affected by a particular source of illumination. Although the light intensity differs among the six images in Figure 6.2, they all employ naturalistic method in lighting depiction, thus having a high modality value in terms of illumination.

Last but not least, the modality marker 'brightness' is a scale that runs from a maximum number of degrees of brightness to only the dark and light versions of a given colour. Kress and van Leeuwen (2006: 162) point out that the difference between the darkest and the lightest areas in an image can be as great as the contrast between deep black and bright white. Towards the other end of the scale, the difference can be minimal and thus a misty, hazy effect is produced. What exceeds the naturalistic standard will be regarded as 'more than real', and hence a lower modality value is assigned. Images 4 and 6 in Figure 6.2 adopt a sharp contrast between pitch dark (i.e. the background and *Jody Williams*' clothes in Image 4, and *Lin Qiaozhi*'s clothes in Image 6) and snow white (i.e. the dog next to *Jody Williams* in Image 4, and the background in Image 6). Nevertheless, this variation of brightness is still within the scope of photographic naturalism. Images 2, 3 and 5 are of higher modality value in brightness, due to the fact that they closely follow the naturalistic standard. On the other hand, the difference in terms of the degrees of brightness in Image 1 is quite small, and hence a vague, misty impression is produced and its brightness value is low.

It should be noted that within a given image, some modality markers may be amplified while others tend to be reduced. For instance, Image 1 in Figure 6.2 has low modality in terms of colour saturation, colour differentiation, colour modulation, contexualization and brightness, at the same time as it is naturalistic in terms of representation, depth and illumination. The overall assessment of modality is generated by the viewer on the basis of the diversity of these modality markers (Kress and van Leeuwen 2006: 163). The effect of the different degrees of amplification or reduction in modality markers may result in a number of 'modality configurations', which cue a viewer's judgements of modality with respect to 'how real' a certain image is to be taken (van Leeuwen 2005: 167). The following section will move on to the discussion of the modality values of different configurations in relation to the preferred visual truth in various contexts.

6.3.2 Coding orientation in other contexts

So far the focus has been on the naturalistic coding orientation, which is the most common standard of visual truth in everyday life. However, configurations with low modality in terms of a naturalistic standard can be of high modality value in other contexts. For example, colour,[2] detail of texture or play of light and shade is seldom found in the figures, diagrams and other technical drawings in scientific and technological discourse; but these images possess higher modality value than a naturalistic photograph as far as their scientific-technological meaning is concerned. Another exemplum comes from the advertising and commercial context. The images in this context are designed to arouse sensations, and thus they are generally sensory, and 'more than real' in many aspects so as to produce an illusion of the benefits that the advertised products claim to bring. As Kress and van Leeuwen remark,

> visual modality rests on culturally and historically determined standards of what is real and what is not, and not on the objective correspondence of the image to a reality defined in some ways independently of it. (Kress and van Leeuwen 2006: 163)

6.3.2.1 *Technological coding orientation*

For technological coding orientation, the reality principle lies in the 'effectiveness' or 'usefulness' of a given image as a 'blue print'. The majority of the images with scientific or instructional purposes, including maps, architectural layouts and instructions for dress-making, accord with this criterion (van Leeuwen 2005:

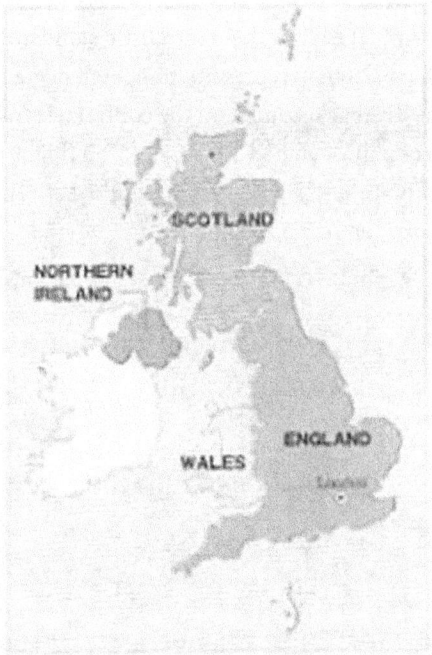

Figure 6.3 Technological coding orientation [New Senior English for China Student's Book 5, 2004: 9].

168). Figure 6.3 is a map from my data showing the contours of the four countries of the UK, which is taken from *Unit 2 The United Kingdom* in *New Senior English for China Student's Book 5* (2004: 9).

In Figure 6.3, most of the modality markers are reduced in articulation. Depth, for instance, is decreased to almost zero degree in the map. In addition, the use of colours has nothing to do with the real colour of the land. The colours are merely conventional 'colour codes' used for denoting different countries in the map so as to facilitate the viewer's understanding. In terms of representation, the map shows only the contours of the four countries. These reduced articulations and flatness do not indicate low modality value. As pointed out by Kress and van Leeuwen (2006: 164), in scientific-technological context what counts as real means what can be known in terms of counting, weighing, measuring and other methods of science. Therefore, in the educational context like that of Figure 6.3, where knowledge of geography is construed, any distracting articulations are reduced to low degrees.

6.3.2.2 Sensory coding orientation

Sensory coding orientations are primarily used in the contexts where the pleasure principle dominates, such as advertising, art, fashion and interior decoration (Kress and van Leeuwen 2006: 165). It is often realized through high degrees of articulation that exceed the naturalistic standard – for example, high colour saturation, sharp detail in representation, high degree of illumination and brightness and so on. The background, on the contrary, is frequently represented as out of focus or roughly sketched in, so as to highlight what is represented in the foreground. Figure 6.4 is taken from *Unit 3 Let's Paint* in *PEP Primary English Students' Book I for Year 3* (2003: 27).

Figure 6.4 Sensory coding orientation [PEP Primary English Students' Book I for Year 3, 2003: 27].

The image depicts a game designed for the purpose of practising the expressions of '*Hi. How are you?*' '*Fine, thank you.*' in primary EFL classrooms. As shown in the image, the characters (i.e. students in an English class) line up, one student greeting the next immediately after responding to the one before him/her. The represented participants are portrayed as anatomically distorted with disproportionately large heads, thin limbs, large eyes and wide smiles. It is noteworthy that three out of the four represented participants in the image are depicted as 'two-headed' people, representing the dual role of one single student taking turns to initiate as well as respond to greetings. Although this exaggerated representation may strike the viewer who holds naturalistic standards as 'more than real', the primary goal of sensory coding orientation is to create pleasure and arouse emotions. The background of the image is totally absent, and thus the represented participants in the foreground are even more eye-catching. In short, all the pictorial techniques in the image are designed as sources 'of pleasure and affective meanings', and consequently Figure 6.4 is regarded as an image of high modality in a sensory coding orientation.

6.3.2.3 *Abstract coding orientation*

In an abstract coding orientation, the standard for visual truth is the 'essence' or 'general truth' that underlies the concrete and specific variations on the surface. This coding orientation is commonly adopted by sociocultural elites in the contexts of 'high' art and academia, where the reduction of diversified, individual differences to the general, essential quality is considered to be of high modality. In these contexts, the ability to identify and produce the texts that are based on this coding orientation is a mark of being an 'educated person' or a 'serious artist' (Kress and van Leeuwen 2006: 165). A case in point can be found in the EFL textbooks under examination. Figure 6.5 is an excerpt from *Unit 4 How Do You Get to School?* in the EFL textbook *Go for It Students' Book I for*

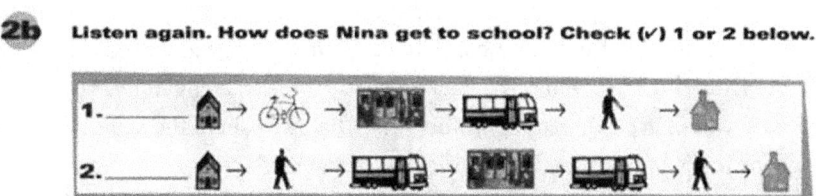

Figure 6.5 Abstract coding orientation [Go for It Students' Book I for Year 8, 2005: 22].

Year 8 (2005: 22); this is a listening comprehension exercise for Year 8 students in junior secondary school.

Students are required to listen to a dialogue and choose the transportation means by which *Nina* gets to school. One of the premises for doing this exercise is the correct reading of the abstract visual symbols that stand for locations including *Nina*'s home (i.e. 🏠) and school (i.e. 🏫), as well as transportation means such as by bike (i.e. 🚲), by subway (i.e. 🚇), by bus (i.e. 🚌) and on foot (i.e. 🚶). In these visual symbols, most of the detail is radically reduced. For example, the human figure is identifiable as a person who is walking, but a viewer cannot tell the gender or age due to the lack of colour, brightness, illumination and representation of details and depth. Other symbols that represent destinations and transportation also employ decreased articulation, for instance, low colour differentiation, low brightness variation with misty impression and so on. In sum, as pointed out by van Leeuwen (2005: 168), from the point of view of the essential or general truth, all details that indicate specific, individual features are irrelevant. The more an image represents the general pattern that underlies the superficially different instances, the higher its modality will be according to an abstract coding orientation.

6.4 A multilevel perspective on visual modality in EFL textbook discourse

Some consideration has so far been given to the eight visual parameters that serve as modality markers in judging what counts as real in a given context or among the members of a certain social group. The reality principles that have been covered include the everyday naturalistic one as well as the technological, sensory and abstract coding orientations adopted in different contexts. The next section will turn to a comparative study of coding orientation in texts for different pedagogic contexts, with the purpose of providing a multilevel perspective on visual modality configurations in primary and secondary EFL textbook discourse in China. The data comprise three teaching units concerning animals, which are comparable in the sense that they share the same field: the 'topic or focus of the activity' in which communicative parties are engaged, or more broadly speaking, the 'institutional focus or social activity type' (Eggins 2004: 9, 103; see also Martin 1984: 23, 1992: 536). In addition, all the EFL textbooks under attention are similar in the register variable of mode, in that they are all edited to be read as formal instructional materials and they all draw upon both linguistic and visual meaning-making resources.

6.4.1 Sensory coding orientation in *We Love Animals*

The unit concerning animals in primary EFL textbooks is *Unit 4 We Love Animals* in *PEP Primary English Students' Book I for Year 3* (2003: 38–47). As indicated in Chapter 5, cartoon is the dominant image style in primary EFL textbooks. The cartoons in the teaching section *Culture* (see Figure 6.6) are taken as an example to examine the coding orientation in the EFL textbooks for primary education.

There are four images in Figure 6.6, each of which depicts one animal considered to be typical in a given country (i.e. *panda* for *CHINA*, *beaver* for *CANADA*, *eagle* for *USA* and *kangaroo* for *AUSTRALIA*), with the name and contour of the country as its background. The visual realization for each modality marker varies in terms of the degree of articulation. Specifically, in terms of colouration, high colour saturation as well as medium colour differentiation and modulation are employed. As for representation, the foregrounded animals are portrayed as 'more than real', in the sense that their emotions and temperament are added into the personified visual displays via facial expressions and gestures. In real life it is usually not easy to tell how an animal feels without specific expertise, but the personification adopted here overtly reveals to us something of the animals' emotions. To be specific, the panda is represented as outgoing with waving

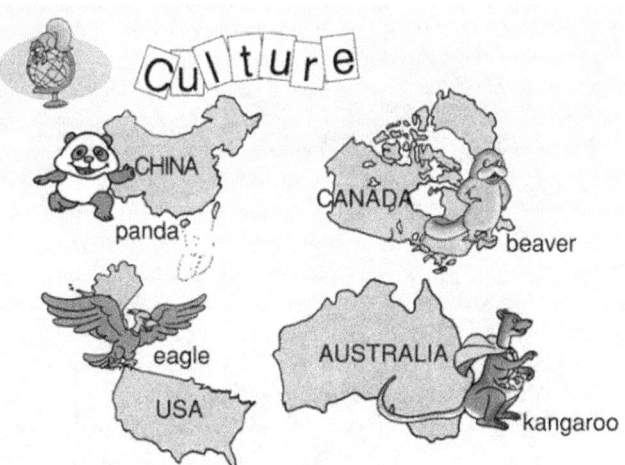

Figure 6.6 Sensory coding orientation in *We Love Animals* [PEP Primary English Students' Book I for Year 3, 2003: 47].

gestures and a wide smile; the beaver seems happy but somewhat cocky with arms akimbo; the eagle appears a bit fierce with wings spread; and the kangaroo looks funny but caring, with a superman's cloak on its shoulder and a baby kangaroo in its pouch. In addition, the animals are represented as disproportionately big as compared with the country contours in the monochrome background; this enhances the entertaining effect of the represented participants in the foreground. The pictorial techniques used in these images follow the pleasure principle, realizing a sensory coding orientation.

As analysed earlier, the 'exaggerated' and 'sensational' style is a common criterion of truth in images for primary school students. This sensory visual style is presumed to attract the attention and excite the imagination of the school-aged English learners. It is designed by the textbook editors to establish a solidarity relationship with the school-aged textbook readers.

6.4.2 Abstract-sensory coding orientation in *Why Do You Like Koalas*

There is a strikingly similar instance in the junior secondary EFL textbooks under attention – an exercise section entitled *Match the animals with the countries* (see Figure 6.7) in *Unit 3 Why Do You Like Koalas* of *Go for It Students' Book II for Year 7* (2005: 13–18). Both the primary school text and the junior secondary school text include images depicting animals and the relevant contours of countries. Their difference lies in the fact in Figure 6.6 the contours of countries serve as the background, whereas in Figure 6.7 the images of animals and countries are

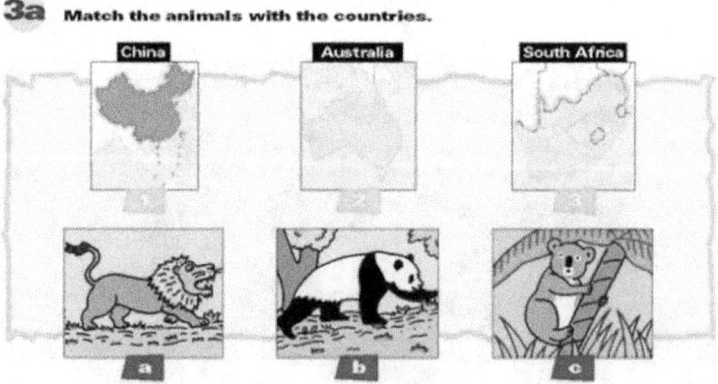

Figure 6.7 Abstract-sensory coding orientation in *Why Do You Like Koalas* [Go for It Students' Book II for Year 7, 2005: 15].

divided into two sets. The lower set represents three animals (i.e. lion, panda and koala), each of which is deemed a recognizable, representative animal of a certain country. The upper set depicts three countries with names as captions: *China*, *Australia* and *South Africa*. Here the junior secondary students are no longer provided with the correct match between animals and countries. Instead, they are required to match the animals with the corresponding countries by themselves. It may be that the repeated use of similar teaching materials across levels complies with the requirement of 'high reappearance rate for language teaching materials', as is stipulated in the *Curriculum Standards for English*. Furthermore, the transition from simple to complex instructional designs reflects the principle of 'proceeding in an orderly way and advancing step by step' (Ministry of Education of the People's Republic of China 2001a: 48).

As for the coding orientation in Figure 6.7, reduced articulation is employed in terms of representation, contextualization, illumination and depth. To be specific, simple line drawing is adopted to capture what makes the animals identifiable. For example, the long heavy mane around the top and sides of the neck, which is the symbol of a male lion, allows the viewer to easily recognize this animal. Nonetheless, the shapes of the three animals and the textures of their fur are brought down to the essential quality. Unlike Figure 6.6, these animals are not depicted without background. Instead, they are represented as snapshotted in their typical habitat. For instance, the koala is described as clinging to a eucalyptus tree. Nonetheless, the background is not articulated in great detail, leaving out details such as the texture of tree bark. The abstract style is also reflected in the low articulation of illumination and depth, in that there is no play of light and shade or perspectival foreshortening in the images. The three maps above the animal images further enhance abstractness. In these maps most of the modality markers are greatly reduced in articulation. Although colour differentiation can be found, the purpose of using various colours in the maps is to distinguish the countries under discussion from the adjacent countries and oceans. Underlying the abstract modality of Figure 6.7 is the truth criterion which holds that the more an image arrests the essential quality or the general truth of what is represented, the higher the modality value will be.

However, it is noteworthy that there is a tension between the abstract modality and an emotive orientation in these images. Unlike the typical abstract images such as scientific diagrams, the animal images in Figure 6.7 draw on the pleasure principle to some degree. A high degree of colour saturation is applied, and subtle nuances of a given colour can be identified. Take the colour green for instance. The variations of green include the bright green for twigs and new leaves, the brownish green for meadow, and dark green for leaves on the eucalyptus tree.

It can be inferred from the analysis above that the criterion for truth in the junior secondary EFL textbooks is both abstract and sensory. In other words, the coding orientation of Figure 6.7 is abstract-sensory. The adoption of this abstract-sensory coding orientation in the junior secondary educational context could be explored by looking at the special role of abstract modality in education and the pleasure principle that continues into adolescent education. Abstract modality goes beyond the surface to capture the underlying essence of phenomena (cf. realism in art and literature as discussed by van Leeuwen 2005: 168). It is used among sociocultural elites (Kress and van Leeuwen 2006: 165), and understandings about producing and reading images with an abstract coding orientation is part of the education of 'cultivated' people. An abstract coding orientation is more evident in textbooks on natural science, where diagrams and figures are widely applied. As shown earlier, the tendency towards the 'conceptual', 'abstract' coding orientation gains momentum in junior secondary context, while the sensory style is still retained. The tension between the educational purpose and pleasure principle accounts for the coding orientation in the junior secondary EFL textbooks, which is 'abstract', 'conceptual' with respect to representation and contextualization, but pleasure-eliciting in terms of colouration.

6.4.3 Naturalistic coding orientation in *Wildlife Protection*

The teaching unit concerning animals in junior secondary EFL textbooks deals with a more serious topic, that is *Wildlife Protection*, which is the fourth unit in *New Senior English for China Student's Book 2* (2004: 25–32) for Year 10 students. The discussion here focuses on the *Warming Up* section (see Figure 6.8) of the unit, which describes three animals (i.e. *panda, milu deer* and *South China tiger*) that were once endangered in China due to lack of food supply or over-hunting. The corresponding verbal texts also introduce some measures that have been taken to protect these species from extinction and the resulting achievements.

Images of the three animals are inserted into a table dealing with the causes of the near extinction, the animals' habitat, as well as the contrast between the previous worsening condition and the current improved situation. These images are photographs with a naturalistic coding orientation, representing the real-

Wild plants and animals have to look after themselves. They have to find food and a good environment. But very often they can't find enough food. They have **enemies** that kill and eat them. **As a result**, many of them have **died out**. They need help. That is what wildlife protection is about.

A REPORT ON SOME WILDLIFE IN CHINA

There has been some progress in saving endangered wildlife in China.

Animal	Problem	One home in China	Number before concern	Number after concern
Panda	not enough food: **loss** of bamboo growing areas	Wolong Nature **Reserve**, Sichuan Province	nearly all disappeared	about 70 after bamboo **areas** set up to help them grow
Milu deer	disappeared from China	Nanhaizi Milu Park, Beijing	none	about 500 after brought back from UK
South China tiger	too much **hunting** in the 1950s	Baishanzu National Natural Protection **Zone**, Zhejiang Province	very few	about 30–60 after being left **in peace** with no hunting

What other endangered species do you know? Why are they **in danger** of disappearing? Do you know of any wildlife that has disappeared? Why does this happen? In pairs talk about these problems.

Figure 6.8 Naturalistic coding orientation in *Wildlife Protection* [New Senior English for China Student's Book 2, 2004: 25].

life situation of the wild animals in natural environment: two pandas eating in a bamboo grove, a number of milu deer drinking by a river and a South China tiger running on meadow. The relevant truth criterion here is the naturalistic standard.

As noted earlier, the naturalistic coding orientation is the shared, dominant truth criterion for the general public. When it comes to public concerns such as pressing environmental problems and corresponding, the use of cartoons can be viewed as downplaying the seriousness of the issue; alternatively the use of schematic drawings that represent animals as symbols or specimens might result in distancing the viewer from instances of an endangered species urgently in need of help. Naturalistic photographs, on the other hand, follow the coding orientation that all members of a given culture share, regardless of their educational levels or special training (Kress and van Leeuwen 2006: 165–6). Here it positions the viewer as involved in an environmental protection campaign in which all members in the shared culture are expected to participate.

So far I have considered the 'interdependence' (Hodge and Kress 1988: 161) between modality and social relations by examining multimodal texts about animals in the context of EFL education. The previous analysis and discussion illustrate that modality is 'pervasive, appearing everywhere in an utterance or text' (Hodge and Kress 1988: 127), and the resources that convey modality value in a text are multimodal.

6.5 A note on visual style within a macrogenre

So far our focus has been on the criteria for truth in different visual styles in EFL textbook discourse and the appropriateness of a given visual style in educational settings. In this regard it is important to note that members of a social group that normally share the same coding orientation have access to more than one style of visual display. With reference to the EFL textbooks under discussion, various visual styles are employed in different elemental genres that constitute the macrogenre of a teaching unit.

6.5.1 The teaching unit as macrogenre

The term 'genre' has been approached in a great variety of disciplines; this discussion draws on the approach to genre developed by the 'Sydney School'.[3] In SFL genre is interpreted for practical purposes as a staged, goal-oriented social process (Martin 1984). More technically speaking is the stratum of contextual semiosis above stratum of register (Martin 1992: 504–7; Martin and Rose 2008: 16).[4] In this model a culture is interpreted as a system of genres.

Genre analysis can be applied to both longer texts that spread across several pages, including several 'elemental' genres realized as shorter texts. Martin (1994) proposes the concept of 'macrogenre' to deal with longer texts in which various participating genres can be identified. Each teaching unit in the EFL textbooks under discussion can be treated as a macrogenre, in that the entire unit is used to accomplish a specific educational goal and is divided into a number of staged sections. Each of the sections belongs to a specific genre. Take *Unit 2 The Olympic Games* in *New Senior English for China Student's Book 2* (2004: 9–16) for instance. As indicated in the corresponding *New Senior English for China Student's Book 2* (2007: 29), the goal of that teaching unit encompasses 'topic (Ancient and modern Olympic Games; Olympic spirit), vocabulary,

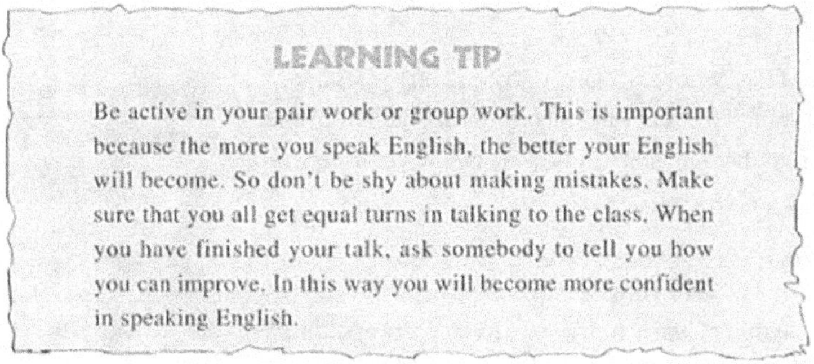

> **LEARNING TIP**
>
> Be active in your pair work or group work. This is important because the more you speak English, the better your English will become. So don't be shy about making mistakes. Make sure that you all get equal turns in talking to the class. When you have finished your talk, ask somebody to tell you how you can improve. In this way you will become more confident in speaking English.

Figure 6.9 *New Senior English for China Student's Book 2*, [2004: 16].

function (Talking about interests and hobbies), and grammar (simple future tense)'. To achieve this goal, the whole unit consists of eight teaching sections: *Warming Up, Pre-reading, Reading, Comprehending, Learning about Language, Using Language, Summing up* and *Learning Tip*, and these sections constitute different types of genre. For instance, the *Reading* section (see Figure 6.10 in Section 6.5.2) in that unit is an description of modern Olympic Games that takes the form of an interview; the reading material of *Using Language* (see Figure 6.11 in Section 6.5.3) on the other hand is a narrative concerning two figures in Greek mythology; and the *Learning Tip* section of that teaching unit is an exposition explaining why the students should be active in pair work or group work.

Martin and his colleagues (Martin 1994; Martin and Rose 2008: 216–23) draw on Halliday's concept of logico-semantic relations to account for the relations between componential genres within a macrogenre. The examination of the relations between different sections within a teaching unit is beyond the scope of this study. The focus here is on the features of the different visual styles in *Reading* and *Using Language* within the macrogenre of the teaching unit *The Olympic Games*, with the purpose of explaining the underlying reasons for the different choices.

6.5.2 Photograph for representing actual scene

The *Reading* section considered here (see Figure 6.10) is a report on the Olympic Games, with an emphasis placed on the similarities and differences between the ancient and modern Olympics. The whole section spreads across two pages. The original layout and typeface can be found in Appendix III.

AN INTERVIEW

Pausanias, who was a Greek writer 2,000 years ago, has come on a magical journey to find out about the present day Olympic Games. He is now interviewing Lili, a Chinese girl.

P: My name is Pausanias, I lived in what you call 'Ancient Greece' and I used to write about the Olympic Games more than 2,000 years ago. I have come to your time to find out about the present day Olympic Games because I know that in 2004 they are to be held in my hometown of Athens. Please can I ask you some questions?

L: Of course you can. What would you like to know?

P: How often do you hold your Games?

L: Every four years athletes from all over the world are admitted as competitors. There are two sets of Games – the Summer and the Winter Olympics and both are held every four years. The Winter Olympics are usually held two years before the Summer Olympics.

P: Winter Games? How can the runners enjoy competing in winter? And what about the horses?

L: Oh no! No running races or horse riding are included. There are events like skiing and ice skating which need snow and ice. That is why they are called the Winter Olympics.

P: Athletes competing from all over the world? Do you mean the Greek world? Our Greek cities used to compete against each other for the honour of winning. No other country could join in, nor could slaves or women.

L: All countries can take part if their athletes reach the standard to be admitted to the games. There are over 250 sports and each one has its own standard. Women are not only allowed to join in but play a very important role, especially in . . .

P: Please stop! All those events, all those countries and even women taking part! Where will all the competitors be staying?

L: A special village is built for the competitors to live in, a stadium for competitions, a very large swimming pool, a gymnasium as well as seats for those who watch the games.

P: It must be expensive. Does anyone want to host the Olympic Games?

L: As a matter of fact, everyone wants to. It's a great honour. It's just as much a competition among countries to host the Olympics as to win an Olympic medal. The 2008 Olympics will be held in China. Did you know that?

P: Oh yes! You must be very proud. Did you say medals? So even the olive wreath has been replaced! Oh dear! Do you compete for money too?

L: No, we don't. It's still all about being able to run faster, jump higher and throw further.

P: That's good news! Thank you for your time. Goodbye.

Figure 6.10 Photograph for representing actual scene (a, b, c) [New Senior English for China Student's Book 2, 2004: 9–10].

A report is a kind of factual genre that is concerned with generic facts about some phenomenon (Martin and Rose 2008: 5–6). In Figure 6.10, a Chinese girl named *Lili* is interviewed by *Pausanias*, an ancient Greek who had written about the ancient Olympics and is now assumed to take a magical journey to the present day with the purpose of figuring out the modern Olympic Games. The specific information about the modern and ancient Olympics is as follows:

Frequency of modern Olympics:
    Every four years athletes from all over the world are admitted as competitors
    The Summer and the Winter Olympics . . . both are held every four years
    The Winter Olympics are usually held two years before the Summer Olympics

Sports events in Winter Olympics:
    Skiing and ice skating, which need snow and ice

Participants of ancient Olympics:
    Greek cities used to compete against each other
    No other country could join in
    Slaves or women (could not join in)

Scale of modern Olympics:
  All countries can take part if their athletes reach the standard to be admitted to the Games
  There are over 250 sports and each one has its own standard
  Women are not only allowed to join in but play a very important role
  A special village is built for the competitors to live in, a stadium for competitions, a very large swimming pool, a gymnasium as well as seats for those who watch the Games
Host of modern Olympics:
  A competition among countries to host the Olympics
Award of modern Olympics:
  Olympic medals
  Still all about being able to run faster, jump higher and throw further
Award of ancient Olympics:
  The olive wreath

From the perspective of the register variable mode, this report genre is an imaginary interview conducted by Lili. *Pausanias* interrupts *Lili* each time he is shocked by the great changes that have taken place in the modern Olympics, and *Lili* in return comments on what has been replaced and clarifies what remains. Accordingly, a report on the major characteristics of modern Olympic Games is presented, as compared with those of the ancient ones.

There are three images accompanying this description: a photograph of the sculpture representing *Pausanias*' head and shoulders, a photograph showing a scene of the opening ceremony of the modern Olympic Games, and a photograph capturing a moment in a speed skating competition in the modern Olympics. These three photographs comply with a naturalistic standard. Although the photograph of *Pausanias*' sculpture might be seen as a borderline case due to its plain background, its naturalistic way of representing the colour, texture and the play of light and shade encode a naturalistic coding orientation.

It can be inferred that the choice of naturalistic visual style in Figure 6.10 reflects the influence of the field of the discourse: the topic of the description. Although the interview is an imaginary one, *Pausanias* was a real writer in Greek history, as revealed in the written text (*a Greek writer . . . 2,000 years ago*). The corresponding image represents the naturalistic sculpture of *Pausanias*, which is the evidence of his former presence that can be traced in our modern times. Here *Pausanias* is represented as a historical figure rather than in an imaginary comic style character, which helps focus the reader's attention on the factual account of the similarities and differences between the ancient and modern

Olympics instead of on the fanciful story about a miraculous journey enabling the interview mode. *Lili* is a fictitious character, and yet what she reports are facts about the Games – and in this respect it is appropriate that none of the images that accompany the interview represents *Lili*. Both photographs represent actual scenes of modern Olympic Games, which link with the nouns in the verbal text, including *the Summer Olympics, the Winter Olympics* and *ice skating*. This choice of visual style thus foregrounds the factual information about the modern Olympics described in the verbal text.

To summarize, the factual orientation of the topic (i.e. field) determines the choice of the naturalistic visual style. The corresponding images in a naturalistic style enhance the factual positioning of the discourse that the intended reader is supposed to assume.

6.5.3 Drawing for illustrating mythology

Another elementary genre in the teaching unit is a myth entitled *The Story of Atlanta*, which tells the story about *Atlanta* and *Hippomenes*, two mythological Greek figures. The story is divided into two parts in the teaching section of *Using Language*. The first part of the story is presented as a reading material, while the second part is recorded as listening material. The two parts are presented as Figure 6.11.

THE STORY OF ATLANTA

Atlanta was a Greek princess. She was very beautiful and could run faster than any man in Greece. But she was not allowed to run in the Olympic Games. She was so angry that she said to her father she would not marry anyone who could not run faster than her. Her father said she must marry and asked her if she wanted to marry a king or prince. But Atlanta replied, 'I will only be married to a man who can run faster than me. When a man says he wants to marry me, I will run against him. If he cannot run as fast as me, he will be killed. No one will be pardoned.'

Many kings and princes wanted to marry Atlanta but when they heard of her rules, some of them sadly went home. Other men stayed to run the race. There was a man called Hippomenes who was amazed when he heard of Atlanta's rules. 'Why are these men so foolish? Why will they let themselves be killed because they cannot run as fast as this princess?' Then when he saw Atlanta come out of her house to run, Hippomenes changed his mind, 'I will marry Atlanta – or die!' he said.

The race started and although the men ran very fast, Atlanta ran faster. As Hippomenes watched, he thought, 'How can I run as fast as Atlanta?' He went to ask for help from the Greek Goddess of Love. She promised to help him and gave him three golden apples. She said, 'Throw an apple in front of Atlanta when she is running past and she will be relaxed. When she stops to pick it up, you will be able to run on and win.'

Hippomenes took the apples and went to the King. He said, 'I want to marry Atlanta.' The King was sad to see another man die, but Hippomenes said, 'I will marry her – or die!' So the race began.

Figure 6.11 Drawing for illustrating mythology (a, b, c) [New Senior English for China Student's Book 2, 2004: 14].

LISTENING TEXT
THE RACE

So the next day the race began. Hippomenes was standing waiting and when Atlanta came out she thought, 'I do not want this man to die. His death will not be caused by me!' So she said to her father, 'Tell him to go away. The race will not be run today.' But Hippomenes said, 'She has said it: she will be married to the man who runs faster than her. Come on now! Let's run!'

Atlanta ran and Hippomenes ran too. He ran very fast but even so Atlanta ran faster. Soon she was in front of him. Then Hippomenes threw one of the golden apples. It went over her head and fell to the side of Atlanta. She stopped and had to run to get it. Hippomenes ran by. Atlanta looked up and she saw him in front. So she ran faster than the fastest bird. She came near! Then she flew past him and was in front again. Again he threw another apple over her head and to the side. Again she stopped to pick it up.

When she reached Hippomenes the third time, he threw the third apple so far to the side that she had further to go. She saw it and wanted it. So she ran and picked it up. By that time Hippomenes was tired and could not run so fast. He was not so far in front. Atlanta ran fast but the apples were heavy and she could not catch up with him. So Hippomenes won the race and married Atlanta. Thanks to the Goddess they lived happily ever after.

(*New Senior English for China Teacher's Book 2* 2007: 44–5)

Labov and Waletsky (1967/1997) propose a schema that consists of the stages of Orientation, Complication, Evaluation, Resolution and Coda to refer to the generalized structure for narratives of personal experience, with Complication and Resolution as obligatory stages while the others optional. In SFL researchers have taken Labov and Waletsky's narrative analysis as the point of departure for one type of story genre and carried out a more discourse-oriented approach to the analysis of story types (Martin and Plum 1997; see also Martin and Rose 2008: 49–90). Martin and Rose (2008: 51–2) identify recount, anecdote, exemplum and observation along with narrative in the story genre family. Narrative proper involves a 'generic pattern that resolves a complication', and the type evaluation of complications includes variation along AFFECT, JUDGEMENT and APPRECIATION, which are regularly employed to 'suspend the action, increasing the narrative tension, and so intensifying the release when tension is resolved' (Martin and Rose 2008: 52). The narrative structure of *The Story of Atlanta* is analysed in Table 6.1, in which generic stages and phases[5] within each stage (Martin and Rose 2008: 79–89) are specified.

In the beginning the Orientation (i.e. from *Atlanta was a Greek princess* to *Other men stayed to run the race*) presents the heroine *Atlanta*'s identity (i.e. *a Greek princess*), the location of the story (i.e. *in Greece*), her speciality (i.e. *very beautiful and could run faster than any man*) and the rule that gives rise to a problem (i.e. *not allowed to run in the Olympic Games*). It is followed by *Atlanta*'s reaction to the rule (i.e. *so angry*), and another problem for *Atlanta* (i.e. *Her father said she must marry and asked her if she wanted to marry a king or prince*). The counter-expectancy signalled by 'but' creates tension and leads to another problem for suitors, that is *Atlanta*'s insistence that any man who wants to marry her must run faster than her or will be killed, preceding the suitors' different reactions. The Complication (i.e. from *There was a man called Hippomenes who was amazed when he heard of Atlanta's rules* to *Soon she was in front of him*) describes how *Hippomenes* decides to enter the race. The hero *Hippomenes* is introduced. The story then describes him seeking advice from

Table 6.1 The Narrative Structure of *The Story of Atlanta*

Orientation	
Setting	Atlanta was a Greek princess. She was very beautiful and could run faster than any man in Greece.
Problem	But she was not allowed to run in the Olympic Games.
Reaction	She was so angry that she said to her father she would not marry anyone who could not run faster than her.
Problem (for Atlanta)	Her father said she must marry and asked her if she wanted to marry a king or prince.
Problem (for suitors)	But Atlanta replied, 'I will only be married to a man who can run faster than me. When a man says he wants to marry me, I will run against him. If he cannot run as fast as me, he will be killed. No one will be pardoned.'
Reaction	Many kings and princes wanted to marry Atlanta but when they heard of her rules, some of them sadly went home. Other men stayed to run the race.
Complication	
Setting	There was a man called Hipppomenes who was amazed when he heard of Atlanta's rules. 'Why are these men so foolish? Why will they let themselves be killed because they cannot run as fast as this princess?' Then when he saw Atlanta come out of her house to run, Hippomenes changed his mind, 'I will marry Atlanta – or die!' he said.
Problem	The race started and although the men ran very fast, Atlanta ran faster.
Solution	As Hippomenes watched, he thought, 'How can I run as fast as Atlanta?' He went to ask for help from the Greek Goddess of Love. She promised to help him and gave him three golden apples. She said, 'Throw an apple in front of Atlanta when she is running past and she will be relaxed.
Setting	When she stops to pick it up, you will be able to run on and win.'
Problem	Hippomenes took the apples and went to the King. He said, 'I want to marry Atlanta.' The King was sad to see another man die, but Hippomenes said, 'I will marry her – or die!' So the race began. (So the next day the race began.)
Reaction	Hippomenes was standing waiting and when Atlanta came out she thought, 'I do not want this man to die. His death will not be caused by me!'
Problem (for Atlanta)	So she said to her father, 'Tell him to go away. The race will not be run today.'
	But Hippomenes said, 'She has said it: she will be married to the man who runs faster than her. Come on now! Let's run!'
Problem (for Hippomenes)	Atlanta ran and Hippomenes ran too. He ran very fast but even so Atlanta ran faster. Soon she was in front of him.

Table 6.1 (Continued)

Resolution	
Solution	Then Hippomenes threw one of the golden apples. It went over her head and fell to the side of Atlanta. She stopped and had to run to get it. Hippomenes ran by.
Problem	Atlanta looked up and she saw him in front. So she ran faster than the fastest bird. She came near! Then she flew past him and was in front again.
Solution	Again he threw another apple over her head and to the side. Again she stopped to pick it up. When she reached Hippomenes the third time, he threw the third apple so far to the side that she had further to go. She saw it and wanted it. So she ran and picked it up.
Problem	By that time Hippomenes was tired and could not run so fast. He was not so far in front.
Solution	Atlanta ran fast but the apples were heavy and she could not catch up with him. So Hippomenes won the race and married Atlanta.
Coda	
Comment	Thanks to the Goddess they lived happily ever after.

I am grateful for Dr David Rose's comments on the phase analysis of *The Story of Atlanta*, though all mistakes are mine.

the *Greek Goddess of Love* and his marriage proposal. Though *Atlanta* does not want *Hipponemes* to die because of losing the race, *Hipponemes*' insistence creates tension again.

The Resolution (i.e. from *Then Hippomenes threw one of the golden apples* to *So Hippomenes won the race and married Atlanta*) clarifies *Hippomenes*' success with the help of the three golden apples given by the *Greek Goddess of Love*. Every time a problem arises and *Hipponemes* looks like losing the race, he throws an apple, which distracts *Atlanta* and the tension is resolved. *Hipponemes* eventually wins the race, and the Coda (i.e. *Thanks to the Goddess they lived happily ever after*) presents the narrator's comment on the happy ending.

There are two images in THE STORY OF ATLANTA, one depicting *Atlanta*'s negotiation with her father about her marriage and the other illustrating *Hippomenes* receiving the three golden apples from the *Greek Goddess of Love* (see Figure 6.11). Both images are colour drawings. From the point of view of the naturalistic standard, they have high modality in terms of colour saturation, colour differentiation, colour modulation, representation and brightness. For instance, an effort has been made to depict skin colour, the texture of people's hair and clothes in a subtle way – relatively close to what we see with the naked eye. Nevertheless, the images depart from the naturalistic coding orientation in terms of illumination, depth and contextualization. To be specific, there is no play of light and shade in the images, and the simple overlapping leads to the absence of depth. In terms of contextualization, the decoration of the palace and the scenery outside the palace that serve as the background in the first image are selectively simplified, and what is preserved is confined to those architectural features that iconically represent ancient Greek buildings. As for the background in the second image, the drifting clouds around the lady enhance her identity as a Goddess from on high.

The targeted viewers of the aforementioned two images are senior secondary students, and naturalistic coding orientation is retained in the representations of certain modality markers as analysed earlier. This complies with the general truth criteria in the whole senior secondary EFL textbooks. However, the deviations from this naturalistic standard are observed in illumination, depth and contextualization. As previously discussed, the topic of the whole discourse (i.e. field) is Greek mythology related to the Olympic Games. The mythology is no doubt intended to enhance students' appreciation of the culture and traditions of Ancient Greece, in which the Olympics is developed; at the same time the event themselves and those characters involved in them do not constitute actual history. The mixed messaging of the more and less naturalistic styles in the drawings resonates well with the myth – a fictional account which nevertheless bears significantly on contemporary and historical reality.

From this discussion of images within different genres in the textbook macrogenre, it can be inferred that the register variable of field is one of the important factors that exerts influence on the choice of visual style. Certain modality markers may be adjusted to some extent due to the topic or focus of the social activity, and the relevant coding orientation will be modified accordingly – resulting in the style variations in photographs and drawings targeting the same group of viewers.

6.6 Summary

This chapter has focused on the issue of truth criteria in the multimodal EFL textbook discourse. After a brief review of relevant studies on modality in both monomodal and multimodal discourse, it presented examples of the visual parameters that express modality and the coding orientations that provide criteria for modality judgements in different contexts. A comparative analysis was then conducted to examine the coding orientations in three teaching units (for primary, junior and senior secondary EFL education) – to investigate the 'interdependence' (Hodge and Kress 1988: 161) between modality and social relations from a multilevel perspective. The last part of this chapter has also considered the influence of field on the choice of visual style within the same teaching unit as a macrogenre.

The analysis has shown that what counts as real is culturally defined and specific to a given communicative context and members of a certain social group. In the primary EFL textbook discourse, the pictorial techniques used in cartoons follow the pleasure principle, and hence a sensory coding orientation is adopted. It was also noted that abstractness increases as students move through the school years from primary to junior secondary education. On the one hand, the vibrant, exciting colouration still acts as a source of pleasure, while on the other, the abstract representation and contextualization of the images capture the underlying essence of what is represented. An abstract-sensory coding orientation is increasingly adopted in junior secondary EFL textbook discourse.

In addition it was noted that the photographs in senior secondary EFL textbook adopt a naturalistic coding orientation in the teaching units on animals. In this context the viewers are treated as members of the general public who share the dominant cultural norms.

Based on the analysis and discussion earlier, we can say that the resources that convey modality value in EFL textbook discourse are multimodal, and the way these multimodal meaning-making resources are deployed both reflects and constructs the solidarity relationship between textbook editors and different groups of English learners.

7

Conclusions and recommendations

7.1 Introduction

The overall aim of this book has been to account for the multimodal construal of interpersonal meaning in China's EFL context, with a special focus on the multimodal resources in EFL textbooks for primary and secondary education. In order to understand the ways in which meanings are created verbally and visually, this study draws upon APPRAISAL theory, a model developed within SFL for analysing interpersonal meaning at the level of discourse semantics, and the Systemic Functional semiotic approach when examining verbal and visual semiotic systems. This chapter is intended to bring together the major findings of the three sub-studies reported in the previous chapters, and to discuss the implications of the work in terms of its theoretical and pedagogic contributions. The book will conclude with the identification of some areas that require further research.

7.2 A retrospective of the research findings

As mentioned in the introductory chapter, the current research grows out of the emerging research of multimodality. Textbooks for China's EFL context, which have been less frequently studied as compared with multimodal pedagogic materials for other school subjects, are chosen as the focus of this study. The Systemic Functional approach, which provides the theoretical foundations on which the current work is grounded, has proven to be effective in dealing with texts that involve more than one semiotic system. In Chapter 1 the following research questions are formulated to specify the research focus:

1. Reader-writer alignment and the graded engagement meanings: (1) How are linguistic and visual meaning-making resources deployed to mediate

the heteroglossic space in the multi-voiced EFL textbook discourse? (2) To what degree can the alignment of voices be graded by utilizing multimodal resources?
2. Attitudinal construction and intermodal relations: (1) How is the attitudinal stance in multimodal EFL textbook discourse construed through linguistic and visual semiotic resources? (2) What kinds of verbiage-image relations are there in the intermodal construal of attitudinal meanings?
3. Modality and pedagogical implications: (1) In what way are multimodal messages presented as real in the EFL textbooks targeting different groups readers? How is it conditioned by and construing the pedagogic context?

Analyses in Chapters 4 to 6 encompass three sub-studies: 'heteroglossic harmony', 'accumulative attitude' and 'contestable reality', to tackle three different facets of interpersonal management in EFL textbook discourse. Responses to these research questions are summarized in the sections that follow.

7.2.1 Multimodal ENGAGEMENT devices and their gradability

To answer the first research question, Chapter 4 has identified and examined the multimodal meaning-making resources enabling dialogic engagement in EFL textbook discourse, and discussed how these multimodal resources scale up or down engagement values. It has been found that along with the authorial editor voice, a given proposition or evaluation can be attributed to other sources, that is, character voice and reader voice, through the use of multimodal ENGAGEMENT devices. Analysis of five types of ENGAGEMENT devices (i.e. labelling, dialogue balloon, jointly constructed text, illustration and highlighting) has revealed that they realize the ENGAGEMENT meanings of [disclaim], [proclaim], [entertain] and [attribute] (Martin and White 2005: 97–8). Specifically, labelling enables editor voice to negotiate meanings with character voice by fending off alternative positions, hence insisting upon the prescribed teaching goals and realizing [proclaim]. Dialogue balloon and illustration bring in character voice, and thus the proposition or viewpoint is 'attributed' to character(s). Jointly constructed text opens up space to introduce reader voice, encoding [attribute] as well. Although the editor-reader alignment does not mean a total agreement between the communicative parties, jointly constructed text construes a compliant reading position, in that its completion requires some shared knowledge and cooperative performance from the ideal reader. Within certain illustrations, editor voice and character voice may go against one another and hence [disclaim] is realized. Highlighting in image may function to [entertain] other possibilities that are grounded within the contingent subjectivity of the multimodal text itself.

The gradability of ENGAGEMENT values (Martin and White 2005: 135) realized by the multimodal resources has also been considered. It has been argued that dialogue balloon may realize different degrees of [attribute] values based on the amount (i.e. FORCE) of responsibility that characters undertake in instructing the reader. Different degrees of reader involvement are closely related to the degree of completion or fulfilment (Hood and Martin 2007) of a jointly constructed text: its prototypicality (i.e. FOCUS) as a co-construction. The higher degree of completeness a jointly constructed text possesses, the less heteroglossic space it opens up to reader voice. In terms of illustration, the intensity of [attribute] meaning can be approached by looking at the role of images in linking different components of a verbal text.

After the identification and analyses of the aforementioned five ENGAGEMENT devices, I further examined the interaction between multiple voices in EFL textbook discourse in relation to three parameters in visual interaction: contact, social distance and point of view. It is shown that while the majority of images belong to the 'observe' type, eye contact between character and viewer is established in those images where reader's action is required. The various choices of social distance demonstrate a wide range of social relations between characters and the reader. The frontal and eye-level angle is frequently adopted due to the engagement of characters represented as peers of the reader.

7.2.2 Intermodal construal of the 'emotion and attitude' goal

As indicated in Chapter 3, the exploration of interpersonal meaning also calls for an examination of the 'personal' dimension. In an attempt to arrive at the answer to the second research question, Chapter 5 was devoted to the way that multimodal meaning-making resources are deployed to achieve the 'emotion and attitude goal' in EFL education (Cheng 2002; Zhong 2006; Zhu 2006), with particular attention paid to the intersemiotic relations of complementarity and co-instantiation in the construal of attitudinal meanings.

The various styles of images (i.e. cartoon, portrait and photograph) in EFL textbooks are grouped into two categories according to whether they describe human participants or inanimate things and landscapes. It is found that the frequently adopted cartoon style in primary and junior secondary textbooks is often indicative of positive affectual meanings, and the happiness of English learning is thus directly inscribed. The corresponding verbiage, however, hardly commits any attitudinal meanings but simply informs the reader of the teaching content. The image-verbiage relation is thus complementary, in that the attitudinally hypo-committed verbal texts explain to the reader what is supposed to be learned, whereas cartoons visually construe an evaluative stance that is assumed to be taken during the process of learning. Some cartoons may also function to invoke APPRECIATION through logogenetic recontextualization (Martin 2002). It can be inferred from the analysis that the visual semiotic system bears much of the responsibility for encoding attitudinal meanings in the textbooks for primary and junior secondary schooling. The trend for explicit affectual inscriptions gradually declines in the textbooks for secondary education. In other words, AFFECT and FORCE are 'coupled' (Martin 2008b) in different ways at these two levels of education. The emerging images signal a transition from the playful childhood to serious adolescence, where a sense of social responsibility is to be cultivated. As for senior secondary textbooks, the 'serious' portraits and photographs with implicit JUDGEMENT or APPRECIATION invocations (Martin and White 2005: 66–7) work in concert with the verbal attitudinal inscriptions and invocations. In this case, both language and image commit attitudinal meanings and thus the image-verbiage relation is co-instantiation. The two semiotic systems echo and reinforce one another in establishing the overall evaluative stance assumed in the putative readership. Image and verbiage also work in tandem with each other in guiding the reader in the completion of jointly constructed texts. It is shown that an overall evaluative stance can be established in the verbiage, whereas the images visualize the ideational tokens as well as invoke positive APPRECIATION, which reinforces the verbal attitudinal orientation. In terms of the amount of meaning potential instantiated in different types of images, it is contended that indirect invocations commit less attitudinal meanings than overt inscriptions.

Based on the studies of the ontogenesis of ATTITUDE system, this sub-study has concluded by accounting for how attitudinal meanings are institutionalized and accumulated as students progress all the way from primary to secondary education. It is argued that a gradual shift in ATTITUDE encoding can be identified – from a personal emotional release to a more institutionalized method of evaluation, which reflects as well as contributes to the accumulation of institutionalized feelings stipulated in the curriculum standards.

7.2.3 Influence of register variables on coding orientation

While Chapter 5 dealt with the attitudinal aspect of interpersonal meaning, the third study in Chapter 6 focuses on the issue of modality (Hodge and Kress 1988; Kress and van Leeuwen 2006, 2020; van Leeuwen 2005), that is the question of 'truth' that a message producer wants a representation to induce in the intended receiver. One of the important tenets in SFL is the close relation between text and context, and the third research question asks about the influence of tenor and field on the criteria for modality judgements in multimodal texts. Drawing on the eight modality markers and four types of coding orientation developed by Kress and van Leeuwen (2006, 2020), the third sub-study provides a multilevel, comparative analysis of coding orientation in three teaching units on a similar topic for different educational contexts.

It was found that the way in which multimodal resources are deployed to convey modality values in pedagogic context is both conditioned by and construing the solidarity between textbook editors and different groups of learners. Specifically, the cartoons in primary EFL textbooks follow the 'pleasure principle' and adopt a sensory coding orientation (Kress and van Leeuwen 2006, 2020). Though sensation remains in junior secondary textbooks, the sense of abstractness tends to increase as education progresses. It is suggested that the amount of cartooning in the primary and junior secondary materials is excessive from the perspective of educational theory on pedagogic discourse and nature of knowledge (Bernstein 1990, 2000). The photographs in senior secondary textbooks, on the other hand, employ a naturalistic coding orientation, positioning the viewers as members of the general public who share the dominant cultural norms.

In addition to the multilevel view on modality in three different EFL educational contexts, the third study also considers various degrees of deviation from the accepted truth criterion in multimodal texts targeting the same group of viewers. It is shown that another register variable – field – may exert some influence on the choice of visual style in different constituent genres within the same teaching unit as a macrogenre. This choice of visual design, on the other hand, helps to enhance an intended reading position. The examination has shown that what counts as real in multimodal texts is culturally defined and specific to a given communicative context.

7.2.4 Summary

In sum, it can be inferred from the three studies that multimodal meaning-making resources play a significant role in encoding interpersonal meaning.

The visual semiotic system in multimodal EFL textbook discourse is by no means redundant with language in meaning-making. In terms of editor-reader alignment, linguistic and visual semiotic systems combined to enable the interpolation of character voice and offer diverse means for editor voice to engage the reader with the proposition put forward in a text. As for the 'emotion and attitude' goal highlighted in the *Curriculum Standards for English* (2001), the intermodal construal contributes to the accumulative attitudinal meanings in primary and secondary education. Lastly, the intended truth value of a multimodal message is closely related to the socially defined truth criterion within a specific social group, though deviation is allowed to cater for different topics within a teaching unit. Nevertheless, it is argued that the nature of pedagogic discourse should also be taken into account when designing visual display for pedagogic materials.

As outlined in Chapter 1, this book is theoretically and pedagogically motivated. The ensuing section will outline some contributions this study has tried to make to the research on interpersonal semantics in multimodal texts, as well as its pedagogic implications for EFL education.

7.3 Contributions and implications

The theoretical and practical relevance of the current research is twofold. One is to work towards a comprehensive model of APPRAISAL (Martin 2000a; Martin and White 2005) that accounts for both linguistic and visual semiotic systems. The other is to address pedagogic concerns closely related to multimodality.

7.3.1 Theoretical contributions

The APPRAISAL system (Martin 1997, 2000a; Martin and White 2005) is a functional model that accounts for interpersonal meaning at the level of discourse semantics. As stated in Chapter 3, a review of the literature on APPRAISAL reveals that while a growing body of work in this area has covered visual semiotic systems, most of the studies have been oriented to the sub-system of ATTITUDE (e.g. Economou 2006), leaving the aspects of ENGAGEMENT and GRADUATION under-theorized. This book has attempted to explore new ground by identifying and analysing multimodal resources that may realize ENGAGEMENT values. It can be inferred from the findings that, on the one hand, one type of ENGAGEMENT meaning may be realized through different multimodal devices (e.g. [Attribute] can be realized by dialogue balloon or illustration). On the other hand, one type of multimodal resource may encode different ENGAGEMENT meanings (e.g. illustration may function to encode [attribute] or [disclaim]).

Another contribution of this study to the understanding of multimodal APPRAISAL resources lies in the examination of the ways in which the attitudinal meanings (i.e. AFFECT, JUDGEMENT, and APPRECIATION) are realized through intersemiotic co-instantiation and complementarity. It has been demonstrated that attitudinal meanings are realized in verbal texts and images via both explicit inscription and implicit invocation. In those multimodal texts where verbiage is attitudinally under-committed (see Martin 2008b, Hood 2008 for an introduction to the concept of 'commitment'), images may 'step up' to reinforce the evaluative stance. When image and verbiage work together in the construal of value positions, these two semiotic systems co-articulate with one another in establishing the attitudinal orientation.

A further theoretical contribution developed in this research is the exploration of how the options from ATTITUDE and ENGAGEMENT can be 'coupled' (Martin 2008b) with the options from GRADUATION (i.e. FORCE and FOCUS), and thus various degrees of attitudinal meanings and ENGAGEMENT values can be encoded in visual communication. It was found that different degrees of the FORCE of inscribed AFFECT can be realized through a variety of depictions of facial expressions and behavioural manifestations that imply different degrees of affectual intensity. It was also found that the ways in which ENGAGEMENT values can be scaled are strongly associated with the intrinsic property of a multimodal resource, such as the projective structure of a dialogue balloon that mediates a character's utterance, the co-constructedness of jointly constructed text, or the elucidative and supportive role of illustration.

7.3.2 Pedagogic implications

Along with the contributions to the theoretical model that underpins this research, this book has set for itself a pedagogic goal that aims at providing some implications for EFL education and textbook design. As articulated in the summarizing remarks of Chapter 2, fives gaps have been recognized in the previous pedagogic research. Each of the three sub-studies in the current research has attempted to provide some answers to at least one aspect of these five areas. The investigation into the heteroglossic nature of EFL textbook discourse demonstrates from a semiotic perspective the way in which multiple semiotic resources are involved in the 'dialogic process' advocated in the classroom teaching (e.g. Chen and Ye 2006), showing how multiple semiotic resources can be manipulated to bring in voices other than the editor's and align the intended reader with propositions and viewpoints.

As has been reiterated throughout this book, the curriculum reform in China points to the significance of emotions, attitudes and values education (Zhu 2006). The current research has strived to anchor the discussion onto linguistic and semiotic analysis, which is intended to reveal the role that multiple semiotic systems can play in realizing the 'emotion and attitude' goal. From the perspective of genre-based literacy (e.g. Martin and Rose 2007b, 2008), critiques are made of the primary and junior secondary EFL textbooks for their neglect of generic/schematic structure in the verbal texts, which might risk reversing the course of language learning. While showcasing the importance of multimodal resources in managing heteroglossic space and encoding attitudinal meanings, the work undertaken here offers a reminder that language teaching should start from the level of genre through discourse semantic patterns downwards to specific lexicogrammatical features.

Another pedagogic implication of the current research is concerned with the choice of coding orientation in relation to the register variables of field and tenor. There is a clear association between image style and social relations. Therefore, it is argued that textbook editors and designers should bear in mind the fact that EFL textbooks is a kind of pedagogic discourse when designing visual arrangement for textbook discourse. It is hoped from this research that we may have one step further towards a comprehensive and critical understanding of multimodal EFL pedagogic materials.

7.4 Suggestions for future studies

The work undertaken in this book is among the first efforts to probe into the multimodal nature of EFL pedagogic materials in China from a Systemic Functional semiotic perspective. This final section outlines some pedagogic and theoretical aspects requiring further exploration.

7.4.1 Multimodality research in educational context

While the focus of this book is on primary and secondary textbooks, it also points to the need for a similar examination of multimodal tertiary textbooks. Furthermore, within pedagogic contexts there are undoubtedly other types of multimodal communication outside textbook discourse. The multimodal teaching and learning resources widely used in China's educational context, such as pictures, maps, three-dimensional objects and audio-visual devices, demand attention from multimodal analysts.

7.4.2 A metafunctionally diversified view

Theoretically speaking, the adoption of the metafunctional principle within SFL reminds us that there are two other functional diversifications to be explored, in addition to the interpersonal metafunction. Ideationally, the process types involved in narrative representation or conceptual representation (Kress and van Leeuwen 2006: 45–113) can be further analysed when examining multimodal pedagogic materials. The depiction of circumstantial elements such as setting is also worth investigating. Moreover, a discourse semantic perspective could be adopted by looking at the ideational meanings in visual media in terms of the relations between elements (i.e. 'taxonomic relations'), the configuration of elements (i.e. 'nuclear relations'), and the relations between processes (i.e. 'activity sequence') (Martin and Rose 2007a: 76). Textually or compositionally, modern printing and digital technologies make possible a great diversity of layout designs. A Systemic Functional semiotic approach may provide an effective analytical tool when addressing issues that arise from various visual compositions (e.g. horizontal polarization, vertical polarization and triptych; see Kress and van Leeuwen 2006, 2020). Of course, the possible realms mentioned here are merely part of the picture, which may give us a glimpse of the great potential of social-semiotic theory in the examination and explanation of multimodal texts.

7.4.3 Inspiration from other contexts

Looking beyond the pedagogic setting, researchers may find that other communicative contexts can provide testing grounds for the expansion and elaboration of social-semiotic theory. Take the elaboration of ENGAGEMENT and GRADUATION systems in the current research for instance. It is identified in Chapter 4 that there are five types of multimodal resources serving as ENGAGEMENT devices (i.e. labelling, dialogue balloon, jointly constructed text, illustration and highlighting). These findings are based on the examination of EFL textbook discourse. Other types of multimodal meaning-making resources encoding ENGAGEMENT meanings may be recognized in analysing multimodal texts in other contexts. With the identification of more ENGAGEMENT devices and the specification of their different functions, the GRADUATION network for the scaling of values in multimodal discourse may accordingly be established and expanded. Addressing these theoretically oriented issues calls for considerable data and in-depth discussions, while at the same time will bring us closer to a comprehensive understanding of linguistic and semiotic theories.

7.5 Envoi

The research reported in this book has endeavoured to bring a knowledge of linguistic and visual semiotic systems to an understanding of multimodal pedagogic materials for teaching English as a foreign language in China. Both multimodality and English-language teaching warrant close attention from linguists. This book has sought to systematically investigate visual semiotic systems along with language, which will hopefully offer insights into future research. The site of EFL education, as has been shown in this work, proves to be an important context for a close examination of multiple semiotic systems. The exploration of multimodal construal of meanings, on the other hand, may address some of the practical issues arising from the current attitudes towards, and demands for, English teaching. It is expected that multimodality and pedagogic materials will continue to constitute part of the ongoing linguistic and semiotic agenda for the foreseeable future.

Appendices

Appendix I A multimodal page introducing major characters in primary textbooks

[*PEP Primary English Students' Book I for Year 6*]

Appendix II The exact layout of *SIGHTSEEING IN LONDON*

Unit 2 The United Kingdom

5 On my way to the station my car **broke down**. When I got to the repair shop I _____ (it / close).
6 The computer doesn't seem to work well. You'd better _____ (it / repair)?
7 Jill and Eric _____ (all their money / steal) while they were on holiday.
8 Chris _____ (some flowers / send) to Sarah on her birthday. Then Chris asked Sarah to marry him and they _____ (it / announce) in the newspaper. They had no time to **arrange** their own **wedding**, so they _____ (it / organize) by a company.

3 Play the game: "What did they find?" Write one sentence about what Mr and Mrs Smith found when they came home from work one day. Remember to use the past participle as the object complement.

EXAMPLE: *They found the window broken.*
Divide your class into groups of five. Give a piece of paper to the first person in each group who **folds** the paper over his / her writing, so the next person cannot see it. Pass the paper to the next person in the group. When the last one in the group has finished writing, he / she comes to the front of the class to read all the ideas of his / her group. The one with the most interesting ideas wins.

SIGHTSEEING IN LONDON

Worried about the time **available**, Zhang Pingyu had made a list of the sites she wanted to see in London. Her first **delight** was going to the **Tower**. It was built long ago by the Norman invaders of AD 1066. Fancy! This solid, stone, square tower had remained standing for one thousand years. Although the buildings had expanded around it, it remained part of a **royal** palace and prison combined. To her great surprise, Zhang Pingyu found the Queen's jewels guarded by special royal soldiers who, on special occasions, still wore the four-hundred-year-old **uniform** of the time of Queen Elizabeth I.

There followed St Paul's Cathedral built after the terrible fire of London in 1666. It looked **splendid** when first built! Westminster Abbey, too, was very interesting. It contained **statues** in memory of dead poets and writers, such as Shakespeare. Then just as she came out of the abbey, Pingyu heard the famous sound of the clock, Big Ben, ringing out the hour. She finished the day by looking at the outside of Buckingham Palace, the Queen's house in London. Oh, she had so much to tell her friends!

The Tower of London

Unit 2 The United Kingdom

St Paul's Cathedral

Westminster Abbey

The second day the girl visited Greenwich and saw its old ships and famous clock that sets the world time. What interested her most was the longitude line. It is an imaginary line dividing the eastern and western halves of the world and is very useful for navigation. It passes through Greenwich, so Pingyu had a photo taken standing on either side of the line.

The last day she visited Karl Marx's statue in Highgate Cemetery. It seemed strange that the man who had developed **communism** should have lived and died in London. Not only that, but he had worked in the famous reading room of the Library of the British Museum. Sadly the library had moved from its original place into another building and the old reading room was gone. But she was **thrilled** by so many wonderful treasures from different cultures displayed in the museum. When she saw many visitors enjoying looking at the beautiful old Chinese **pots** and other objects on show, she felt very proud of her country.

The next day Pingyu was leaving London for Windsor Castle. "Perhaps I will see the Queen?" she wondered as she fell asleep.

Karl Marx

Royal Observatory in Greenwich

Make a list of Zhang Pingyu's tour of London and a comment on each place she visited.

Day 1	Comments	Day 2 and comment	Day 3 and comment
1	1		
2	2		
3	3		
4	4		

[*New Senior English for China Student's Book 5* 2004: 13–14]

Appendix III The original layout and typeface of *AN INTERVIEW*

AN INTERVIEW

Pausanias, who was a Greek writer 2,000 years ago, has come on a **magical** journey to find out about the present day Olympic Games. He is now **interviewing** Lili, a Chinese girl.

P: My name is Pausanias. I lived in what you call "Ancient **Greece**" and I used to write about the Olympic Games more than 2,000 years ago. I have come to *your* time to find out about the

present day Olympic Games because I know that in 2004 they are to be held in my hometown of Athens. Please can I ask you some questions?
L: Of course you can. What would you like to know?
P: How often do you hold your Games?
L: Every four years **athletes** from all over the world are **admitted** as competitors. There are two **sets** of Games – the Summer and the Winter Olympics and both are held every four years. The Winter Olympics are usually held two years before the Summer Olympics.
P: Winter Games? How can the runners enjoy competing in winter? And what about the horses?
L: Oh no! No running races or horse riding are included. There are events like skiing and ice skating which need snow and ice. That is why they are called the Winter Olympics.
P: Athletes competing from all over the world? Do you mean the Greek world? Our Greek cities used to compete against each other for the honour of winning. No other country could join in, nor could **slaves** or women.
L: All countries can take part if their athletes reach the standard to be admitted to the games. There are over 250 sports and each one has its own standard. Women are not only allowed to join in but play a very important role, especially in ...
P: Please stop! All those events, all those countries and even women taking part! Where will all the competitors be staying?
L: A special village is built for the competitors to live in, a **stadium** for competitions, a very large swimming pool, a **gymnasium as well as** seats for those who watch the games.
P: It must be expensive. Does anyone want to host the Olympic Games?
L: As a matter of fact, everyone wants to. It's a great honour. It's just as much a competition among countries to host the Olympics as to win an Olympic medal. The 2008 Olympics will be held in China. Did you know that?
P: Oh yes! You must be very proud. Did you say medals? So even the olive wreath has been **replaced**! Oh dear! Do you compete for money too?
L: No, we don't. It's still all about being able to run faster, jump higher and throw further.
P: That's good news! Thank you for your time. Goodbye.

[*New Senior English for China Student's Book 2* 2004: 9–10]

Notes

Chapter 1

1 This study follows the view in social semiotics that the terms 'discourse' and 'text' represent two complementary perspectives on the same phenomenon. Specifically, 'discourse' is used to refer to 'the social process in which texts are embedded', while 'text' is adopted when mentioning 'the concrete material object produced in discourse' (Hodge and Kress 1988: 6).
2 This book follows SFL conventions (e.g. Martin 2000a; Kress and van Leeuwen 2006, 2020) in using small capitals to indicate systems (e.g. ENGAGEMENT, APPRAISAL), square brackets for system choices (e.g. [proclaim], [attribute]) and initial letters capitalized when talking about functional labels (e.g. Actor, Goal).
3 Macrogenre is a concept developed in the Sydney School's genre studies (Martin 1994), which deal with longer texts where various participating genres are identified.

Chapter 2

1 The term 'Sydney School' is proposed by Green and Lee (1994). The studies carried out by the functional linguists and educational linguists in the Department of Linguistics at the University of Sydney have influenced work around and well beyond Australia, reaching Indonesia, Singapore, Hong Kong, Britain, Argentina, South Africa and many other places in the world. Martin (2000b) uses the term 'action research' to refer to this work because it 'involved an interaction of theory and practice which pushed the envelop of the understandings about modelling language in social life and which at the same time led to innovative literacy teaching across sectors in Australia and overseas'.

Chapter 3

1 As pointed out by Matthiessen (1993), there are at least three ways of interpreting the relationship between context of culture and context of situation, which respectively follow three different organizing principles, i.e. rank, stratification

and potentiality. In addition to the multi-stratal model adopted in the present study, other models of context include the single-stratum one that regards context of situation as an instance of the cultural potential (Halliday 1978, 1999), and the macro-micro relationship in which a culture can be viewed as consisting of situation types.

2. In SFL, the term 'register' is initially defined by Halliday (1978: 111) as 'the configuration of semantic resources that the member of a culture typically associates with a situation type. It is the meaning potential accessible in a given social context'. Therefore, it is deemed as located at the semantic level of the linguistic system, whereas the categories of field, mode and tenor are regarded as the features of the context of situation and thus belong to one level up (Halliday in Thibault 1987: 610). The contextual model adopted here (Martin 1985a, 1992, 1999a) extends the notion of register to refer to the semiotic system metafunctionally organized and independently located between language and genre as one of the contextual strata.

3. In addition to realization and instantiation, another hierarchy that plays the complementary role in the SFL framework when exploring semantic variations is individuation (e.g. Martin 2008b). Individuation deals with the relationship between the reservoir of meanings in a given culture and the repertoire deployed by individuals in texts. The three hierarchies complement each other in that all systems along the realization hierarchy instantiate, and all individuate as well (Martin 2008b). To avoid too many foci, the present study primarily concentrates on the hierarchies of realization and instantiation.

4. According to Martin (2008b), coupling in its narrow sense involves those meanings that enter directly into semantic relations with one another, while broadly speaking it might refer to the meanings that co-occur more frequently than expected in a text or set of texts with reference to specifiable norms. Here the discussion focuses on the narrow reading of the concept of coupling.

5. According to Halliday (1992), there are two kinds of categories in the analysis of language: theoretical and descriptive. Those categories like 'metafunction', 'system' and 'realization' belong to the former, while those such as 'material process', 'theme' and 'preposition' which are language-specific and have evolved in the description of particular languages belong to the latter.

6. See, however, the searing critique of this attribution by Bota and Bronckart 2011.

7. The semantic system that is currently and widely referred to as GRADUATION was termed AMPLIFICATION in some early works (Eggins and Slade 1997, Martin 1997).

8. Based on the observation of our data, it can be inferred that the reading direction in most of the images under discussion follows the conventional reading direction in the contemporary society of China, i.e. from left to right rather than from right to left as was in the ancient times (cf. Jewitt and Oyama 2001).

Chapter 4

1. Considering the fact that the main purpose and function of EFL textbooks is for language teaching, I use 'reader' in the term 'reader voice' to refer to both reader of verbal texts and viewer of images. Nevertheless, the term 'viewer' is sometimes adopted in the current research when the analysis mainly centres on images (e.g. Section 4.3.2.3).
2. For more discussion on the notion of 'putative', 'ideal' or 'imagined' reader/audience, see Eco (1984), Coulthard (1994), Martin and White (2005), and Thompson (2001).

Chapter 5

1. In addition to the studies on the relations between different parts of a multimodal text, social-semiotic approaches to verbiage-image relations also include studies on the relations between whole multimodal texts. Iedema's (2001, 2003) concept of 'resemiotization' and Martinec and van Leeuwen's (2008) work on translating different text types into different kinds of diagrams fall into this category.
2. This study on gradability of attitudinal meanings follows Martin and White's (2005: 48) view that the high, median and low degrees do not imply discrete values but are used to describe the emotions graded along a clined scale.
3. A system network representing the possibilities of the sub-systems coupling with each other could be produced with more visual instances analysed in future research.
4. *Nelson Mandela*'s photograph may be interpreted as slightly impassioned, and yet I consider that it aims at capturing the temperament of *Nelson Mandela* instead of expressing affectual meaning. Actually whether the affectual meaning encoded in this image is joy or anger or some other feelings is difficult to nail down.

Chapter 6

1. An additional category of modulation is ability, which we set aside here since it is not concerned with degrees of polarity.
2. There is application of colour in visual displays in certain scientific and technological texts. Nevertheless, this use of colour is 'more or less arbitrary to facilitate the reading of complex diagrams' rather than the actual colour that is encountered in reality (Kress and van Leeuwen 2006: 169).
3. According to Hyon (1996), within linguistic studies two other main perspectives on genre are English for specific purposes (ESP) and North American New Rhetoric studies.

4   Within SFL there are alternative viewpoints on the status of genre. Halliday (1978: 145) treats genre as 'an aspect of what we here call the "mode"'. As for the concept of generic structure, he articulates that it 'can be brought within the general framework of the concept of register, the semantic patterning that is characteristically associated with the "context of situation" of a text' (Halliday 1978: 134). Hasan (1985: 63–9) emphasizes the relationship between text structure, genre and field. These perspectives tend to relate genre to one of the contextual variables, rather than viewing genre as a more abstract semiotic stratum that is above register.

5   When analysing generic structure of story, Martin and Rose (2007b) suggest adopting both perspectives of generic stages and phases. Story phases have to do with 'a common set of resources' that the story family (i.e. narrative, recount, anecdote, exemplum and observation) share in 'moving sequences forward and engaging readers' (Martin and Rose 2007b: 79). Each phase type has a specific function and may occur in any stage of a story.

References

Alexander, R. (2000), *Culture and Pedagogy: International Comparisons in Primary Education*, Oxford: Blackwell.

Bakhtin, M. (1981), *The Dialogic Imagination*, ed. M. Holquist, trans. C. Emerson and M. Holquist, Austin: University of Texas Press.

Bakhtin, M. (1986), 'The problem of speech genres', in C. Emerson and M. Holquist (eds), V. W. McGee (trans), *Speech Genres and Other Late Essays*, 60–102, Austin: University of Texas Press.

Baldry, A. P. (2000), 'English in a visual society: Comparative and historical dimensions in multimodality and multimediality', in A. P. Baldry (ed.), *Multimodality and Multimediality in the Distance Learning Age*, 41–89, London: Equinox.

Baldry, A. P. (2004), 'Phase and transition, type and instance: Patterns in media texts as seen through a multimodal concordancer', in K. L. O'Halloran (ed.), *Multimodal Discourse Analysis: Systemic Functional Perspectives*, 83–108, London: Continuum.

Baldry, A. P. and P. J. Thibault (2006), *Multimodal Transcription and Text Analysis*, London: Equinox.

Barthes, R. (1977), 'Rhetoric of the image', in R. Barthes and S. Heath (trans), *Image-Music-Text*, 32–51, London: Fontana.

Barthes, R. (1981), *Camera Lucida*, New York: Farrar, Straus and Giroux Inc.

Barthes, R. (1985), *The Fashion System*, trans. M. Ward and R. Howard, London: Jonathan Cape.

Bateman, J. A. (2008), *Multimodality and Genre: A Foundation for the Systematic Analysis of Multimodal Documents*, New York: Palgrave Macmillan.

Bateman, J. A. (2014), *Text and Image: A Critical Introduction to the Visual/Verbal Divide*, London: Routledge.

Bateman, J. A. (2017), 'Triangulating transmediality: A multimodal semiotic framework relating media, modes and genres', *Discourse, Context & Media*, 20: 160–74.

Bateman, J. A. and C. Tseng (2013), 'The establishment of interpretative expectations in film', *Review of Cognitive Linguistics*, 11 (2): 353–68.

Bateman, J. A., C. Tseng, O. Seizov, A. Jacobs, A. Ludtke, M. G. Muller and O. Herzog (2016), 'Towards next-generation visual archives: Image, film and discourse', *Visual Studies*, 31 (2): 131–54.

Bednarek, M. (2008), *Emotion Talk across Corpora*, New York: Palgrave Macmillan.

Ben kan bianji (本刊编辑, 'Editorial team of Ethnic Education of China') (2017), 'Xin xueqi, san ke jiaokeshu dabianyang-quanzhongguo zhongxiaoxue qishi nianji xinsheng tongyi shiyong yuwen, lishi, daode yu fazhi "bu bian ben" jiaocai (新学期、三科教科书大变样——全国中小学起始年级新生统一使用语文、历史、道德

与法治"部编本"教材, 'Great changes in the new semester—Textbooks on Chinese, history, and moral education compiled by Ministry of Education are to be used nationwide')', *Zhongguo minzu jiaoyu (*中国民族教育,*' Ethnic Education of China'),* 9: 7–8.

Bernstein, B. (1975), *Class Codes and Control, Vol. 3: Towards a Theory of Educational Transmissions*, 2nd edn, London: Routledge.

Bernstein, B. (1981), 'Codes, modalities and the process of cultural reproduction: A model', *Language and Society*, 10: 327–63.

Bernstein, B. (1990), *Class, Codes and Control, Volume 4: The Structuring of Pedagogical Discourse*, London: Routledge and Kegan Paul.

Bernstein, B. (1999), 'Vertical and horizontal discourse: An essay', *British Journal of Sociology of Education*, 2 (2): 157–73.

Bernstein, B. (2000), *Pedagogy, Symbolic Control and Identity: Theory, Research, Critique*, Rev. edn, Lanham: Rowman and Littlefield.

Bo, T. (博涛) (2000), 'Qianxi dili jiaocai zhong ditu de sheji sixiang (浅析地理教材中地图的设计思想, 'Analysis of the map design in geography textbooks')', *Kecheng·jiaocai·jiaofa* (课程·教材·教法, '*Curriculum, Teaching Material and Method'),* 12: 40–3.

Bogatyrev, P. (1938), 'Semiotics in the Folk Theatre', in L. Matejka and I. R. Titunik (eds), *Semiotics of Art: Prague School Contributions*, 33–49, Cambridge: Massachusetts Institute of Technology Press.

Borke, H. (1975), 'Piaget's mountain revisited: Changes in the egocentric landscape', *Developmental Psychology*, 11 (2): 240–3.

Bota, C and J. P. Bronckart (2011), *Bakhtine démasqué: histoire d'un menteur, d'une escroquerie et d'un délire collectif*, Geneva: Librarie Droz.

Broadbent, G. (1977), 'A plain man's guide to the theory of signs in architecture', *Architecture Design*, 47 (7–8): 474–82.

Burke, K. (1969), *A Grammar of Motives*, Englewood Cliffs, NJ: Prentice-Hall.

Caldwell, D. (2014), 'The interpersonal voice: Applying appraisal to the rap and sung voice', *Social Semiotics*, 24 (1): 40–55.

Caple, H. (2013), *Photojournalism: A Social Semiotic Approach*, New York: Palgrave Macmillan.

Caple H. and J. Knox (2017), 'Genre(less) and purpose(less): Online news galleries', *Discourse, Context and Media*, 20: 204–17.

Castillo-Ayometzi, C. (2007), 'Storying as becoming: Identity through the telling of conversion', in A. De Fina and M. Bamberg (eds), *Selves and Identities in Narrative and Discourse*, 41–70, Philadelphia: John Benjamins.

Chen, H. X. and B. Y. Zhang, (陈红香、张必隐) (1997), 'Xiaoxue san wu nianji xuesheng yuedulijie zhong chatu xiaoying de yanjiu (小学三、五年级学生阅读理解中插图效应的研究, 'A study of the influence of illustration on Years 3 and 5 students' reading comprehension')', *Xinli kexue (*心理科学, *'Psychological Science'),* 5: 464–5.

Chen, W. J. (陈文婕) (2006), 'Dui jiaocai zhong chatu peizhi de fenxi yu sikao. (对教材中插图配置的分析与思考, An analysis of and reflections on illustration arrangement in textbooks)', *Xiandai yuwen (Jiaoxue yanjiu ban)* (现代语文(教学研究版), 'Modern Chinese (Teaching and Research Edition)')*, 10: 21–2.

Chen, Y. M. (2010a), 'Exploring dialogic engagement with readers in multimodal EFL textbooks in China', *Visual Communication*, 9 (4): 485–506.

Chen, Y. M. (2010b), 'The semiotic construal of attitudinal curriculum goals: Evidence from EFL textbooks in China', *Linguistics and Education*, 21 (1): 60–74.

Chen, Y. M. (2017), 'Comparing the semiotic construction of attitudinal meanings in the multimodal manuscript, original published and adapted versions of *Alice's Adventures in Wonderland*', *Semiotica*, 215: 341–64.

Chen, Y. M. and X. Y. Qin (陈瑜敏、秦小怡) (2007), 'Jiaokeshu yupian duomoshi fuhao de jieru yiyi yu duosheng hudong (教科书语篇多模式符号的介入意义与多声互动, 'Multimodal engagement resources and voice interaction in textbook discourse')', *Waiyu yu waiyu jiaoxue* (外语与外语教学, 'Foreign Languages and Their Teaching')*, 12: 15–18.

Chen, Y. M. and H. Y. Wang (陈瑜敏、王红阳) (2008), 'Duomotai yupian tuxiang de gainian yiyi yu tuwen guanxi (多模态语篇图像的概念意义与图文关系, 'Ideational meaning of images and text-image relations')', *Ningbo daxue xuebao (Jiaoyu kexue ban)* (宁波大学学报 (教育科学版), 'Journal of Ningbo University (Education Edition)')*, 1: 124–9.

Chen, Y. R. (陈月茹) (2005), 'Jiaokeshu Neirong Shuxing Gaige Yanjiu (教科书内容属性改革研究, 'Study on the reform of textbook content attributes')', Unpublished PhD thesis, East China Normal University.

Chen, Y. R. and L. X. Ye (陈月茹、叶丽新). (2006), 'Jiaokeshu: duihua zhong shengcheng de kaifang wenben (教科书: 对话中生成的开放文本, 'Textbook: The open discourse in dialogue')', *Dangdai Jiaoyu Kexue (*当代教育科学, 'Contemporary Educational Science')*, 23: 34–6.

Cheng, X. T. (程晓堂) (2002), 'Guanyu yingyu kecheng biaozhun de jidian renshi (关于《英语课程标准》的几点认识, 'Reflections on the Curriculum Standards for English')', *Jiaoxue yuekan (Zhongxue ban)* (教学月刊(中学版), 'Teaching Monthly (Middle School Edition)')*, 11: 29–33.

Cheng, X. T. and Y. F. Gong (程晓堂、龚亚夫) (2005), 'Yingyu kecheng biaozhun. (《英语课程标准》的理论基础, 'On the theoretical basis of English curriculum standards')', *Kecheng·jiaocai·jiaofa* (课程·教材·教法, 'Curriculum, Teaching Material and Method')*, 3: 66–72.

Christie, F. (2002), *Classroom Discourse Analysis. A Functional Perspective*. London: Continuum.

Christie, F. (2004), 'Authority and its role in the pedagogic relationship of schooling', in L. Young and C. Harrison (eds), *Systemic Functional Linguistics and Critical Discourse Analysis: Studies in Social Change*, 173–201, London: Continuum.

Christie, F. (2007), 'Ongoing dialogue: Functional linguistic and Bernsteinian sociological perspectives on education', in F. Christie and J. R. Martin (eds), *Language, Knowledge and Pedagogy: Functional Linguistic and Sociological Perspectives*, 3–13, London: Continuum.

Christie, F. and J. R. Martin, eds (2007), *Language, Knowledge and Pedagogy: Functional Linguistic and Sociological Perspectives*, London: Continuum.

Christie, F. and K. Maton, eds (2011), *Disciplinarity: Functional Linguistic and Sociological Perspectives*, London: Continuum.

Coates, J. (1983), *The Semantics of the Modal Auxiliaries*, London: Croom Helm.

Coffin, C. (2000), 'History as discourse: Construals of time, cause and appraisal', PhD diss., University of New South Wales.

Cope, B. and M. Kalantzis, eds (2000), *Multiliteracies: Literacy Learning and the Design of Social Futures*, London: Routledge.

Cortazzi, M. and L. Jin (1999), 'Cultural mirrors materials and methods in the EFL classroom', in E. Hinkel (ed.), *Culture in Second Language Teaching and Learning*, 196–219, Cambridge: Cambridge University Press.

Coulmas, F. (2003), *Writing Systems: An Introduction to Their Linguistic Analysis*, Cambridge: Cambridge University Press.

Coulthard, M. (1994), 'On analysing and evaluating text', in M. Coulthard (ed.), *Advances in Written Text Analysis*, 1–11, London: Routledge.

Cui, J. and D. J. Ren (崔军、任大吉) (2001), 'Jiaokeshu chatu de zuoyong (教科书插图的作用, 'The function of textbook illustrations')', *Shengwuxue jiaoxue (*生物学教学, 'Biology Teaching')*, 12: 15–16.

de Saint Georges, I. (2014), 'Mediated discourse analysis, 'embodied learning' and emerging social and professional identities', in S. Norris and C. D. Maier (eds), *Interactions, Images and Texts: A Reader in Multimodality*, 347–56, Boston: de Gruyter.

de Saint Georges, I. and S. Norris (1999), 'Literate design and European identity: Visual practices of an imagined community', Paper presented at *International* Visual Sociology Association Annual Conference, Antwerp: University of Antwerp.

de Saussure, F. ([1983] 1916). *Course in General Linguistics*, eds. C. Bally and A. Sechehaye (with the collaboration of A. Riedlinger), trans. and annotated, R. Harris, London: Duckworth.

Ding, C. P. (丁朝蓬) (2001), 'Jiaokeshu jiegou fenxi yu neirong zhiliang pingjia (教科书结构分析与内容质量评价, 'Analysis of textbook structure and evaluation of content quality')', *Jiaoyu lilun yu shijian (*教育理论与实践, 'Theory and Practice of Education')*, 8: 61–4.

Ding, J. X. (丁建新) (2007), 'Shijue de yufa: Tonghua chatu zhong qingtai de shehui fuhaoxue yanjiu (视觉的语法: 童话插图中情态的社会符号学研究, 'Visual grammar: Social semiotic perspectives on the modality of fairy tale illustrations')', *Zhongshan daxue xuebao (Shehui kexue ban) (*中山大学学报 (社会科学版), 'Journal of Sun Yat-sen University (Social Science Edition)')*, 5: 39–42.

Diringer, D. (1968), *The Alphabet: A Key to the History of Mankind*, 3rd edn, London: Hutchinson.

Dixon, J. (1967), *Growth through English*, London: National Association for the Teaching of English and Oxford University Press.

Djonov, E. and T. van Leeuwen (2018), 'The power of semiotic software: A critical multimodal perspective', in J. Flowerdew and J. E. Richardson (eds), *The Routledge Handbook of Critical Discourse Studies*, 566–81, New York: Taylor & Francis.

Djonov, E. (2007), 'Website hierarchy and the interaction between content organization, webpage and navigation design: A systemic functional hypermedia discourse analysis perspective', *Information Design Journal*, 15 (2): 144–62.

Donaldson, M. (1978), *Children's Explanations: A Psycholinguistic Study*, Cambridge: Cambridge University Press.

Dondis, D. A. (1972), *A Primer of Visual Literacy*, Cambridge: Massachusetts Institute of Technology Press.

Doran, Y. J. (2018), *The Discourse of Physics: Building Knowledge through Language, Mathematics and Image*. London: Routledge.

Doran, Y. J. (2019), 'Building knowledge through images in physics', *Visual Communication*, 18 (2): 251–77.

Du, G. Y. (杜广友) (1982), 'Luetan lishi jiaoxue zhong shiyong chatu de wenti (略谈历史教学中使用插图的问题, 'A brief comment on the use of illustration in teaching history')', *Lishi Jiaoxue (*历史教学*, 'History Teaching')*, 1: 50–1.

Eco, U. (1972), 'A componential analysis of the architectural sign/column/', *Semiotica*, 5 (2): 92–117.

Eco, U. (1984), *The Role of the Reader: Explorations in the Semiotics of Texts*, Bloomington: Indiana University Press.

Economou, D. (2006), 'The big picture: The role of the lead image in print feature stories', in I. Lassen, J. Strunck and T. Vestergard (eds), *Mediating Ideology in Text and Image: Ten Critical Studies*, 211–33, Amsterdam: Benjamins.

Eggins, S. (2004), *An Introduction to Systemic Functional Linguistics*, 2nd edn, London: Continuum.

Eggins, S. and D. Slade (1997), *Analysing Casual Conversation*, London: Cassell.

Fairclough, N. (1992), *Discourse and Social Change*, Cambridge: Polity Press.

Fairclough, N. (1995), *Critical Discourse Analysis*, London: Longmans.

Fairclough, N. (2000), 'Multiliteracies and language: Orders of discourse and intertextuality', in B. Cope and M. Kalantzis (eds), *Multiliteracies: Literacy Learning and the Design of Social Futures*, 162–81, London: Routledge.

Feng, D. (2017), 'Infusing moral education into English language teaching: An ontogenetic analysis of social values in EFL textbooks in Hong Kong', *Discourse: Studies in the Cultural Politics of Education*, 40 (4): 458–73.

Fernandez-Fontecha, A., K. L. O'Halloran, P. Wignell and S. Tan (2020), 'Scaffolding CLIL in the science classroom via visual thinking: A systemic functional multimodal approach', *Linguistics and Education*, 55. doi:10.1016/j.linxged.2019.100788.

Field, T. M. and N. Fox, eds. (1985), *Social Perception in Infants*, Norwood, NJ: Ablex.

Forceville, C. (1999), 'Educating the eye?: Kress and Van Leeuwen's *Reading Images: The Grammar of Visual Design* (1996)', *Language and Literature*, 8 (2): 163–78.

Freebody, P., K. Maton and J. R. Martin (2008), 'Talk, text, and knowledge in cumulative, integrated learning: A response to "intellectual challenge"', *Australian Journal of Language and Literacy*, 31 (2): 188–201.

Fryer, D. L. (2019), 'Engagement in medical research discourse: A multisemiotic discourse-semantic study of dialogic positioning', PhD diss., Faculty of Arts at the University of Gothenburg, Sweden.

Fu, Y. (傅莹) (2005), 'Yingxiang de jiaoyu liliang (影像的教育力量, 'The educational power of visual images')', *Guangdong jiaoyu (*广东教育*, 'Guangdong Education'*), 7: 60–1.

Fuller, G. (1998), 'Cultivating science: Negotiating discourse in the popular texts of Stephen Jay Gould', in J. R. Martin and R. Veel (eds), *Reading Science: Critical and Functional Perspectives on Discourses of Science*, 35–62, London: Routledge.

Gelb, I. J. (1963), *A Study of Writing*, 2nd edn, Chicago: University of Chicago Press.

Green, B. and A. Lee (1994), 'Writing geography lessons: Literacy, identity and schooling', in A. Freedman and P. Medway (eds), *Learning and Teaching Genre*, 207–24, Portsmouth, NH: Boynton/Cook.

Guijarro, A. J. M. (2011), 'Engaging readers through language and pictures: A case study', *Journal of Pragmatics*, 43: 2982–91.

Guo, L. B. (2004), 'Multimodality in a biology textbook', in K. L. O'Halloran (ed.), *Multimodal Discourse Analysis: Systemic Functional Perspectives*, 196–219, London: Continuum.

Guo, S. and D. Feng (2015), 'The Visual Construction of Knowledge in English Textbooks from an Ontogenetic Perspective', *Linguistics and Education*, 31: 115–29.

Hall, E. (1964), 'Silent assumption in social communication', *Disorders of Communication*, 42: 41–55.

Hall, E. (1966), *The Hidden Dimension*, New York: Doubleday.

Halliday, M. A. K. (1973), *Explorations in the Functions of Language*, London: Arnold.

Halliday, M. A. K. (1975), *Learning How to Mean: Explorations in the Development of Language*, London: Arnold.

Halliday, M. A. K. (1976), *System and Function in Language*, ed. G. R. Kress, London: Oxford University Press.

Halliday, M. A. K. (1978), *Language as Social Semiotic: The Social Interpretation of Language and Meaning*, London: Arnold.

Halliday, M. A. K. (1979/2002), 'Modes of meaning and modes of expression: Types of grammatical structure and their determination by different semantic functions', in D. J. Allerton, E. Carmey and D. Hodcroft (eds), *Function and Context in Linguistic Analysis: A Festschrift for William Haas*, 57–79, Cambridge: Cambridge University Press. / in J. Webster (ed.), *On Grammar*, 196–218, London: Continuum.

Halliday, M. A. K. (1985), 'Part A', in M. A. K. Halliday and R. Hasan (ed.), *Language, Context and Text: Aspects of Language in a Social-semiotic Perspective*, 1–49, Geelong, VIC: Deakin University Press.

Halliday, M. A. K. (1992), 'Systemic grammar and the concept of a "science of language"', *Journal of Foreign Languages* 2: 1–9.

Halliday, M. A. K. (1994), *An Introduction to Functional Grammar*, 2nd edn, London: Arnold.

Halliday, M. A. K. (1999), 'The notion of 'context' in language education', in M. Ghadessy (ed.), *Text and Context in Functional Linguistics*, 1–24, Amsterdam: Benjamin.

Halliday, M. A. K. and C. M. I. M. Matthiessen (1999), *Construing Experience through Meaning: A Language-based Approach to Cognition*, London: Cassell.

Halliday, M. A. K. and C. M. I. M. Matthiessen (2004), *An Introduction to Functional Grammar*, 3rd edn, London: Arnold.

Halliday, M. A. K. and C. M. I. M. Matthiessen (2014), *Halliday's Introduction to Functional Grammar*, 4th edn, Oxon: Routledge.

Halliday, M. A. K. and J. R. Martin (1993), *Writing Science: Literacy and Discursive Power*, London: Falmer.

Halliday, M. A. K. and R. Hasan (1976), *Cohesion in English*, London: Longman.

Halliday, M. A. K. and R. Hasan (1985), *Language, Context and Text: Aspects of Language in a Social-semiotic Perspective*, Geelong, VIC: Deakin University Press.

Hao, J. and S. Hood (2018), 'Valuing science: The role of language and body language in a health science lecture', *Journal of Pragmatics*, 25 (4): 503–35.

Hasan, R. and J. R Martin, eds (1989), *Language Development: Learning Language, Learning Culture*, Norwood, NJ: Ablex.

Hjelmslev, L. (1961), *Prolegomena to a Theory of Language*, Madison: University of Wisconsin Press.

Hodge, R. and D. Tripp (1986), *Children and Television*, Cambridge: Polity Press.

Hodge, R. and G. Kress (1988), *Social Semiotics*, Cambridge: Polity Press.

Honzl, J. (1940), 'Dynamics of the sign in the theater', in L. Matejka and I. R. Titunik (eds), *Semiotics of Art: Prague School Contributions*, 74–93, Cambridge: Massachusetts Institute of Technology Press.

Hood, S. (2004), 'Appraising research: Taking a stance in academic writing', PhD diss., University of Technology, Sydney.

Hood, S. (2007), 'Embodying language: Bringing gesture in from the paralinguistic cold', Paper presented at *Semiotic margins: Reclaiming Meaning*, Sydney: The University of Sydney.

Hood, S. (2008), 'Summary writing in academic contexts: Implicating meaning in processes of change', *Linguistics and Education*, 19 (4): 351–65.

Hood, S. (2011), 'Body language in face-to-face teaching: A focus on textual and interpersonal meaning', in S. Dreyfus, S. Hood and M. Stenglin (eds), *Semiotic Margins: Meaning in Multimodalities*, 31–52, London: Continuum.

Hood, S. and J. R. Martin (2007), 'Invoking attitude: The play of graduation in appraising discourse', in R. Hasan, C. M. I. M. Matthiessen and J. Webster (eds), *Continuing Discourse on Language. Vol. 2*, 739–64, London: Equinox.

Hood, S. and S. Shay, eds (2016), *Knowledge-building: Educational Studies in Legitimation Code Theory*, London: Routledge.

Hu, Z. L. (胡壮麟) (2007), 'Shehui fuhaoxue yanjiu zhong de duomotaihua. (社会符号学研究中的多模态化, 'Multimodalization in social semiotics')', *Yuyan jiaoxue yu yanjiu* (语言教学与研究, *Language Teaching and Linguistic Studies*), 1: 1–10.

Hu, Z. L. (胡壮麟) (2010), 'Duomotai xiaopin de wenshi yu fazhan (多模态小品的问世与发展, 'The growth and development of multimodal essays')', *Waiyu dianhua jiaoxue* (外语电化教学, *Computer-Assisted Foreign Language Education*), 4: 3–9.

Hu, Z. L. (胡壮麟) (2011), 'Lun duomotai xiaopin zhong de zhuti motai (谈多模态小品中的主体模态, 'On principal modals of multi-mode short essays')', *Waiyu jiaoxue* (外语教学, *Foreign Language Education*), 32 (4): 1–5.

Hu, Z. L., Y. S. Zhu, D. L. Zhang and Z. Z. Li (胡壮麟、朱永生、张德禄、李战子) (2005), *Xitong gongneng yuyanxue gailun* (系统功能语言学概论, *A Survey of Systemic Functional Linguistics*). Beijing: Peking University Press.

Huang, G. W. and M. Ghadessy (2006), *Functional Discourse Analysis*, Shanghai: Shanghai Foreign Language Education Press.

Huang, G. W. (黄国文) (2003), 'Gongneng yupian fenxi gailun (功能语篇分析概论, 'A Survey of functional discourse analysis')', in B. Wang (ed.) *Yuyan de xiangdu* (语言的向度, *Language Dimensions*). Guangzhou: Sun Yat-sen University Press, 89–116.

Huang, G. W. (黄国文) and M. Ghadessy (2006), *Functional Discourse Analysis*. Shanghai: Shanghai Foreign Language Education Press.

Huang, Y. H. (黄熠华) (1999), 'Liyong chatu shanghuo sixiang pinde ke (利用插图上活思想品德课, 'Utilizing illustration to teach moral education')', *Xiaoxue jiaoxue yanjiu* (小学教学研究, *Primary School Teaching Research*), 10: 33–3.

Hyon, S. (1996), 'Genre in three traditions: Implications for ESL', *TESOL Quarterly*, 30 (4): 693–722.

Iedema, R. (1995), *Literacy of Administration (Write it Right Literacy in Industry Research Project - Stage 3)*, Sydney: Metropolitan East Disadvantaged Schools Program.

Iedema, R. (2001), 'Resemiotization', *Semiotica*, 137 (1/4): 23–39.

Iedema, R. (2003), 'Multimodality, resemiotization: Extending the analysis of discourse as multi-semiotic practice', *Visual Communication*, 2 (1): 29–57.

Iedema, R., S. Feez and P. R. R. White (1994), *Media Literacy. Write it Right Literacy in Industry Research Project – Stage 2*, Sydney Metropolitan East Disadvantaged Schools Program, NSW Department of School Education.

Jencks, C. (1984), *The Language of Post-Modern Architecture*, 4th edn, London: Academy Editions.

Jewitt, C. (2002), 'The move from page to screen: The multimodal reshaping of school English', *Visual Communication*, 1 (2): 171–95.

Jewitt, C. (2017), 'Multimodal discourses across the curriculum', in S. L. Thorne and S. May (eds), *Language, Education and Technology*, 31–43, Boston: Springer.

Jewitt, C. and K. L. Kerstin (2018), 'Methodological dialogues across multimodality and sensory ethnography: Digital touch communication', *Qualitative Research*, 19 (1): 90–110.

Jewitt, C. and R. Oyama (2001), 'Visual meaning: A social semiotic approach', in van T. Leeuwen and C. Jewitt (eds), *Handbook of Visual Analysis*, London: Sage, 134–56.

Jewitt, C., A. Xambó and S. Price (2016), 'Exploring methodological innovation in the social sciences: The body in digital environments and the arts', *International Journal of Social Research Methodology*, 20: 105–20.

Jiang, C. Y. (姜朝义) (1984), 'Qiantan shengwu jiaoxue zhong shiyong chatu wenti (浅谈生物教学中使用插图问题, 'Using illustrations in teaching biology')', *Shengwuxue jiaoxue (生物学教学, 'Biology Teaching')*, 3: 31–2.

Jocuns, A. (2009), 'Participation structures as mediational means: Learning Balinese Gamelan in the United States through intent participation, mediated discourse, and distributed cognition', *Mind, Culture and Activity*, 16 (1): 48–63.

Johns, A. (1998), 'The visual and the verbal: A case study in macroeconomics', *English for Specific Purposes*, 17 (2): 183–97.

Johnson, A. (2002), 'Modalities of identity negotiation in U.S. immigration interviews', Paper presented at Sociolinguistics Symposium 14, Ghent, Belgium: University of Ghent.

Jones, R. (1999), 'Mediated action and sexual risk: Searching for "culture" in discourses of homosexuality and AIDS prevention in China', *Culture, Health & Sexuality*, 1 (2): 161–80.

Jones, R. (2002), 'A walk in the park: Frames and positions in AIDS prevention outreach among gay men in China', *Journal of Sociolinguistics*, 6 (3): 575–88.

Jones, R. (2014), 'Mediated discourse analysis', in S. Norris and C. D. Maier (eds), *Interactions, Images, and Texts: A Reader in Multimodality*, 39–52, New York: de Gruyter.

Jones, R. (2020), 'Mediated discourse analysis', in S. Adolphs and D. Knight (eds), *The Routledge Handbook of English Language and Digital Humanities*, 202–19. London: Routledge.

Kalantzis, M. and B. Cope (2001), 'Introduction', in M. Kalantzis and B. Cope (eds), *Transformations in Language and Learning: Perspectives on Multiliteracies*, 9–18, Melbourne: Common Ground.

Knox, J. (2007), 'Visual-verbal communication on online newspaper home pages', *Visual Communication*, 6 (1): 19–53.

Kress, G. (2000), 'Multimodality: Challenges to thinking about language', *TESOL Quarterly*, 34 (2): 337–40.

Kress, G. R. and R. Hodge (1979), *Language as Ideology*, London: Routledge and Kegan Paul.

Kress, G., C. Jewitt, J. Ogborn and C. Tsatsarelis (2001), *Multimodal Teaching and Learning: The Rhetorics of the Science Classroom*, London: Continuum.

Kress, G. and T. van Leeuwen (1996), *Reading Images: The Grammar of Visual Design*, London: Routledge.
Kress, G., R. Leite-Garcia and T. van Leeuwen (1997), 'Discourse semiotics', in T. A. van Dijk (ed.), *Discourse as Structure and Process: Discourse Studies: A Multidisciplinary Introduction Vol 1*, 257–91, London: Sage.
Kress, G. and T. van Leeuwen (2001), *Multimodal Discourse: The Modes and Media of Contemporary Communication*, London: Arnold.
Kress, G. and T. van Leeuwen (2002), 'Color as a semiotic mode: Notes for a grammar of color', *Visual Communication*, 1 (3): 343–68.
Kress, G. and T. van Leeuwen (2006), *Reading Images: The Grammar of Visual Design*, 2nd edn, London: Routledge.
Kress, G. and T. van Leeuwen (2020), *Reading Images: The Grammar of Visual Design*, 3rd edn, London: Routledge.
Kristeva, J. (1986), 'Word, dialogue and novel', in T. Moi (ed.), *The Kristeva Reader*, 34–61, Oxford: Blackwell.
Kuang, L. Z. (邝丽湛) (2002), 'Jiaocai pingjia de benzhi jiqi jiazhi fenxi (教材评价的本质及其价值分析, 'Analysis of the essence and value of textbook assessment')', *Jiaoyu yanjiu (教育研究, Educational Research)*, 7: 33–6.
Labov, W. and J. Waletzky (1967/1997), 'Narrative analysis: Oral versions of personal experience', in J. Helm (ed.), *Essays on the Verbal and Visual Arts: Proceedings of the 1966 Annual Spring Meeting of the American Ethnological Society*, 12–44, Seattle: University of Washington Press. / in M. G. W. Bamberg (ed.), *Journal of Narrative and Life History: Special Issue. Oral Versions of Personal Experience: Three Decades of Narrative Analysis*, 7(1–4): 3–38, London: Lawrence Erlbaum Associates.
Larochelle, M. and N. Bednarz (1998), 'Constructivism and education: Beyond epistemological correctness', in M. Larochelle, N. Bednarz and J Garrison (eds), *Constructivism and Education*, 3–20, Cambridge: Cambridge University Press.
Larochelle, M., N. Bednarz and J Garrison, eds (1998), *Constructivism and Education*, Cambridge: Cambridge University Press.
Lemke, J. (1998b), 'Introduction: Language and other semiotic systems in education', *Linguistics and Education*, 10 (3): 245–6.
Lemke, J. L. (1984), *Semiotics and Education*, Toronto: Victoria College / Toronto Semiotic Circle Monographs.
Lemke, J. L. (1995), *Textual Politics: Discourse and Social Dynamics*, London: Taylor & Francis.
Lemke, J. L. (1998a), 'Multiplying meaning: Visual and verbal semiotics in scientific text', in J. R. Martin and V. R. eel (eds), *Reading Science: Critical and Functional Perspectives on Discourses of Science*, 87–113, London: Routledge.
Lemke, J. L. (2000), 'Multimedia literacy demands of the scientific curriculum', *Linguistics and Education*, 10 (3): 247–71.
Lemke, J. L. (2002), 'Multimedia semiotics: Genres for science education and scientific literacy', in M. J. Schleppegrell and M. C. Colombi (eds), *Developing Advanced*

Literacy in First and Second Languages: Meaning with Power, 21–44, London: Lawrence Erlbaum Associates.

Lemke, J. L. (2012), 'Multimedia and discourse analysis', in J. P. Gee and M. Handford (eds), *The Routledge Handbook of Discourse Analysis*, 79–89, London: Routledge.

Levie, W. H. and R. Lentz (1982), 'Effects of text illustration: A review of research', *Education Communication and Technology Journal: A Journal of Theory, Research, and Development*, 30 (4): 195–232.

Lewis, C., P. Enciso and E. B. Moje (2007), *Reframing Sociocultural Research on Literacy: Identity, Agency, and Power*. Mahwah, NJ: Lawrence Erlbaum.

Li, Z. Z. (李战子) (2003), 'Duomoshi de shehuifuhaoxue fenxi (多模式话语的社会符号学分析, 'Social semiotic approach to multimodal discourse')', *Waiyu yanjiu (外语研究, 'Foreign Languages Research')*, 5: 1–8.

Liao, Y. (廖鹰) (2004), 'Jiaokeshu ruhe chongfen de tixian kecheng biaozhun: Jiyu xin kecheng xiaoxue yuwen jiaokeshu ge banben bijiao (教科书如何充分地体现课程标准: 基于新课程小学语文教科书各版本比较, How textbook embodies curriculum standards: A comparative study of different editions of Chinese textbooks based on the new curriculum standards for elementary level)', Unpublished MA thesis, Hunan Normal University.

Lim, F. V. (2019) 'Investigating intersemiosis: A systemic functional multimodal discourse analysis of the relationship between language and gesture in classroom discourse', *Visual Communication*, 20 (1): 34–58.

Lim, F. V. and W. Toh (2020), 'Children's digital multimodal composing: Implications for learning and teaching', *Learning, Media and Technology*, 45 (4): 422–32.

Luke, A. (2000), 'Critical literacy in Australia: A matter of context and standpoint', *Journal of Adolescent & Adult Literacy*, 43: 448–61.

Macken-Horarik, M., (2003), 'Appraisal and the special instructiveness of narrative', *Text*, 32 (2): 285–312.

Macken-Horarik, M., K. Love, C. Sandiford and L. Unsworth (2017), *Functional Grammatics: Re-conceptualizing knowledge about language and image for school English*, London: Routledge.

Martin, J. R. (1984), 'Language, register and genre', in F. Christie (ed.), *Language Studies: Children Writing. Reader*, 21–9, Geelong, VIC: Deakin University Press.

Martin, J. R. (1985a), 'Process and text: Two aspects of human semiosis', in J. D. Benson and W. S. Greaves (eds), *Systemic Perspectives on Discourse vol. 1: Selected Theoretical Papers from the 9th International Systemic Workshop*, 248–74, Norwood, NJ: Ablex.

Martin, J. R. (1985b), *Factual Writing: Exploring and Challenging Social Reality*, Geelong, VIC: Deakin University Press.

Martin, J. R. (1986), 'Grammaticalising ecology: The politics of baby seals and kangaroos', in T. Threadgold, E. A. Grosz, G. Kress and M. A. K. Halliday (eds), *Semiotics, Ideology, Language*, 225–68, Sydney: Sydney Association for Studies in Society and Culture (Sydney Studies in Society and Culture).

Martin, J. R. (1989), *Factual Writing: Exploring and Challenging Social Reality*, 2nd edn, Oxford: Oxford University Press.

Martin, J. R. (1991), 'Intrinsic functionality: Implications for contextual theory', *Social Semiotics*, 1 (1): 99–162.

Martin, J. R. (1992), *English Text: System and Structure*, Amsterdam: Benjamins.

Martin, J. R. (1994), 'Modelling big texts: A systemic functional approach to multi-genericity', *Network*, 21: 29–52.

Martin, J. R. (1997), 'Analysing genre: Functional parameters', in F. Christie and J. R. Martin (eds), *Genre and Institutions: Social Processes in the Workplace and School*, 3–39, London: Cassell.

Martin, J. R. (1999a), 'Modelling context: A crooked path of progress in contextual linguistics', in M. Ghadessy (ed.), *Text and Context in Functional Linguistics*, 25–61, Amsterdam: Benjamins.

Martin, J. R. (1999b), 'Mentoring semogenesis: "Genre-based" literacy pedagogy', in F. Christie (ed.), *Pedagogy and the Shaping of Consciousness: Linguistic and Social Processes*, 123–55, London: Cassell (Open Linguistics Series).

Martin, J. R. (2000a), 'Beyond exchange: Appraisal systems in English'. in S. Hunston and G. Thompson (eds), *Evaluation in Text: Authorial Stance and the Construction of Discourse*, 142–75, Oxford: Oxford University Press.

Martin, J. R. (2000b), 'Grammar meets genre: Reflections on the "Sydney School"', *Inaugural lecture*, Sydney University Arts Association.

Martin, J. R. (2001), 'Fair trade: Negotiating meaning in multimodal texts', in P. Coppock (ed.), *The Semiotics of Writing: Transdisciplinary Perspectives on the Technology of Writing*, 311–38, Bloomington: Indiana University Press.

Martin, J. R. (2002), 'Blessed are the peacemakers: Reconciliation and evaluation', in C. Candlin (ed.), *Research and Practice in Professional Discourse*, 187–227, Hong Kong: City University of Hong Kong Press.

Martin, J. R. (2003), 'Instantiating appraisal: Key and stance', Paper presented at Australian Systemic Functional Linguistics Association Conference, Adelaide.

Martin, J. R. (2004), 'Sense and sensibility: Texturing evaluation', in J. Foley (ed.), *New Perspectives on Education and Discourse*, 270–304, London: Continuum.

Martin, J. R. (2007), 'Construing knowledge: A functional linguistic perspective', in F. Christie and J. R. Martin (eds), *Language, Knowledge and Pedagogy: Functional Linguistic and Sociological Perspectives*, 34–64, London: Continuum.

Martin, J. R. (2008a), 'Intermodal reconciliation: Mates in arms', in L. Unsworth (ed.), *New Literacies and the English Curriculum: Multimodal Perspectives*, 112–48, London: Continuum.

Martin, J. R. (2008b), 'Tenderness: Realisation and instantiation in a Botswanan town', in N. Nørgaard (ed.), *Odense Working Papers in Language and Communication (Special Issue of Papers from 34th International Systemic Functional Congress)*, 30–62.

Martin, J. R. (2008c), 'Chaser's war on context: Making meaning', Paper presented at the 35th International Systemic Functional Congress, Sydney: Macquarie University.

Martin, J. R. (2011), 'Nominalization in science and humanities: Distilling knowledge and scaffolding text', in E. Ventola (ed.), *Functional and Systemic Linguistics: Approaches and Uses*, 307–38, New York: De Gruyter Mouton.

Martin, J. R. (2017), 'The discourse semantics of attitudinal relations: Continuing the study of lexis', *Russian Journal of Linguistics Vestnik RUDN (Special Issue on Discourse Analysis in the 21st Century: Theory and Practice)*, 21 (1): 22–47. [republished as 'Attitudinal relations: Continuing the study of lexis', in L. Barbara, A. S. Rodriques-Júnior and G. M. V. Hoy, eds (2017), *Estudos e Pesquisas em Linguística Sistêmico-Funcional*. São Paulo: Mercado de Letras: 53–87].

Martin, J. R. (2019), 'Once more with feeling: Negotiating evaluation', *Language, Context and Text*, 1 (2): 234–59.

Martin, J. R. (2020), 'Metaphors we feel by: Stratal tension', *Journal of World Languages*, 6 (1–2), 8–26.

Martin, J. R., K. Maton and Y. J. Doran, eds. (2020) *Accessing Academic Discourse: Systemic Functional Linguistics and Legitimation Code Theory*, London: Routledge.

Martin, J. R. and D. Rose (2007a), *Working with Discourse: Meaning beyond the Clause*, 2nd edn, London: Continuum.

Martin, J. R. and D. Rose (2007b), 'Interacting with text: The role of dialogue in learning to read and write', *Foreign Languages in China*, (5): 66–80.

Martin, J. R. and D. Rose (2008), *Genre Relations: Mapping Culture*, London: Equinox.

Martin, J. R. and G. Plum (1997), 'Construing experience: Some story genres', *Journal of Narrative and Life History (Special Issue: Oral Versions of Personal Experience: Three decades of narrative analysis)*, 7(1/4): 299–308.

Martin, J. R. and M. Stenglin (2007), 'Materialising reconciliation: Negotiating difference in a post-colonial exhibition', in T. Royce and W. Bowcher (eds), *New Directions in the Analysis of Multimodal Discourse*, 215–238, Mahwah, New Jersey: Lawrence Erlbaum Associates.

Martin, J. R. and P. R. R. White (2005), *The Language of Evaluation: Appraisal in English*, London: Palgrave.

Martin, J. R. and M. Zappavigna (2019), 'Embodied meaning: A systemic functional perspective on body language', *Functional Linguistics*, 6 (1): 1–33.

Martinec, R. (1998), 'Cohesion in action', *Semiotica*, 120 (1/2): 161–80.

Martinec, R. (2000), 'Types of process in action', *Semiotica*, 130 (3/4): 243–68.

Martinec, R. (2005), 'Topics in multimodality', in R. Hasan, C. M. I. M. Matthiessen and J. Webster (eds), *Continuing Discourse on Language: A Functional Perspective, Vol. 1*, 157–81, London: Equinox.

Martinec, R. and A. Salway (2005), 'A system for image-text relations in new (and old) media', *Visual Communication*, 4 (3): 337–71.

Martinec, R. and T. van Leeuwen (2008), *The Language of New Media Design: Theory and Practice*, London: Routledge.

Maton, K. (2014), *Knowledge and Knowers: Towards a Realist Sociology of Education*. London: Routledge.

Maton, K. and J. Muller (2007), 'A sociology for the transmission of knowledges', in F. Christie and J. R. Martin (eds), *Language, Knowledge and Pedagogy: Functional Linguistic and Sociological Perspectives*, 14–33, London: Continuum.

Maton, K., J. R. Martin and Y. J. Doran, eds. (2021) *Teaching Science: Language, Knowledge and Pedagogy*, London: Routledge.

Matthiessen, C. M. I. M. (1993), 'Registers in the round: Diversity in a unified theory of register analysis', in M. Ghadessy (ed.), *Register Analysis: Theory and Practice*, 221–92, London: Pinter.

Matthiessen, C. M. I. M. (2007), 'The multimodal page: A systemic functional exploration', in T. Royce and W. L. Bowcher (eds), *New Directions in the Analysis of Multimodal Discourse*, 1–62, Mahwah, NJ: Lawrence Erlbaum Associates.

Messaris, P. and S. Moriarty (2005), 'Visual literacy theory', in K. Smith, S. Moriarty, G. Barbatsis and K. Kenney (eds), *Handbook of Visual Communication: Theory, Methods and Media*, 479–502, Mahwah, NJ: Lawrence Erlbaum Associates.

Messer, D. J. (1994), *The Development of Communication: From Social Interaction to Language*, Chichester: Wiley.

Metz, C. (1974), *Language and Cinema*, The Hague: Mouton.

Mills, K. A., B. G. Stone, L. Unsworth and L. Friend (2020), 'Multimodal language of attitude in digital composition', *Written Communication*, 37 (2): 135–66.

Ministry of Education of the People's Republic of China (2001a), *Curriculum Standards for English*, Beijing: Beijing Normal University Press.

Ministry of Education of the People's Republic of China (2001b), *Curriculum Standards for Mathematics*, Beijing: Beijing Normal University Press.

Mosley, M. (2010), 'That really hit me hard: Moving beyond passive anti-racism to engage with critical race literacy pedagogy', *Race Ethnicity and Education*, 13 (4), 449–71.

Mukarovsky, J. (1978), *Structure, Sign and Function*, eds. and trans. J. Burbank and P. Steiner, New Haven: Yale University Press.

Muller, J. (2000), *Reclaiming Knowledge: Social Theory, Curriculum and Education Policy*, London: Rougledge Falmer.

Myskow, G. (2018), 'Calibrating the 'right values': The role of critical inquiry tasks in social studies textbooks', *Visual Communication*, 18 (1): 31–54.

Murray, L. and C. Trevarthen (1985), 'Emotional regulation of interactions between two-month-olds and their mothers', in T. M. Field and N. A. Fox (eds), *Social Perception in Infants*, 177–97, New Jersey: Ablex.

Nesbitt, C. and G. Plum (1988), 'Probabilities in a systemic-functional grammar: The clause complex in English', in R. P. Fawcett and D. Young (eds), *New Developments in Systemic Linguistics, Vol. 2: Theory and Application*, 6–38, London: Pinter.

New London Group (1996), 'A pedagogy of Multiliteracies: Designing social futures', *Harvard Educational Review*, 66 (1): 60–92.

Ngo, T., S. Hood, J. R. Martin, C. Painter, B. Smith and M. Zappavigna (in press) *Modelling Paralanguage Using Systemic Functional Semiotics*, London: Bloomsbury.

Nodelman, P. (1988), *Words about Pictures: The Narrative Art of Children's Picture Books*, Athens: The University of Georgia Press.

Norris, S. (2002), 'A theoretical framework for multimodal discourse analysis presented via the analysis of identity construction of two women living in Germany', PhD diss., Georgetown University.

Norris, S. (2004), 'Multimodal discourse analysis: A conceptual framework', in P. LeVine and R. Scollon (eds), *Discourse and Technology: Multimodal Discourse Analysis*, 101–15, Washington, DC: Georgetown University Press.

Norris, S. (2005), 'Habitus, social identity, the perception of male domination—and agency?' in S. Norris and R. H. Jones (eds), *Discourse in Action: Introducing Mediated Discourse Analysis*, 183–96, London: Routledge.

Norris, S. and R. H. Jones (2005), *Discourse in Action: Introducing Mediated Discourse Analysis*, London: Routledge.

O'Halloran, K. L. (1999b), 'Interdependence, interaction and metaphor in multisemiotic texts', *Social Semiotics*, 9 (3): 317–54.

O'Halloran, K. L. (2000), 'Classroom discourse in mathematics: A multi-semiotic analysis', *Linguistics and Education*, 10 (3): 359–88.

O'Halloran, K. L. (2005), *Mathematical Discourse: Language, Symbolism and Visual Image*, London: Continuum.

O'Halloran, K. L. (2008), 'Systemic functional-multimodal discourse analysis (SF-MDA): Constructing ideational meaning using language and visual imagery', *Visual Communication*, 7 (4): 443–75.

O'Halloran, Kay, Sabine Tan and Peter Wignell (2016), 'Intersemiotic translation as resemiotisation: A multimodal perspective', *Signata*, 7(7): 199–229.

O'Halloran, K. L. (1999a), 'Towards a systemic-functional analysis of multi-semiotic mathematics text', *Semiotica*, 124(1/2): 1–29.

O'Halloran, K. L. (2015), 'The language of learning mathematics: A multimodal perspective', *The Journal of Mathematical Behavior*, 40: 63–74.

O'Toole, M. (1994), *The Language of Displayed Art*, London: Leicester University Press.

O'Toole, M. (2004), 'Opera Ludentes: The Sydney Opera House at work and play', in O'Halloran, K. L. (ed.), *Multimodal Discourse Analysis: Systemic Functional Perspectives*, 11–27, London: Continuum.

O'Toole, M. (1990), 'A systemic-functional semiotics of art', *Semiotica*, 82 (3/4): 185–209.

Ong, W. J. (1982), *Orality and Literacy: The Technologizing of the Word*, Methuen: London.

Page, R. E. (2003), 'An analysis of APPRAISAL in childbirth narratives with special consideration of gender and storytelling style', *Special Issue of Text*, 23 (2): 211–37.

Painter, C. (1984), *Into the Mother Tongue: A Case Study in Early Language Development*, London: Pinter.

Painter, C. (1999), *Learning through Language in Early Childhood*, London: Cassell.

Painter, C. (2003), 'Developing attitude: An ontogenetic perspective on APPRAISAL', *Special Issue of Text*, 23 (2): 183–209.

Painter, C. (2007), 'Children's picture book narratives: Reading sequences of images', in A. McCabe, M. O'Donnell and R. Whittaker (eds), *Advances in language and education*, 40–59, London: Continuum.

Painter, C. and J. R. Martin (1986), *Writing to Mean: Teaching Genres Across the Curriculum*, Bundoora, VIC: Applied Linguistics Association of Australia.

Painter, C., J. R. Martin and L. Unsworth (2013), *Reading Visual Narratives: Image Analysis of Children's Picture Books*, London: Equinox.

Palmer, F. R. (1990), *Modality and the English Modals*, 2nd edn, London: Longman.

Piaget, J. (1976), *Judgement and Reasoning in the Child*, trans. M. Warden, Totowa, NJ: Littlefield Adams.

Piaget, J. (1977), *The Essential Piaget*, eds. H. E. Gruber and J. J. Vonèche, London: Routledge and Kegan Paul.

Quirk, R., S. Greenbaum, G. Leech and J. Svartvik (1985), *A Comprehensive Grammar of the English Language*, London: Longman.

Ravelli, L. (2006), *Museum Texts: Communication Frameworks*, Abingdon, Oxon: Routledge.

Ravelli, L. J. and R. J. McMurtrie (2016), *Multimodality in the Built Environment: Spatial Discourse Analysis*, Oxon: Routledge.

Rish, R. (2015), 'Researching writing events: Using mediated discourse analysis to explore how students write together', *Literacy*, 49 (1): 12–19.

Rish, R. (2017), 'Mediated discourse analysis', in K. Peppler (ed.), *The SAGE Encyclopedia of Out-of-School Learning*, 476–9, Thousand Oaks: Sage.

Rogers, R. (2011), 'Becoming discourse analysts: Constructing meanings and identities', *Critical Inquiry in Language Studies*, 8 (1), 72–104.

Rothery, J. and M. Stenglin (2000), 'Interpreting literature: The role of appraisal', in L. Unsworth (ed.), *Researching Language in Schools and Communities: Functional Linguistic Perspectives*, 222–44, London: Cassell.

Royce, T. (1998), 'Synergy on the page: Exploring intersemiotic complementarity in page-based multimodal text', in N. Yamaguchi and W. Bowcher (eds), *Japan Association Systemic Functional Linguistics Occasional Papers*, 1 (1): 25–49.

Royce, T. (2002), 'Multimodality in the TESOL classroom: Exploring visual-verbal synergy', *TESOL Quarterly*, 36 (2): 191–205.

Samuel, J. and P. E. Bryant (1984), 'Asking only one question in the conservation experiment', *Journal of Child Psychology and Psychiatry*, 25: 315–18.

Scollon, R. (1997), 'Handbills, tissues, and condoms: A site of engagement for the construction of identity in public discourse', *Journal of Sociolinguistics*, 1 (1): 39–61.

Scollon, R. (1998), *Mediated Discourse as Social Interaction*, London: Longman.

Scollon, R. (2001), *Mediated Discourse: The Nexus of Practices*, London: Routledge.

Scollon, R. (2008), *Analyzing Public Discourse: Discourse Analysis in the Making of Public Policy*, London and New York: Routledge.

Scollon, R. (2013), 'Geographies of discourse: Action across layered spaces', in I. Saint-Georges and J.-J. Weber (eds), *Multilingualism and multimodality: Current challenges for Educational Studies*, 183–98, Rotterdam: Sense Publishers.

Scollon, R. and S. Scollon (2004), *Nexus Analysis: Discourse and the Emerging Internet*, London: Routledge.

Seppänen, J., ed. (2006), *The Power of the Gaze: An Introduction to Visual Literacy*, New York: Peter Lang.

Sharp, R. and A. Green (1975), *Education and Social Control: A Study in Progressive Primary Education*, London: Routledge and Kegan Paul.

Sheldon, L. (1988). 'Evaluating ELT textbooks and materials', *ELT Journal*, 42 (2): 237–46.

Shen, D. L. and Y. Tao (沈德立、陶云) (2001), Chuzhongsheng youwu chatu kewen de yandong guocheng yanjiu. (初中生有无插图课文的眼动过程研究, 'A study of eye movement in reading texts with or without illustration for junior high school students'). *Xinli kexue* (心理科学, 'Psychological Science'), 4: 385–8.

Sinclair, H. (1974), 'Recent Piagetian research in learning studies', in M. Schwebel and J. Raph (eds). *Piaget in the Classroom*, 57–72, London: Routledge and Kegan Paul.

Smith, B. E., M. B. Pacheco and C. R. de Almeida (2017) 'Multimodal codemeshing: Bilingual adolescents' processes composing across modes and languages', *Journal of Second Language Writing*, 36: 6–22.

Song, Z. S. (宋振韶) (2005), 'Jiaokeshu chatu de renzhixinlixue yanjiu (教科书插图的认知心理学研究, 'A study of illustrations in textbooks from the perspective of cognitive psychology'). Beijing shifan daxue xuebao (Shehui kexue ban) (北京师范大学学报(社会科学版)', *Journal of Beijing Normal University (Social Science Edition)*, 6: 22–6.

Stenglin, M. (2004), 'Packaging curiosities: Towards a grammar of three-dimensional space', PhD diss., University of Sydney.

Tang, J. B. (汤金波) (2007), 'Sukeban wuli shiyan jiaocai chatu de gongneng (苏科版物理实验教材插图的功能, 'The role of illustrations in a physics textbook')', *Jiaoxue yu guanli* (教学与管理, 'Teaching and Administration'), 10: 75.

Tao, Y. and J. L. Shen (陶云、申继亮) (2003), 'Gaoer xuesheng yuedu chatu kewen de jishi jiagong yanjiu (高二学生阅读插图课文的即时加工研究, 'The immediate processing study on reading picture texts for Grade 11 students')', *Xinli fazhan yu jiaoyu* (心理发展与教育, 'Psychological Development and Education'), 2: 43–6.

The Encyclopaedia of China·Education (2004), Beijing: Encyclopaedia of China Publishing House.

The Encyclopedia Americana·Volume 26, International Edition, ([1829] 2000), Danbury, CT: Grolier Incorporated.

Thibault, P. (1987), 'An interview with Michael Halliday', in R. Steele and T. Threadgold, *Language Topics: Essays in Honor of Michael Halliday*, Vol. II, 602–27, Amsterdam: Benjamins.

Thibault, P. J. (2000), 'The multimodal transcription of a television advertisement: Theory and practice', in A. P. Baldry (ed.), *Multimodality and Multimediality in the Distance Learning Age, Campobasso*, 311–85, Italy: Palladino Editore.

Thibault, P. J. (2001), 'Multimodality and the school science textbook', in C. Torsello G. Brunetti and N. Penello (eds), *Corpora Testuali per Ricerca, Traduzione e Apprendimento Linguistico. Studi Linguistici Applicati*. Padova: Unipress, 293–335.

Thompson, G. (1996), *Introducing Functional Grammar*, London: Arnold.

Thompson, G. (2001), 'Interaction in academic writing: Learning to argue with the reader', *Applied Linguistics*, 22 (1): 58–78.

Tian, P. (2007), 'Co-articulating "worry" in children's picture books', Paper presented at Semiotic Margins: Reclaiming Meaning, Sydney: The University of Sydney.

Trevarthen, C. (1980), 'The foundations of intersubjectivity: Development of interpersonal and cooperative understanding in infants', in D. R. Olson (ed.), *The Social Foundations of Language and Thought: Essays in Honor of Jerome S. Bruner*, 316–42, New York: Norton.

Tsakona, V. (2009), 'Language and image interaction in cartoons: Towards a multimodal theory of humor', *Journal of Pragmatics*, 41: 1171–88.

Tseng, C. (2016), 'Revisiting dynamic space in film from a semiotic perspective', *Semiotica*, 210: 129–49.

Tseng, C. (2018), 'The impact of new visual media on discourse and persuasion in the war film', *Film Studies*, 19: 34–57.

Unsworth, L. (2001), *Teaching Multiliteracies across the Curriculum: Changing Contexts of Text and Image in Classroom Practice*, Buckingham: Open University Press.

Unsworth, L. (2005), *E-Literature for Children: Enhancing Digital Literacy Learning*, London: Routledge.

Unsworth, L., ed. (2008), *New Literacies and the English Curriculum: Multimodal Perspectives*, London: Continuum.

Unsworth, L. and C. Cleirigh (2009), 'Multimodality and reading: The construction of meaning through image-text interaction', in C. Jewitt (ed.) *Handbook of Multimodal Analysis*, London: Routledge, 151–64.

Unsworth, L. (2017), 'Image-language interaction in text comprehension: Reading reality and national reading tests', in C. Ng and B. Bartlett (eds), *Improving Reading and Reading Engagement in the 21st Century*, Singapore: Springer, 99–118.

Unsworth, L. and A. Thomas (2014), *English Teaching and New Literacies Pedagogy: Interpreting and Authoring Digital Multimedia Narratives*, New York: Peter Lang.

van Leeuwen, T. (1999), *Speech, Music, Sound*, New York: Palgrave Macmillan.

van Leeuwen, T. (2005), *Introducing Social Semiotics*, London: Routledge.

van Leeuwen, T. and C. Jewitt, eds. (2001), *Handbook of Visual Analysis*, London: Sage.

von Glasersfeld, E. (1998), 'Why constructivism must be radical', in M. Larochelle, N. Bednarz and J. Garrison (eds), *Constructivism and Education*, 23–8, Cambridge: Cambridge University Press.

Vygotsky, L. S. (1978), *Mind in Society: The Development of Higher Psychological Processes*, eds. M. Cole, V. John-Steiner, S. Scribner and E. Souberman, Cambridge, MA: Harvard University Press.

Wang, J. M. and Y. Z. Lu (王金梅、路云芝). (2006), 'Ruhe zhengque yunyong lishi chatu (如何正确运用历史插图, 'How to use history illustration correctly')', *Shandong Jiaoyu (山东教育, 'Shandong Education')*, 11: 36.

Wang, T. (王婷) (2000), 'Jiaokeshu de fumianxing ji duice yanjiu (教科书的负面性及对策研究, 'Negativity of textbooks and countermeasures')', *Jiaoyu kexue yanjiu (教育科学研究, 'Educational Science Research')*, 1: 68–72.

Wang, X. H., X. W. Gao and J. Li (王秀红、高晓伟、历晶) (2006), 'Xin kebiao huaxue jiaokeshu chatu sheji fenxi ji yunyong celue (新课标化学教科书插图设计分析及运用策略, 'Analysis and utilization of illustrations in chemistry textbooks based on new curriculum standards')', *Huaxue jiaoyu (化学教育, 'Chemical Education')*, 7: 23–6.

Wang, Y. (汪莹) (2000), 'Zuguo neidi yu xianggang, aomen, taiwan diqu zhongxiaoxue jiaokeshu zhidu bijiao yanjiu (祖国内地与香港、澳门、台湾地区中小学教科书制度比较研究, 'A comparative study of the primary and secondary textbook system in China mainland, Hong Kong, Macao, and Taiwan')', *Kecheng, jiaocai, jiaofa (课程·教材·教法, 'Curriculum, Teaching Material and Method')*, 9: 49–51.

Wang, Y. S. (王有升) (2000), 'Woguo xianxing jiunian yiwu jiaoyu jieduan yuwen jiaokeshu (renjiaoban) de wenhua goucheng fenxi (我国现行九年义务教育阶段语文教科书(人教版)的文化构成分析, 'Analysis of cultural composition of Chinese textbooks for compulsory education')', *Jiaoyu yanjiu yu shiyan (教育研究与实验, 'Educational Research and Experiment')*, 1: 34–8.

Weninger, C and T. Kiss (2013), 'Culture in English as a foreign language (EFL) textbooks: A semiotic approach', *TESOL Quarterly*, 47 (4): 694–716.

Wertsch, J. V. (1991), *Voices of the Mind: A Sociocultural Approach to Mediated Action*, Cambridge, MA: Harvard University Press.

Wertsch, J. V. (1998), *Mind as Action*, New York: Oxford University Press.

White, P. R. R. (1998), 'Telling media tales: The news story as rhetorics', PhD diss., University of Sydney.

White, P. R. R. (2003), 'Beyond modality and hedging: A dialogic view of the language of intersubjective stance', *Text (Special Edition on Appraisal)*, 23 (2): 259–84.

White, P. R. R. (2006), 'Multimodal Appraisal – verbal and visual evocation of attitude in the print media', Paper presented at Australian Systemic Functional Linguistics Association Conference, Armidale: The University of New England.

Wignell, P., K. L. O'Halloran, S. Tan, R. Lange and K. Chai (2018), 'Image and text relations in ISIS materials and the new relations established through recontextualisation in online media', *Discourse & Communication*, 12 (5): 535–59.

Wohlwend, K. E. (2009), 'Mediated discourse analysis: Researching young children's non-verbal interactions as social practice', *Journal of Early Childhood Research*, 7 (3): 228–43.

Wohlwend, K. E. (2014), 'Mediated discourse analysis: Tracking discourse in action', in P. Albers, T. Holbrook and A. S. Flint (eds), *New Methods in Literacy Research*, 56–69, New York: Routledge.

Wohlwend, K. E. and L. Handsfield (2012), 'Twinkle, twitter little stars: Tensions and flows in interpreting social constructions of the techno-toddler', *Digital Culture Education*, 4: 185–202.

Xiao, L. F. (肖龙福) (2004), 'Qianxi woguo zhongxue yingyu jiaokeshu zhong de wenhua xinxi (浅析我国中学英语教科书中的文化信息, 'Analysis of the cultural information in EFL textbooks in China')', *Guowai waiyu jiaoxue (*国外外语教学, 'Foreign Language Teaching Abroad')', 1: 31–7.

Xie, H. J. and N. Q. Song (谢华均、宋乃庆) (2003), 'Xin jiaocai bianxie de jiaoyu linian tanxi (新教材编写的教育理念探析, 'Exploration of the educational principles underlying the compilation of the new textbook series')', *Kecheng·jiaocai·jiaofa (*课程·教材·教法, 'Curriculum, Teaching Material and Method')', 5: 9–12.

Xiong, T. and Y. Peng (2020), 'Representing culture in Chinese as a second language textbooks: A critical social semiotic approach', *Language Culture and Curriculum*, 34 (2), 163–82.

Xu, R. (徐润) (1997), 'Shuxue jiaoxue zhong ruhe yonghao chatu (数学教学中如何用好插图, 'How to use illustrations effectively in mathematics education')', *Shanxi jiaoyu (*陕西教育, *Shanxi Education*), 3: 25–6.

Yan, P., Q. Li and H. Zhang (阎苹、李群、张红) (2003), 'Dui chuzhong yuwen jiaokeshu chatu gongneng de sikao (对初中语文教科书插图功能的思考, 'Reflections on the functions of illustrations in junior secondary Yuwen textbooks')', *Zhongxiaoxue jiaocai jiaoxue (*中小学教材教学, 'Pedagogic Materials and Teaching in Primary and Secondary Education')', 35: 14–17.

Yang, Q. L. (杨启亮) (2002), 'Jiaocai de gongneng: Yizhong chaoyue zhishiguan de jieshi (教材的功能: 一种超越知识观的解释, 'Functions of textbooks: An explanation that transcends the notion of knowledge')', *Kecheng·jiaocai·jiaofa (*课程·教材·教法, 'Curriculum, Teaching Material and Method')', 12: 10–13.

Ye, Q. C. (叶起昌) (2006), 'Chaowenben duoyushi de shehuifuhaoxue fenxi (超文本多语式的社会符号学分析, 'A social semiotic analysis of hypertext's multimodality')', *Waiyu jiaoxue yu yanjiu (*外语教学与研究, 'Foreign Language Teaching and Research')', 6: 437–42.

Yuan, C. Y. and E. L. Chen (袁春艳、陈恩伦) (2007), 'Guanyu jianli woguo yiwujiaoyu jiaokeshu xuanyong zhidu de sikao (关于建立我国义务教育教科书选用制度的新思考, 'Reflections on the establishment of textbook selection principles for China's compulsory education')', *Jichu jiaoyu cankao (*基础教育参考, 'Basic Education Review')', 4: 60–2.

Zammit, K. and J. Callow (1999), 'Ideology and technology: A visual and textual analysis of two popular CD-ROM programs', *Linguistics and Education*, 10 (1): 89–105.

Zappavigna, M. (2012), *Discourse of Twitter and Social Media*, London: Continuum.

Zeng, L. (曾蕾) (2006), 'Dongtai duofuhao yupian de zhengti yiyi goujian: guoji xueshu jiaoliu yanjiang jiaoxue moshi tantao (动态多符号语篇的整体意义构建, 'Constructing semiotics in dynamic multimodal discourse')', *Waiyu yishu jiaoyu yanjiu (*外语艺术教育研究, *'Educational Research on Foreign Languages and Arts')*, 3: 42–8.

Zhang, D. L. (张德禄) (2009), 'Duomotai huayu fenxi zonghe lilun kuangjia tansuo (多模态话语分析综合理论框架探索, 'On a synthetic theoretical framework for multimodal discourse analysis')', *Zhongguo waiyu (*中国外语, *'Foreign Languages in China')*, 1: 24–30.

Zhang, D. L. (张德禄) (2009), 'Duomotai huayu lilun yu meiti jishu zai waiyu jiaoxue zhong de yingyong (多模态话语理论与媒体技术在外语教学中的应用, 'The application of multimodal theory and media technology in foreign language education')', *Waiyu jiaoxue (*外语教学, *'Foreign Language Education')*, 4: 15–20.

Zhang, D. L. (张德禄) (2010), 'Duomotai waiyu jiaoxue de sheji yu motai diaoyong chutan (多模态外语教学的设计与模态调用初探, 'Preliminary Investigation into the Concept of Design and the Selection of Modalities in Multimodal Foreign Language Teaching')', *Zhongguo waiyu (*中国外语, *'Foreign Languages in China')*, 3: 48–53.

Zhang, D. L. (张德禄) (2012), 'Lun duomotai huayu sheji (论多模态话语设计, 'On Design in Multimodal Discourse')', *Shandong waiyu jiaoxue (*山东外语教学, *'Shandong Foreign Language Teaching Journal')*, 1: 9–15.

Zhang, D. L. (张德禄) (2018), 'Waiyu benkesheng duoyuan nengli peiyang jiaoxue xuanze moshi tansuo (外语本科生多元能力培养教学选择模式探索, 'Exploring the teaching mode for cultivating foreign language majors' multiple competences')', *Waiyu jie (*外语界, *'Foreign Language World')*, 1: 28–35.

Zhang, D. L. and Y. X. Li (张德禄、李玉香) (2012), 'Duomotai ketang huayu de motai peihe yanjiu (多模态课堂话语的模态配合研究, 'A study of the multimodal configuration in classroom discourse')', *Waiyu yu waiyu jiaoxue (*外语与外语教学, *'Foreign Languages and Their Teaching')*, 1: 39–43.

Zhang, D. L. and T. Qu (张德禄、瞿桃) (2015), 'Duomotai huayu zhong de zhuanyi xianxiang yanjiu – yi cong daxue yingyu keben dao yingyu ketang jiaoxue de zhuanyi wei li (多模态话语中的转译现象研究——以从大学英语课本到英语课堂教学的转译为例, 'Translation in multimodal discourse: From college English textbook to classroom teaching')', *Waiyu dianhua jiaoxue (*外语电化教学, *'Computer-Assisted Foreign Language Education')*, 6: 17–23.

Zhang, D. L. and S. J. Zhang (张德禄、张淑杰) (2010), 'Duomotaixing waiyu jiaocai bianxie yuanze taisuo (多模态性外语教材编写原则探索, 'Exploring the compilation principles of multimodal foreign language textbooks')', *Waiyu jie (*外语界, *'Foreign Language World')*, 5: 26–33.

Zhang, H. K. (张海宽) (2005), 'Neihan fengfu de yifu jixiebo chatu (内涵丰富的一幅机械波插图, 'A meaningful illustration in a physics textbook')', *Wuli jiaoxue tantao (*物理教学探讨, *'Exploration of Physics Teaching')*, 6: 16–17.

Zhang, J. (张静) (1993), 'Tan chatu zai xuesheng lishi xuexi xinli guocheng zhong de zuoyong (谈插图在学生历史学习心理过程中的作用, 'The influence of illustration on students' mentality in learning history')', *Kecheng· jiaocai· jiaofa (*课程·教材·教法, *'Curriculum, Teaching Material and Method')*, 2: 32–35.

Zhang, J. and Y. L. Yang (张洁、杨永林) (2003), 'Xiaoxue yingyu jiaocai jianshe zhongde yuyan xingbie qishi xianxiang (小学英语教材建设中的语言性别歧视现象研究, 'A study on linguistic sexism in English textbooks of China primary schools)', *Qinghua daxue jiaoyu yanjiu (*清华大学教育研究, *'Research On Education Tsinghua University')*, s1: 73–76.

Zhang, S. H. (张三花) (2005), 'Woguo zhongxiaoxue jiaokeshu yanjiu shuping (我国中小学教科书研究述评, 'Review of the studies on primary and secondary school textbooks in China')', *Jiaoyu kexue yanjiu (*教育科学研究, *'Educational Science Research')*, 5: 9–12.

Zhao, S. M. and M. Zappavigna (2017), 'Beyond the self: Intersubjectivity and the social semiotic interpretation of the selfie', *New Media & Society*, 20 (5): 1735–54.

Zhao, S. M., E. Djonov and T. van Leeuwen (2014), 'Semiotic technology and practice: A multimodal social semiotic approach to PowerPoint', *Text & Talk*, 34 (3): 349–75.

Zhong, Q. Q. (钟启泉) (2006), 'Curriculum reform in China: Challenges and reflections', *Frontiers of Education in China*, 3: 370–82.

Zhongguo da baike quanshu· jiaoyu (《中国大百科全书·教育》, 'The Encyclopaedia of China· Education') (2004), Beijing: Encyclopaedia of China Publishing House.

Zhonghuarenmingongheguo jiaoyubu (中华人民共和国教育部, 'Ministry of Education of the People's Republic of China') (2001a), *Yingyu kecheng biaozhun (*英语课程标准, *'Curriculum Standards for English')*, Beijing: Beijing Normal University Press.

Zhonghuarenmingongheguo jiaoyubu (中华人民共和国教育部, 'Ministry of Education of the People's Republic of China'). (2001b), *Shuxue kecheng biaozhun* (数学课程标准, 'Curriculum Standards for Mathematics'), Beijing Normal University Press.

Zhu, Y. S. (朱永生) (2007), 'Duomotai huayu fenxi de lilun jichu yu yanjiu fangfa (多模态话语分析的理论基础与研究方法, 'Theory and methodology of multimodal discourse analysis')', *Waiyu xuekan (*外语学刊, *'Foreign Language Research')*, 5: 82–6.

Zhu, X. M. (朱小曼) (2006), 'Moral education and values education in curriculum reform in China', *Frontiers of Education in China*, 2: 191–200.

Zuo, Y. M. (左育民) (1986), 'Dui chuzhong huaxue keben zhong liangfu chatu de yijian (对初中化学课本中两幅插图的意见, 'Some opinions on two illustrations in a chemistry textbook for junior secondary education')', *Huaxue jiaoyu (*化学教育, *'Journal of Chemical Education')*, 4: 47–9.

Textbooks Cited

Go for it Students' Book II for Year 7 (2005), Beijing: People's Education Press.
Go for it Students' Book I for Year 8 (2005), Beijing: People's Education Press.

New Senior English for China Student's Book 1 (2004), Beijing: People's Education Press.
New Senior English for China Student's Book 2 (2004), Beijing: People's Education Press.
New Senior English for China Student's Book 4 (2004), Beijing: People's Education Press.
New Senior English for China Student's Book 5 (2004), Beijing: People's Education Press.
New Senior English for China Teacher's Book 1 (2006), Beijing: People's Education Press.
New Senior English for China Teacher's Book 2 (2007), Beijing: People's Education Press.
PEP Primary English Students' Book I for Year 3 (2003), Beijing: People's Education Press.
PEP Primary English Students' Book II for Year 3 (2003), Beijing: People's Education Press.
PEP Primary English Students' Book I for Year 4 (2003), Beijing: People's Education Press.
PEP Primary English Students' Book II for Year 4 (2003), Beijing: People's Education Press.
PEP Primary English Students' Book I for Year 5 (2003), Beijing: People's Education Press.
PEP Primary English Students' Book II for Year 5 (2003), Beijing: People's Education Press.
PEP Primary English Students' Book I for Year 6 (2003), Beijing: People's Education Press.
PEP Primary English Students' Book II for Year 6 (2003), Beijing: People's Education Press.
PEP Primary English Teachers' Books Book I for Year 3 (2003), Beijing: People's Education Press.

Index

NOTE: Page numbers in *italics* refer to figures; in **bold** refer to tables.

abstract coding orientation 52, 133–4, 141–2, 146, 159
abstract-sensory coding orientation 144–6, 165
academic communication 24
  'voice' in 59
action process 47, 63
action research 175 n.1
aesthetics. *See* appreciation
affect 40–3, 91, 96, 118–20, 124, 127, 167, 177 n.4
  and cartoons 97–100, 164
  gradability of 100–2
  institutionalized/
    recontextualized 124–7
  and jointly constructed text 122
  and sensory coding orientation 141
  types of 98, **99**
  visual inscription of 95
amplification. *See* graduation
analytical process 48, 71
angular–isometric perspective 137
appraisal 7–9, 18, 39, 93, 108–9
  and commitment 36
  and instantiation 35, **59**
  notion of 37
  research on 166–7
  sub-systems of 39–45
appreciation 40–2, 91, 108, 167
  and cartoons 103–6
  co-instantiation of 116–20
  as institutionalized affect 124–7
  invocation of 114–15, 164
  and jointly constructed text 122
  and portraits 109, 111
attitude 8, 18, 37, 39–44, 55, 126, 162, 166, 167. *See also* emotion and attitude education
  inscription and invocation of 94–6, 111–15, **119**, 122, 164

shift in 9, 127, 128, 164
  in visual interaction 51
attitudinal meanings 7, 36, 39–41, 45. *See also* affect; appreciation; judgement
  in cartoons 97–106
  gradability of **44**, 100, 109, 177 n.2
  institutionalized 164
  in jointly constructed text 121–3
  in multimodal texts 55–6, 91–7, 127–8, 164
attribute 43, **44**, **45**, 90, 162, 163
  and dialogue balloons 65, 66, 69
  and illustration 81, 86
  and jointly constructed texts 72, 75
available designs 21

Bakhtin, M. 42, 57–9
Baldry, A. P. 16
Barthes, R. 92
Bateman, J. A. 15
brightness 52, 133, 138, 140, 142, 157

Callow, J. 17
capacity 42, 108, 124
carrier 48
cartoons
  attitudinal meanings in 97–106
  and dialogue balloons 67–9
  in EFL textbooks for different levels of education 96, **97**, 163–4
  in primary EFL textbooks 61–2, 78, 96–9, 127, 165
CD-ROM 17
central perspective 137
centred composition 53
character focalization 50, 113
character voice 57, 60–2
  and dialogue balloons 66–70, 73, 74, 83–4
  and illustration 79–81

interplay between editor, reader
    and   9, 72, 86–9, 162–3
  and jointly constructed text   73–5
  and thought balloons   73–4
Chen, H. X.   25
Chen, Y. M.   95
classificational process   48
classroom practices
  multimodal approach   18–20
Cleirigh, C.   93
coda   155, 157
coding orientation   52, 56, 159
  register variables influence on   165, 168
  for sound modality   134
  types of   52
  for visual modality   133–4
Coffin, C.   59
cohesive resources   38
co-instantiation   93, 127, 163, 167
  in appreciation   116–20
  in jointly constructed text   121–3
  in judgement invocation   111–14, 164
  and putative reading   106–11
colour differentiation   52, 133, 135, 136, 143, 145, 157
colour modulation   52, 133, 135, 136, 143, 157
colour saturation   52, 133, 135–6, 140, 143, 145–6, 157
commitment   35–6, 122
competencies   25–6
complementarity   93, 100, 123, 163, 167, 176 n.3
compliant reading   77
complication   155, **156**, 157
composition   42, 108
  visual   46, 52–4, 95, 169
conceptual representation   26, 47, 48, 146, 169
contact   9, 49–50, 69–70, 163
'contact' type images   50, 87
content   32–3
content and language integrated thinking (CLIL)   20
context   82
  of culture   7, 24, 33, 175 n.1
  of situation   7, 24, 33–4, 175 n.1, 176 n.2, 178 n.4
  social   32, 33, 38

contextualization   52, 133, 136–7, 145, 158, 159
coupling   35, 176 n.4
culture   60, 61, 148
  context of   7, 24, 33, 175 n.1
curriculum standards   8, 100
  emotion and attitude goals in   4, 9, 104, 106, 123–4, **125**, 128, 166
  reform (2001)   4, 28, 123, 168

demand   49–50
demodalization   60–1
deontic modality   60, 130
depth   52, 133, 137, 140, 145, 158
descriptive categories   176 n.5
dialogic contraction   43, *44*
dialogic expansion   43, *44*
dialogism   42, 55, 59
dialogue/speech balloons   *61*, 62, 64, 65, 89, 90, 115, 162, 163
  gradability of   83–4
  highlighting in   81
  types of   65–70, 83
Ding, J. X.   24
disclaim   43, *44*, **45**, 86, 90, 167
  and illustration   79, 162–3
Doran, Y. J.   16

Economou, D.   94–5
editor-reader alignment   5, 6, 8, 167–8
  and engagement system   57, 161–2
  and jointly constructed texts   71, 73, 75, 76–7
editor voice   57, 60–1
  and dialogue balloons   65–6, 69, 83
  and highlighting   82–3
  and illustration   78–81
  interplay between reader, character and   9, 72, 86–9, 162–3
  and jointly constructed text   72, 74–5
  and labelling   61, 64–5
EFL. *See* English as Foreign Language
electronic and digital media   16–18
e-literary classrooms   17
emotion and attitude education   4–5, 7, 9, 28, 29, 55, 104, 106, 123–4, **125**, 128, 163–4, 168
  and cartoons   100, 102–6
  and socialization   102
emotions. *See* affect

engagement 8, 9, 39, 42–3, **44**, 166–7
engagement devices 55, 57, 59–60, 63, 89–90
   dialogue/speech balloons *61*, 62, 64–70, 81, 83–4, 89, 90, 115, 162, 163
   future studies 169–70
   gradability of 83–6, 90, 162–3
   highlighting 62, 81–3, 87, 90, 162, 163
   illustration 62, 72, 77–81, 85, *86*, 89, 153–8, 162–3
   jointly constructed text 61, 62, 70–7, 84–5, 88, 90, 121–3, 162–4
   labelling 61, 63–5
English as Foreign Language (EFL) education
   goals in 4–5
   research 23, 25–6
English as Foreign Language (EFL) textbooks. *See also* junior secondary EFL textbooks; primary EFL textbooks; senior secondary EFL textbooks
   for college teaching 26
   cultural representation in 16
   emotion and attitude dimension in 4–5
   future studies 168–70
   pedagogical implications for 167–8
enhancement 45
entertain 43, *44*, **45**, 86, 90, 162
   and highlighting 81, 87, 163
epistemic modality 130
ethics. *See* judgement
evaluative meanings 39, 41, 42, 59, 91
   image-text relations 9, 56, 95–6, 109–10, 127
experiential metafunction 36
experiential structure 38
explicit modality 131
extrinsic modality 130
eye contact 49–50, 69–70, 86–7, 90, 163
eye-level angle 51, 163

Feng, D. 26
Fernández-Fontecha, A. 20
field 178 n.4
   influence on choice of visual style 158, 165
   notion of 38
fish-eye perspective 137

focalization 50, 69, 86–7, 113
focus grades 44–5, 167
   of jointly constructed texts 84–5, 163
force grades 44, 45, 167
   of dialogue balloons 84, 163
   of illustrations 85
framing 53–4
frontal angle 88, 90, 113, 120, 163
frontal-isometric perspective 137
function 36
functional grammatics 15–16

GeM model 15
genre 33–4, 177 n.3, 178 nn.4–5
   and modality markers 133
   notion of 148
gesture 24, 98, **99**, 102, 143–4
   and language 20
given-new information value 53
graded engagement meanings 6, 7
graduation 8, 9, 39, 43–5, 167
   in affectual inscription 100–2
   of attitudinal meanings **44**, 100, 109, 177 n.2
   of engagement devices 83–6, 90, 162–3
   notion of 43
group work 60, 69, 100–2, 149
Guijarro, A. J. M. 95–6
Guo, S. 26

Halliday, M. A. K. 2–3, 24, 31, 32, 38, 46, 92, 130–1, 149, 176 nn.2, 5, 178 n.4
heteroglossia/heteroglossic space 42, 58, 167–8
   and dialogue balloons 66, 69
   and highlighting 81–3
   and illustration 79
   and jointly constructed text 74
   and labelling 64
   and multimodal engagement resources 57, 59–60, 62, 63, 89–90, 163
   voice in 59
highlighting 62, 87, 90, 162, 163
   text in image 81–2
   in verbal text 82–3
Hjelmslev, L. 32, 33
Hodge, R. 133
Hood, S. 35–6, 45, 59, 109
Hu, Z. L. 23–4
Hyon, S. 177 n.3

ideal-real information value   53
ideational meaning   33, 35–6, 169
  categories of   36–7
  and image-text relations   92–3
  notion of   36
  in technical images   16, 25
Iedema, R.   58–9, 177 n.1
illumination   52, 133, 137–8, 140, 145, 158
illustration   62, 72, 89, 162–3
  backgrounded and foregrounded   79–81
  fairy-tale   24
  gradability of   85, *86*
  of improper behaviours   78–9
  as link between verbal texts   77–8
  in mythology   153–8
image(s). *See also* illustration
  attitudinal meanings in   95, 127
  'contact' type   50, 87
  and interactive meanings   49–51
  'observe' type   50, *63*, *64*, *66*, *67*, 69–70, 86–7, 163
image-text relations
  attitude in   94–6, 127–8
  from attitudinal perspective   55–6, 91, 164
  interpersonal aspect of   93, 127
  social-semiotic approach to   92–3, 177 n.1
  synergistic model of   93
  types of   77
imperative clauses   60, 68, 69, 72, 74–5, 78–80, 89
implicit modality   131
individuation   176 n.3
information value   53
inscribed attitude
  verbal   94, **119**
  visual   95
instantiation   34–5, **59**, 62, 76, 176 n.3
intensification   109
intensity   45
interaction
  visual   46–7, 49–51, 54
  voice   86–90
interpersonal meaning   8, 33, 38, 93
  interactive dimension of   9, 57
  in multimodal EFL textbooks   4–7, 54–6, 165–6

notion of   37
  personal dimension of   91, 163
  and systemic functional semiotic approach   46–7
interrogative clauses   69
intimate distance   50, 87, 88, 110
intrinsic modality   130
invoked attitude   111–15
  verbal   94, **119**
  visual   94–5
involvement   37

Jewitt, C.   17
jointly constructed drawing exercises   71–2, 84
jointly constructed herald page   72–4, 84, 85
jointly constructed text   61, 90
  with accompanying images   74–5, 84
  attitudinal meanings in   121–3, 164
  gradability of   84–5, 162, 163
  notion of   70
  and reader involvement   88
  and readership construal   76–7
  reader voice in   62, 75
judgement   40–2, 91, 95, 96, 167
  co-instantiation in   111–14
  encoded in cartoons   103–6
  encoded in photographs/portraits   108, 111, 127–8
  and English learning   124
  as institutionalized affect   124–7
junior secondary EFL textbooks
  abstract coding orientation in   141–2, 159
  abstract-sensory coding orientation in   144–6, 165
  affectual inscription in   100–2
  critique on   168
  dialogue balloons in   65, *67*, 68
  emotion and attitude dimension in   102, 124
  labelling in   63–5
  multimodal jointly constructed text in   72–4
  naturalistic coding orientation in   146–8
  research on   5–6, 9
  visual styles in   96–7, 127, 163–5

Kiss, T.   16
Kress, G.   19, 62, 81, 133, 165. *See also* systemic functional semiotic approach
Kristeva, J.   58

labelling   61, 63–5, 71, 90, 162
Labov, W.   155
language   18
   function in SFL   7–8, 31–7
   and gesture   20
   as institution   32
   integrative role of   17
   and register   38
   in SFL   63
   as system   32
Lemke, J. L.   14–15, 18, 92
lexicogrammatical resources   38
Li, Y. X.   25, 26
Li, Z. Z.   23
Lim, F. V.   17
linguistic modality   130–1
linguistic resources   9
logical metafunction   36
logogenetic recontextualization model   102–6, 127, 164

Macken-Horarik, M.   15–16, 59
macrogenre   9, 159, 175 n.3
   teaching unit as   148–9
   visual choices   148–53
Martin, J. R.   16, 25, 33–6, 38, 41–3, 45, 76, 77, 94, 98, 104, 109, 122, 148, 149, 175 n.1, 176 n.4, 177 n.2, 178 n.5
Martinec, R.   92, 177 n.1
mathematical symbolism   18–19, 92
Matthiessen, C. M. I. M.   38
meaning(s)
   'multiplying meaning'   92, 111
   types of   36
mediated discourse analysis   12–13
metafunctional diversification   36–9, 169
metalanguage
   of multiliteracies   21–2
Mills, K. A.   17–18
Ministry of Education   27

modality   7, 37, 46, 51–2, 162, 165
   in multimodal discourse   9, 129, 158–9
   notion of   130
   in other semiotic modes   132–4
   social-semiotic approach to   129, 131–2
   variables in   130–1
modality cues   133
modality markers   56, 133
   for coding orientation   52, 165
   for naturalistic coding orientation   133–8
mode   38, 178 n.4
modulation   130
mood   33, 37, 72
morals and value education   27, 28, 55, 102–6, 123
multiliteracies   8, 20–3, 28–9
multiliteracies pedagogy   22–3
   in early school years   19–20
multiliteracy competence   18
multimedia digital literary activities   17
multimodal communicative competence   19
multimodal discourse analysis   24, 92–3
multimodal documents   15
multimodality   1–2, 8
   in education   2–3, 11–20, 161
   notion of   2, 11
   and semiotics   2–4
multimodality research   14–20, 28
   in China   23–6, 29
   future studies   168–9
multimodalization   23–4, 130
multimodal scaffolding techniques   20
multimodal semiotics   23–5
multimodal texts   25
   analytical practices in China   24
   in Australia   15
   in Hong Kong SAR   26
multiple voices
   dialogic interaction between   55, 57, 60–2, 86–9, 163
mythology   153–8

narrative representation   26, 47–8, 63, 71, 169
   editor voice in   64
   of a story genre   155–7

naturalistic coding orientation 51–2,
    133–8, 146–8, 152–3, 157–9, 165
negotiation 37
Nesbitt, C. 35
New London Group 21–2
nexus analysis. *See* mediated discourse
    analysis
normality 42, 108
novel (fiction) 17

objective modality 131
'observe' type images 50, *63*, *64*, *66*, *67*,
    69–70, 86–7
offers 49–50
O'Halloran, K. L. 15, 92–3
one-point perspective 137
orientation 130–1, 155, **156**

Painter, C. 15, 50, 126
pair work 60, 61, 69, 149
pedagogy as Design 21
Peirce, Charles Sanders 3
People's Education Press (PEP) 5, 27
personal distance 50–1, 88, 110
photographs
    and co-instantiation 110–14
    contextualization and
        decontextualization 136–7
    in EFL textbooks for different levels of
        education 96, **97**
    naturalistic coding orientation 147,
        152–3, 159, 165
    representation of actual scene
        149–53
    truth value of 51–2
Plum, G. 35
point of view 9, 49, 51, 163
    and character engagement 88
portrait
    in EFL textbooks for different levels of
        education 96, **97**
    putative reading 106–10
possessive attributes 48
primary EFL textbooks
    cartoons in 61–2, 78, 96–9, 127,
        163–5
    choice of coding orientations in 9, 52
    critique on 168
    development of 27

dialogue balloons in 65–7, 69–70, 99
emotion and attitude dimension
    in 100, 102–6, 123–4, 127
highlighting in 81–2
illustrations in 77–9
jointly constructed drawing exercises
    in 71–2
labelling in 63
multimodal page in 171
research on 4–6, 28
sensory coding orientation in
    114–15, 140–1, 143–4, 159, 165
visual styles used in 96–7, 126, 127
printed texts 14–16
proclaim 43, *44*, **45**
    and labelling 64, 65, 90, 162
projective structure 62
pronunciation 60, 61
propriety 42, 108, 124
prosodic realization 38
public distance 87–8, 113
putative reading
    of portraits 106–10

Qu, T. 25, 26
quantity 45

reaction 42, **59**, 108
reactional process 47, 63
reader(s)
    dialogue balloons giving directions
        to 69–70
    and editor alignment (*see* editor-reader
        alignment)
reader voice 57, 60, 62
    interaction between character and 89
    interplay between editor, character
        and 9, 72, 75, 86–9, 162–3
    and jointly constructed text 75
reading types 77
realization 35, 38, 40, 176 n.3
register 33–4, **59**, 176 n.2
register variables 38
    influence on coding orientation 165,
        168
representation 46–8, 52, 54, 133, 137,
    140, 143, 145, 157
resistant reading 77
resolution 155, 157

Rose, D.   16, 25, 77, 178 n.5
Royce, T.   19, 92

salience   53, 81
Salway, A.   92
science classrooms   18–20
section titles   89
   and editor voice   60–1
semiotic metaphor   15, 19, 92
semiotics
   and multimodality   1–4
   notion of   3
   stratification within and between   32–4
senior secondary EFL textbooks
   affectual inscriptions in   164
   emotion and attitude dimension in   102, 106–14, 116–23, 164
   highlighting in   82–3
   illustrations in   79–81
   jointly constructed text in   70, 74–5, 121–3
   labelling practices   65
   multimodal pages in   172–4
   naturalistic coding orientation in   135–8, 146–7, *150–1*, 152, 158, 159, 165
   photographs and portraits in   106–7, 159, 164, 165
   research on   5–6, 9
   technological coding orientation in   139–40
   visual styles in   96, **97**, 106, 164
   visual styles within different genres in   148–58
sensory coding orientation   52, 114–15, 140–1, 159, 165
SFL. *See* systemic functional linguistics
Smith, B. E.   18
social context   32, 33
   and metafunctional diversification   38–9
social distance   9, 49–51, 90
   and reader involvement   87–8, 163
social esteem
   judgement of   41–2
social relations. *See also* social distance
   interdependence between modality and   56, 129, 132, 142–8, 159

social sanction
   judgement of   41, 42, 108, 113–14
social semiotics   2–3, 169
   'discourse' and 'text'   175 n.1
   and image-text relations   92–3, 177 n.1
   language use in   7–8, 18, 32
   and modality   13–20, 56, 129, 131–2
   multimodalization in   23–4
sound modality   134
speech functions   68–9
speech process   64
   and character voice   62
story genre   155–7, 178 n.5
story time   60, 61
stratified model of context   33–4
structural resources   38
structured informality   20
subjective modality   131
surrealist illusionism   24
Sydney School   14, 148, 175 n.1, 175 n.3
symbolic attributive process   48
symbolic process   48
symbolic suggestive process   48
systemic functional linguistics (SFL)   3–4, 7–8, 31
   appraisal system within   39–45
   functional-semantic orientation of   8
   genre in   148, 178 n.4
   interpersonal meaning in   8
   perspectives on voice   58–9
   theoretical framework of   9, 31–9
systemic functional semiotic approach   7–9, 169
   components of   46–54

tactical reading   77
task time   60
technological coding orientation   52, 139–40
tenacity   42, 108, 124
tenor   38, 56, 165
textbooks
   editing of   27
   geography   25
   mathematics   15
   research in China   27–9
text-image relations. *See* image-text relations

textual meaning 33, 36, 38, 93
theme 33
theoretical categories 176 n.5
Thomas, A. 17
thought balloons 73-4
three-dimensional modality 134
Tian, P. 95
Toh, W. 17
transitivity 33, 36
translanguaging 18

Unsworth, L. 15-17, 19-20, 93

valuation 42, 108
value 130, 131
Van Leeuwen, T. 62, 81, 133, 165, 177 n.1. *See also* systemic functional semiotic approach
veracity 42, 108
visual communication
   relationships in 54-5
   systemic functional semiotic approach to 9, 46-54
visual composition 46, 52-4, 95, 169
visual demonstration
   and dialogue balloons 66-9, 100
visual display 18, 79
visual focalization 50
visual interaction 46-7, 49-51, 54
visual modality
   modality markers 133-8
   multilevel view of 56, 142-8
visual semiotic resources 9

visual styles
   diversity of 9
   in EFL textbooks for different levels of education 96-7, 129, 143-8, 163-4
   influence of field on 158, 165
   within a microgenre 148-58
visual thinking 20
voice
   abstract sense of 59
   in heteroglossia studies 59
   notion of 57, 58
   studies on 58-60
voice interaction 86-9, 90
voice roles 59

Waletsky, J. 155
Wang, B. Y. 25
Weninger, C. 17
WH-interrogative clauses 68, 72, 115
White, P. R. R. 35, 42-3, 76, 94, 98, 177 n.2
Wignell, P. 93

YouTube video productions 17

Zammit, K. 17
Zeng, L. 24-5
Zhang, D. L. 24-6
Zhang, H. K. 28
Zhang, S. J. 25, 26
Zhu, Y. S. 24

www.ingramcontent.com/pod-product-compliance
Lightning Source LLC
Chambersburg PA
CBHW062226300426
44115CB00012BA/2233